Written by an AIDS "carepartner" and two professional therapists, *When Someone You Know Has AIDS* is a book for anyone who cares about a friend, relative, or lover with AIDS or ARC (AIDS-related complex). Informative and compassionate, this book will help you care in a practical way.

How do you confront the trauma of an AIDS diagnosis? How can you handle your own (and your loved one's) fear, denial, and anger? What questions must you ask the doctor? How do you manage the everyday difficulties AIDS can cause—from diet and therapy to health insurance and stress? In what ways will your relationship with your sick friend start changing?

When Someone You Know Has AIDS answers all these questions and many more. With personal stories and the most up-to-date information about the disease's symptoms and treatments, this book provides the practical facts you need—as well as comfort and solace.

When Someone You Know Has AIDS is a collaboration among LEONARD J. MARTELLI, a writer and AIDS carepartner, who has interviewed hundreds of friends and relatives of people with AIDS; and therapists FRAN D. PELTZ and WILLIAM MESSINA, who specialize in counseling people with AIDS or ARC and those who care about them.

WHEN SOMEONE YOU KNOW HAS A·I·D·S

A PRACTICAL GUIDE

LEONARD J. MARTELLI
WITH FRAN D. PELTZ, C.R.C.
& WILLIAM MESSINA, C.S.W.

INTRODUCTION BY JOYCE WALLACE, M.D.

Crown Publishers, Inc., New York

Copyright © 1987 by Leonard J. Martelli
All rights reserved.
No part of this book may be reproduced
or transmitted in any form or
by any means, electronic or mechanical,
including photocopying, recording,
or by any information storage and retrieval system,
without permission in writing from the publisher.
Published by Crown Publishers, Inc.
225 Park Avenue South, New York, New York 10003
and represented in Canada by the Canadian MANDA Group
CROWN is a trademark of Crown Publishers, Inc.
Manufactured in the United States of America

Library of Congress Cataloging-in-Publication Data

Martelli, Leonard J.
    When someone you know has AIDS.
    Bibliography: p.
    Includes index.
    1. AIDS (Disease)—Social aspects.   2. AIDS (Disease)—
Psychological aspects.   3. AIDS (Disease)—Patients—
Home care.   4. AIDS (Disease)—Patients—Family
relationships.   I. Peltz, Fran D.   II. Messina,
William.   III. Title.   [DNLM: 1. Acquired Immunodeficiency
Syndrome—popular works.   WD 308 M376w]
RC607.A26M36   1987   616.97'92   86-29276
ISBN 0-517-56555-2
        0-517-56556-0 (pbk.)

10 9 8 7 6 5 4

To Evan, the Nipper, who has been brave, courageous, and an inspiration throughout his illness and whose love has made me strong

L.J.M.

CONTENTS

APPENDIXES 197

FOREWORD

A physician friend of mine, who directs a large venereal disease clinic and who is himself gay, has said that AIDS is the end of the world. It is the end of the world for those who have contracted this disease and died. It is horrible for those who have seen their loved ones suffer and die.

Many people are so terrified of this disease that they run from even the mention of its name, and they abandon anyone who suffers from it, be that person husband, wife, son, daughter, lover, or friend. Others cause amazing cruelty by firing persons with AIDS, by keeping them out of school, by isolating them from society and trying to make them feel like social outcasts.

Many others, some of whom you will meet in this book, have assumed the burden of care for their fellows. People are caring for sons and daughters, for husbands and wives, for lovers, and even for relative strangers. All have stretched their energy, ability, and love to the point that is consonant with the very best we can do. The "care giver"—the "carepartner and caring friend"—now needs help. This book is that help.

We have come a long way since the first days of this epidemic when we in the medical profession were then struggling, not only to discover the nature of the problem, but simultaneously trying to save the lives of those who were dying cruel and premature deaths. And we did not know the underlying cause of the disease. Today, we know a great deal more about treating the opportunistic infections related to AIDS, and research is progressing at a furious pace to stop the virus and correct the underlying immune deficiency. But the end is not yet in sight, even though we are beginning to see hopeful signs.

I say this because we know that more people will suffer and more care will be needed before this grave medical problem is solved.

This book will be helpful, not just to those who care for AIDS patients, but to any person who helps another through the difficult experience of being terminally ill and dying.

I wish to earnestly thank Len, Nini, Edam, Karen, Jimmy, Joe, John, and all those who have taken care of my patients. You must be beloved by not only those you care for, but also by God for caring for God's children.

JOYCE I. WALLACE, M.D., F.A.C.P.

PREFACE

AIDS. The very word makes us apprehensive, uneasy, even fearful. A new disease, mysterious, insidious, uncontrolled, and as yet incurable, has appeared. AIDS is a most terrifying disease—like something conjured up for a science fiction novel—because it attacks the body's very ability to defend itself against other diseases. Consequently, people with AIDS can become infected with exotic, bizarre, sometimes deadly diseases: diseases that are all around us, in our bodies, in our food, in our animals, blown through the air—diseases that are not a threat at all to people with normal immune systems, but can be deadly to someone with AIDS.

We feel threatened. We react to protect ourselves. We vow to keep this disease away from ourselves and those we love. And so we take actions that we hope will keep us safe. Some actions, based on medical information, can and do help prevent AIDS. Others, based on fear, rumors, prejudices, and ignorance, do nothing to help us, and can even harm those in greatest danger of the disease. But we feel we must do something.

There are thousands of people with AIDS and there will be many thousands more—fifty thousand per year may be dying by the end of this decade. Preventive actions are too late for them. It doesn't matter what we think of their lives or life-styles; the facts of the disease remain the same. AIDS is a human tragedy of undefined and ominous proportions.

Each person with AIDS is someone's child, perhaps someone's brother or sister, someone's husband or wife, someone's lover or friend—even someone's parent. The number of us whose lives have been touched by this disease, or who will be touched, is indeed huge. If we include all the people related to those at high risk of getting this disease, the number is staggering.

How are we all going to respond when AIDS strikes close to us? Understandably, some of us will turn away, feeling it's not our responsibility, feeling in danger, or that we can't bear the stress or the pain. Many have responded like this in the past; many more will do so in the future.

Understandably, too, some of us will stay. We will be willing to accept the responsibility of helping the person with AIDS, willing to bear the inevitable stress and pain—knowing that, with a little care, we are not in danger, knowing that we are needed.

In any crisis, there are likely to be people who act heroically and humanely. It is the same in the AIDS crisis. Up to now, almost all attention and support has been focused on the persons who are afflicted with this illness; little attention or support has been given to those who are the primary care givers and the caring friends to the person with AIDS. Yet these people find themselves in one of the most stressful, demanding, difficult, and sad situations imaginable—caring for a loved one who has a progressively debilitating and apparently terminal illness. In this book, these people are called *carepartners* and *caring friends*.

This is a book about and for carepartners and caring friends. We hope it will help them understand their situation better and deal with it with a little less pain. It is comforting to know there are other people with the same experience who are coping with it and who are willing to share their experiences with others. It is a relief to learn that the situations we find ourselves in, no matter how strange and painful they seem to us, may be normal and understandable under the circumstances—something we can endure and over which we can even prevail.

This is also a book for friends of people with AIDS. It will help them better understand the disease and how it affects the people afflicted with it both physically and mentally. It will help support and maintain friendships with people with AIDS and friendships with those who are taking care of the afflicted day after day.

Following the progression of the illness, this guidebook is filled with practical advice, intended to help you understand better what is happening not just to you but to your friend with AIDS. Interspersed with the practical advice are stories of loving, intense relationships, filled with every human emotion on an almost exaggerated scale—stories of people learning that every moment of life is precious and can be an occasion for joy, even in the saddest and most difficult circumstances. These stories are here as an example, as a vivid testimony that you are not alone, that someone has been there before, and that you too can help.

LEONARD J. MARTELLI

WHEN SOMEONE YOU KNOW HAS A·I·D·S

1
EVERYBODY'S PROBLEM

Jeffrey and Paul, both in their early thirties, had been together only a few months when Paul's health began to change. Paul said, "I noticed that I started to feel a little run-down, and I was having a little trouble swimming—I used to swim five times a week—and suddenly I was dropping ten pounds on the weights I lifted twice a week. I was falling asleep at my desk. One or two people asked me if I was losing weight. I said that it was conscious on my part, because I was dieting and had been working real hard lately. Finally, I decided I needed a vacation, a rest, so I planned a trip to the Caribbean. While I was in the Caribbean, I not only missed Jeffrey, but wasn't feeling any better, even after doing nothing but sleep for the first two and a half days. I had no energy. I thought, 'There's definitely something wrong.' So with a lot of juggling, I got a flight out early, after three or four days. I called Jeffrey as soon as I got back. We went to a movie that night, and I felt awful. The next day I had an appointment with my doctor."

Tom and Mart had been together for eighteen years. In some ways they grew up together, since they had met in their early twenties and formed a relationship they both valued more than anything else. Both had given up promising acting careers because the demands of theater interfered greatly with this relationship. Mart started a successful business, and Tom put himself through college. They had had many happy years together at the time that Mart became ill. He went into the hospital to have minor surgery of a fistula in his colon, an operation the doctors assumed would also bring under control the high fevers he had been having for several weeks. Tom said, "On the day of Mart's surgery, I went to visit him. Afterward, I ran into his doctor, his GP who was overseeing the surgery. 'How do you think it went with Mart?' I asked him. He was very brusque with me and said, 'Well whatever the problem is with the fevers, it certainly wasn't the fistula. So we're going to have to start testing for AIDS.' Just like that.

" 'AIDS,' I said, my voice rising. 'Why AIDS?' He said, 'Cer-

1

tainly, when someone is running a high fever, that could be the problem.' I said, 'It can't be that.' He just walked away. I was livid. Not just because of the way he had handled it, but that he should have even brought up the subject of AIDS upset me more than I can say."

Stella and David lived in a tiny hamlet in southern Kentucky. They had been married fifteen years, had two daughters, and had only recently built the house they had always dreamed of owning. David, a hemophiliac, had been regularly taking two clotting factors by injection at home since 1973. "The first time we heard anything about AIDS was about March 1983," Stella said in her deep southern accent. "There was a little article in the paper, and it said that hemophiliacs had less than a 1 percent chance of getting it, so we weren't too concerned about it. Less than a 1 percent chance— it's going to happen to someone else, not our family. About the time I started reading up on AIDS in May 1983, David developed symptoms: a sinus infection that wouldn't go away and frequent colds. He was the type that was very, very healthy. Other than the hemophilia, he never had a cold, flu, whatever. He started to have night sweats, too. I discussed it with David, and I said, 'We need to get this checked out, because you know this sinus infection is not going away, even with the antibiotics.' David was a positive person. 'I don't have it,' he said. 'We won't worry about it. I'm not going to get it.' "

Joan and Barry are a successful couple who own several dry-cleaning stores in a midwestern state. Their four children have all graduated from college and left home. Joan tells this story. "My youngest son, David, came home that year [1983] at Christmas, and I knew something was terribly wrong with him. He had no energy, and he always seemed to be running a fever. He looked thin and very pale. He just wanted to sit around the house and rest or sleep. I asked him what was wrong, but he said he didn't know. He told me he had been to a doctor in California, but the doctor told him he was working too hard and needed a vacation.

"I was worried, so I went with him to our family doctor, who called me into his office after he examined David. He told David to wait outside as this matter didn't concern him. Then he told me he thought David had some of the symptoms of AIDS, a new disease that had been recently discovered among homosexual men. I just looked at him, stunned. 'I can't say that to him, Stanley,' I said. 'He and I and his father have never discussed that part of his life.' Stanley told me, 'I'm going to tell him myself, then, but I'm not going to mention that I told you. I know about all this because my son told me about friends of his in San Francisco who are affected,

2

and I've been reading up on it.' So the doctor told him and recommended a doctor for him to see in California. David never mentioned it during that trip and neither did Barry or I. I can't tell you how much I regret that we didn't talk about that with our son back when we might have been able to help him."

Linda is a real estate broker with her own business. She is divorced, with two children, aged seven and nine. She tells about her brother, Gary, twenty-nine, who came to see her one day at her office at closing time and shut the door behind him. "At first I couldn't believe my eyes. I hadn't seen him in two months, even though we lived only about a hundred miles apart, and he looked terrible. He was thin and haggard, and he sort of slumped in the chair. Since college I had known he was gay. He had been living with another man, Bob, for about five years. But there was no way I could have been prepared for what he told me. He said, 'Linda, I'm really scared. The doctors tell me I have ARC, and that it might develop into AIDS. But if I take care of myself, it might not. I'm so screwed up. I barely have the strength to get to work anymore, and you can imagine that Bob is as scared as I am. We're just not making it.' He started to cry at that point, and I got up and went and hugged him. I had been reading about AIDS ever since it broke in the news, because I was afraid for him. I kept thinking, 'How are we going to cope with this? How are we going to tell Mom and Dad?' And I said to him, 'Tell me what you want me to do. Tell me what you need. Do you need to come here where the family can take care of you?' He had come to me, I knew, because he felt that we could help him get well. But he couldn't go to our parents first."

Jeffrey and Paul, Tom and Mart, Stella and David, Joan and Barry, and Linda are all people beginning to discover that something is going terribly wrong in their lives or in the life of someone they love. Some big change is happening. As you read this book, you will be introduced to many people who have grappled with the problems of caring for and caring about a person with AIDS. These are real people who have been interviewed by the authors and who have agreed to share their experiences with you. In some cases their circumstances and names have been changed to protect their privacy, but these people want to do whatever they can to help educate others about this disease.

AIDS CAN BECOME YOUR PROBLEM, TOO

Your involvement in the life of a person with AIDS could happen suddenly. You might get a phone call from a friend in great distress. "I need your help," he says. "I'm very sick." It could happen to you as it did to Linda or Tom.

Or it could happen gradually. You might notice that your friend, lover, son, daughter, brother, sister, husband, or wife hasn't seemed quite up to par lately. He or she seems to lack energy, to be more tired, to catch more colds and flus, to have strange rashes that come and go, and to be losing weight. You wonder what is going on. You may even suspect. If you love this person—if you care enough—you may be on your way to becoming a carepartner or a caring friend. You will not know what this means at first. But you will learn as you go along, and you will choose to do what you do.

A *carepartner* is a person who is providing continuing emotional support and physical care to a person with AIDS or AIDS-Related Complex (ARC), a health condition in which some of the symptoms of AIDS have appeared. A carepartner can be a friend, a parent, a sibling, a lover, anyone who is willing to become the primary care giver for the ill person, who is willing to be responsible for a person with AIDS on an daily basis.

A *caring friend* is involved with the person with AIDS in the same ways as a carepartner, but to a lesser degree, perhaps less intensely or not on a daily basis.

Generally, though, when someone you care about gets AIDS, you have to be willing to accompany him on a journey through a troubled and largely uncharted land of strange and dreadful illnesses and trials. You will find yourself learning about experimental drugs and treatments, confronting undreamed-of prejudice and mean-ness, experiencing anxiety and tears, but always, always hoping that the cure is right around the corner.

For the sake of simplicity in this book, we will call your ill spouse, sibling, child, or lover your *friend.* And we will refer to him or her as *he*, although many persons with AIDS are women. We will refer to you, not as mother or father, brother or sister, husband or wife, or lover, but also as a *friend.* We do this simply to include everyone, because the relationships people have with persons with AIDS are as myriad as human relationships themselves, and we cannot attempt to name them all in every instance.

You probably already know something about the characteristics of AIDS and what it does. Nevertheless, the following sections will define AIDS for you, tell you something about it, and provide you with all the information you are going to need to understand everything covered in this book.

Acquired Immune Deficiency Syndrome, AIDS, is a complex disease—a disease complex—that is characterized by severe damage to the body's natural immune system. When a person has AIDS, he becomes susceptible to unusual opportunistic diseases and cancers that are not ordinarily a threat to people with normal immune systems. The two most common are Pneumocystis carinii pneumonia (PCP) and Kaposi's sarcoma (KS), a cancer.

Researchers have found a virus that can be linked to AIDS, but there is no conclusive proof that this virus is the sole cause of AIDS. There is even some controversy whether it is the most important factor in the onset of AIDS. In the United States this virus is usually called HTLV-III (human T-cell lymphotropic virus, type III). In France, where it was also identified, the virus is called lymphadenopathy-associated virus, or LAV. In this book, we will call this virus HIV, human immunodeficiency virus, a nomenclature adopted in Paris at a conference on AIDS in June 1986. HIV effectively describes the virus without controversy.

There is even an important contention that the virus associated with AIDS has not been properly identified, that it is related to the African Swine Fever virus. See Appendix A for more information about this debate.

Cofactors: Whatever virus or viruses are contributing to the development of AIDS in individuals, they are apparently not enough by themselves to cause disease in most cases. A great deal of evidence has accumulated that cofactors are necessary to bring on the onset of full-blown, or frank, AIDS. Among cofactors named are recreational and prescribed drugs, the general health of the individual, malnutrition, poor sanitation, other infections, such as intestinal parasites, or even the immunological shock that follows surgery. However, no one has conclusively linked a particular cofactor to the onset of a particular case of AIDS. No one has been able to say, "He got this infection, and it triggered AIDS."

The damaged immune system: Apparently HIV first attacks a specific subset of white blood cells called the T-4 cells, or T-helper cells, which are a key component in the body's defense system against invading organisms. The function of these cells is to alert other white blood cells that a foreign organism is in the body and to begin to attack and destroy it. Without sufficient T-4 cells, the body's defense system doesn't recognize and attack these infections as they appear. As a result, certain organisms that our bodies ordinarily destroy almost immediately become life-threatening infections to persons with AIDS.

The virus is in some ways slow-acting. It makes its way into the T-4 cell and becomes part of that cell's DNA where it can lie dormant for at least six months and cause no symptoms whatsoever, except that the infected T-4 cell no longer performs its function. When the virus is activated—perhaps by a cofactor—it turns the T-4 cell into a factory replicating the virus itself. Then millions more of the virus are released into the bloodstream to seek out other T-4 cells, further weakening the immune system. One of the characteristics of the blood of persons infected with HIV is a depletion of the T-4 cells and a reversed ratio of T-4 cells and T-8 cells. T-8 cells are called suppressor cells, and they tell the body when to call off the attack on foreign organisms. Ordinarily there are two T-4 cells for every T-8 cell. In people infected with HIV, this ratio is reversed.

What does infection mean?   Not everyone exposed to HIV, or infected by it, has developed AIDS. At this time, up to 60 or 70 percent of the male homosexual populations of some large cities are testing positive to HIV antibodies. This simply means that these people have been infected by the virus. We don't know how many will come down with AIDS in the long term, or even what percentage will ever show some symptoms. Estimates of the percentage of the infected who will develop AIDS range widely, from 5 percent to 50 percent to 100 percent. There could be as many as one to two million people in the United States who have been exposed to HIV. So no matter which estimate of the percentage who will get sick turns out to be correct, the problem is immense and is going to get much bigger.

Transmission of the disease: AIDS is generally a disease transmitted sexually or intravenously. It takes direct blood-to-blood contact, or direct semen-to-blood contact, to transmit the virus. Although the virus has been found in small amounts in other body fluids, such as saliva, there is no evidence that the virus has been transmitted by these fluids. Further, there is no evidence that AIDS can be transmitted by any casual contact, when normal sanitary procedures are observed. Only theoretically can someone get AIDS from kissing. There is not one documented case.

No one is going to get AIDS from a glass, from a toothbrush, a toilet seat, from someone's soiled clothing, from handling money, or from eating in restaurants. No one is going to get AIDS from living with someone who has AIDS, or because he lives in New

York, or Miami, or San Francisco. Contact of blood to blood, or semen to blood, is the way it is spread.

In areas where the sanitary standard are very different and much lower than in the United States, it is possible that AIDS is spread in other ways, but there are no conclusive studies to prove this either.

There are two cases where nurses who were punctured with needles containing the blood of AIDS patients have become infected. Yet this type of accident with infected needles has occurred hundreds of times, and only two cases of infection have resulted. So even this type of contact is not a very efficient means of spreading the infection.

Risk groups: At present in the United States, there are several risk groups: homosexual men, IV-drug users, newborn children of women infected with HIV, and sex partners—male and female—of persons infected with HIV. Hemophiliacs and recipients of blood products and transfusions before April 1985, when the blood supply began to be tested for antibodies to HIV, are also at risk—including President Reagan, who received blood transfusions in 1981 after the attempted assassination.

The two largest risk groups are homosexual males and IV-drug users. Apparently these groups, at least in the United States, have provided the disease with the easiest means of transmission: the exchange of body fluids and the sharing of contaminated needles. Both of these routes provide the virus with a direct entry into the bloodstream. Anal intercourse between men seems to be by far the most high-risk sexual activity, simply because tears in the lining of the colon caused by the penis can provide direct access to the bloodstream for the virus, which is present in large numbers in the semen.

It is obvious how contaminated needles used by more than one person can spread the disease among IV-drug users.

Vaginal intercourse also provides occasion for infection, although a less probable one, at least in the United States, where we have a limited number of documented cases of AIDS infection through this route. This may well be because the walls of the vagina are less likely to tear during intercourse than the lining of the colon. It seems more likely that men will give AIDS to women than vice versa, but there are documented cases both ways. It is most probable that vaginal secretions in infected women contain HIV because these secretions contain large numbers of white blood cells. A microscropic abrasion on the surface of the penis could provide a route of entry for the virus.

7

In Africa, AIDS occurs mostly among heterosexuals and the risk groups are entirely different. There, highly promiscuous middle-class heterosexuals in large cities form the largest risk group.

The prognosis: The latest statistics show that slightly less than half the people who have been diagnosed with AIDS are still alive. There are, of course, extraordinary cases of people who have survived many years after diagnosis. But in general, the prognosis is not good. Although doctors are getting better at handling most of the opportunistic infections associated with AIDS, over the long run it's a losing battle. About 80 percent of those diagnosed with AIDS die within three years of diagnosis, and most of the remaining 20 percent die within five years. But there are new drugs on the horizon that may prevent the replication of the virus, and those drugs may alter the statistics in years to come.

AIDS is an extremely complicated medical problem to solve, especially because of the nature of the viruses associated with it. HIV can hide in certain cells; it goes into nerve and brain cells too, and it appears in many variations or mutations, which make it more difficult to combat. HIV may work in concert with some of the other viruses found in persons with AIDS.

However, as with many medical challenges over the years, an answer or solution may suddenly appear from the most unexpected quarters.

A DANGER TO ALL

All sexually active people, heterosexual and homosexual, should be worried about contracting AIDS. It is theoretically possible that a single unsafe sex act with an infected person could lead to infection and a chance of contracting the disease. The spread of AIDS infection, as we mentioned earlier, has been most rapid among homosexual men, IV-drug users, recipients of blood products, and people who have sex with members of these groups. But the patterns of risk yesterday are not necessarily the patterns of risk tomorrow.

Homosexuals respond: Most homosexual men know these facts, and they have been heeding the warnings about promiscuity and anonymous sex. As anyone in contact with the homosexual community knows, there is very much less anonymous sex and promiscuity than there was in the first years after gays developed their own visible subculture. Such behavior is no longer something that people brag and joke about.

A study reported at the Conference on AIDS in Atlanta in 1985 showed that in San Francisco there had been a 70 percent drop in the cases of rectal gonorrhea over a three-year period since the onset of AIDS. More recent studies have shown similar startling drops in the incidence of sexually transmitted diseases among homosexual men. All this, together with the mobilization of gay people to deal with the disease, indicates the tremendously positive and responsible reaction of homosexual men to the AIDS crisis. The vast majority of men are not risking their lives for the pleasures of a chance sexual encounter.

Jack and Bruce met on Montrose Avenue in Houston on a summer afternoon in August 1983. They were walking from one bar to another when they passed each other on the sidewalk. Both were big men dressed in jeans and T-shirts. Bruce was in his early thirties, and Jack his late twenties. The attraction was instant. Jack tells the story. "Bruce just stuck out his hand and said, 'My name's Bruce. Let's both go in the same direction and have a drink together.' I remember laughing and saying something like, 'You're a man of few words. Let's go.'" So they went to a bar together and sat outside in the late evening heat. At one point Bruce explained, "You know I haven't been tricking around for a long time now, so I'd like to make a date with you. Get to know you better. Then I'll trick with you." He laughed.

"I was surprised and pleased," Jack continued. "I hadn't met such a straightforward man in years. But his honesty let me be honest. I said, 'I haven't been doing much of that either. I got the shit scared out of me in L.A. a couple of years ago. They told me I had GRID. But I'm all right now.'

"Bruce put his arm around me. 'Imagine that. An honest man. Gay Related Immune Deficiency. Sounds familiar to me. Just been eating right, taking my vitamins, getting my sleep, working out, and not screwing around. I was living in San Francisco. You came home to Texas, too?' 'That's right,' I replied."

Heterosexuals respond: Most heterosexuals still believe that AIDS is a gay disease or a disease of drug addicts. Not enough has been done outside the homosexual community to educate the American people about the danger of AIDS. Quoted in the *New York Times* on June 17, 1986, Dr. Walter Dowdle, the AIDS coordinator for the Public Health Service, said in an interview, "The public needs to understand this [AIDS] can be transmitted sexually, whether homo or hetero. And information must be disseminated in areas where AIDS transmission among heterosexuals is most likely, including certain larger cities and in high schools and colleges."

9

Dr. Dowdle's warning becomes even more urgent in the light of study reported in Paris at an international meeting on AIDS in June 1986. This continuing study, conducted in Haiti, has shown a dramatic shift in the population groups in Haiti that are affected by AIDS. Dr. Warren Johnson of Cornell Medical College reported that this study showed, in 1983, 71 percent of the cases of AIDS in Haiti came from the same groups that are at high risk today in the United States: homosexual men, IV-drug users, and recipients of blood products. By 1986, the pattern had shifted. Only 11 percent of the new cases came from these groups. Now, 72 percent of the cases occur among promiscuous heterosexuals. Dr. Peter Piot, an AIDS expert at the Institute of Tropical Medicine in Antwerp, Belgium, quoted in the *New York Times* on June 29, 1986, said the Haitian study showed "how rapidly and dramatically the AIDS virus can be spread in a promiscuous heterosexual population."

"We have to undo the general perception that this is a gay disease," Dr. Dowdle said. "It is a sexually transmitted disease."

TOO LATE FOR SOME

By the time the Centers for Disease Control defined AIDS in 1981, preventive actions were already too late for many people. More than 25 percent of sexually active, homosexual men in such cities as New York and San Francisco had already been infected by the virus that is associated with AIDS, and the virus had not yet been identified. Different studies indicate that the percentage infected today may be as high as 70. Among IV-drug users, some studies show close to 60 percent infected, and among hemophiliacs, about 90 percent. Studies of prostitutes in major cities also indicate that up to 50 percent are infected.

A great many of these people were infected long before anyone knew what was causing the problem, or before anyone outside the homosexual community was sounding the alarm. They may become sick at some time in the future. The Public Health Service expects a tenfold increase in AIDS deaths by 1991, to 54,000 in that year alone, with a cumulative total by 1991 of 270,000 cases and 179,000 deaths. New York City will have a cumulative total of 40,000 cases by 1991 and 30,000 deaths. These numbers stagger the imagination.

Richard and Jose had been a more or less monogamous couple for almost ten years. They had few sexual encounters outside the relationship, perhaps once or twice a year, and they did not keep these encounters secret from each other. Jose says, "You know, they had been taking my blood since 1979 for a Hepatitis B study and freezing it. So just two months ago, they went back and ran those tests for HIV antibodies and discovered that my blood had turned positive between 1981 and 1982. Do you believe it? I could name the guy I got it from. I had one sexual contact during that time. And my blood is positive every year after that. I don't have any symptoms though, and Richard still tests negative. Neither of us has had sex outside the relationship in over two years. So you figure it? We still have a very active sex life. But now we're scared. We've even started practicing safer sex, using condoms, even though it seems that whatever was going to happen between Richard and me should already have happened. But who knows? We're not going to take any chances."

Suzanne describes her fears for her daughter Michelle, an IV-drug user. "As her drug problem increased, so did my fear for her health. She was not a candidate to be a drug addict. She wasn't strong. I used to say that to her, 'Michelle, your body just won't support your life-style. Maybe some of the people you know can do this and get away with it for a number of years.' Of course, I chose to think that she would outgrow this, that she would eventually take care of her health. She might have. It's not that unusual to be doing drugs at age twenty-four. But it wrecks your immune system; you just leave yourself wide open.

"Michelle loved us. We loved her. She drove us crazy, and her drug problem created chaos in our lives. . . . We did everything we could to try to manipulate her into going through a drug program. As soon as I started hearing about AIDS, something clicked in my brain. I was beside myself that this would happen to her. She was like a profile of someone who would get AIDS. It was as if she had said, 'Well, I guess I'll go out and get AIDS.' "

AIDS-RELATED COMPLEX (ARC)

It may take months or even years after infection for symptoms of AIDS or ARC to appear, if they appear at all. Here are some early signs of trouble we need to watch for:

- Tiredness, a very low energy level, an inability to be as active as before, without any apparent reason, over a period of several months.

- Loss of weight, perhaps fifteen pounds or more, or 10 percent of body weight, over a three-month period, without any dieting or change of eating habits.

- Swollen lymph glands in the groin, the neck, underarms, that last for several months and have no apparent cause.

11

- Fevers, persisting over several months, for which there is no apparent cause. Sometimes these fevers "spike" or shoot up suddenly.
- Chronic diarrhea.
- Night sweats, waking up in the night with the bed soaked from sweat.
- Flu or coldlike symptoms that last for a month or more.
- Rashes and other strange skin irritations that appear over a period of time and then may disappear or persist.

Howard and Alex had been together for seven years. Both in their forties, Howard was a successful businessman and Alex an architect. They lived in a huge loft they had created from raw space in an industrial building. Howard said, "Alex had been feeling run-down and had a fever for a long time, since about a year ago Thanksgiving. But it really started last May. He went for a haircut, and the barber noticed a bump on his head and told him that he should look into it. Alex had been to the dermatologist a number of times. He even went to a second dermatologist, because he was getting skin eruptions and irritations and rashes, and he wasn't getting well. So after the business with the barber, he went back to the dermatologist who did a biopsy."

Albert and Melvin had been friends for over five years. During that time they had lived together off and on, but they didn't get along well living under the same roof. Finally, Melvin joined the Navy, but left after only a year. He returned to Albert's apartment sick. Albert said, "He went to the doctor here. The doctor told him he had a hole in the lining of his colon . . . but no one said anything about AIDS. I wasn't thinking AIDS at all. But I knew he was sick, and I didn't know what the long haul would bring. That's why I went out on a limb and got him a job in the same agency where he worked before. He needed medical insurance.

"He kept going to doctors, back and forth, taking all kinds of medication. He had the night sweats and he had fevers. But the doctors said he didn't have AIDS. They thought the night sweats came from the infection in his colon. I didn't know any better."

Talk to your doctor: If two or more of the symptoms described above appears in your friend, urge him to go to a doctor. Your friend may have ARC—AIDS-Related Complex—a health condition in which some of the symptoms of AIDS have appeared, but no major opportunistic infection is evident. ARC encompasses a great variety of conditions, as noted above, from swollen glands to persistent fevers. Many people with ARC are not sick at all and continue to function normally at the same energy level as before. Others are very sick and may be unable to function normally. People with ARC are, however, considered to be contagious with the virus associated with AIDS.

Some cases of ARC progress to full-blown AIDS, but many do not. The percentage that does progress is not known at this time, because the discovery of the disease has been so recent, there has not been enough time to complete thorough research and tracking of a sufficient number of cases.

However, the behavior of your infected friend can influence his condition, especially if his symptoms are mild and his health is basically good. So now is the time to act. Ask your friends, or even your regular physician, but be sure to help your friend find a doctor who works with AIDS patients. Why? Knowledge about AIDS symptoms, infections, and treatments varies among all doctors. Many will not know what to look for or what to do.

Howard encountered this problem. "At that time we were both seeing an internist, and Alex had been complaining to the internist repeatedly. Finally the internist told us that Alex was suffering from chronic depression. The idiot! He knew Alex was gay. He knew all about him. Two years before all this happened, Alex had been so sick that his mother and sister came to stay with us. But the doctors never figured out what was wrong with him then." A doctor familiar with AIDS might have seen early symptoms and come to different conclusions.

If the doctor that you and your friend choose recommends blood tests, have them. It's better to know the status of your own and your friend's health as indicated in the blood tests than to stick your head in the sand. But remember, the results of these blood tests are only an indication of overall health. This is especially true of the T-4, T-8 cell ratios. This ratio is not a predictor of disease. Urge your friend not to agree to the HIV-antibody test until you both have carefully considered all the pros and cons. See Appendix B at the end of this book for some of these arguments. Keep in mind the controversy at this time about whether HIV is the sole cause of AIDS.

"I went back to see our family doctor," Joan said, "after my son David returned to California. I had been reading everything I could find about AIDS, but it was very confusing. So one evening I went to see Stanley after all his other patients had left. I didn't have an appointment, I just dropped by. I said, 'Tell me what your diagnosis of David means. I'm really worried. Does this mean that David is going to die?'

"Stanley and I had been friends for years, and he had taken care of all my children, so I felt I could trust him. But his answer didn't really help me. 'I don't know what it means,' he said. 'It's such a new thing no one seems to know a lot. Some people with David's symptoms just stay that way. Sort of sickly. Others get AIDS and die. Some have gotten better, my son tells me.' He stopped a minute and looked at me. 'Does David live alone?' I thought the question was very odd, but I said, 'Yes, I think so.' 'That's too bad,' he said. 'It's going to be harder for him to take care of himself and his health.'

"For just a moment the thought went through my mind that Stanley was telling me to get David home. But a lot of other thoughts crowded in. 'I have to think about what to tell Barry,' I said. I got up to leave, and Stanley came around his desk and hugged me. He never did that. 'This is an awful thing to have to face,' he said. But I felt very confused and depressed. On the one hand something told me that this was a terrible and serious situation. On the other hand something inside me just wanted to believe that it would all go away."

Further symptoms: Other symptoms are more directly related to the opportunistic infections related to AIDS:

- A dry, persistent, heavy cough that lasts for a month or more (this could be related to Pneumocystis carinii pneumonia, PCP).

- Shortness of breath (related to PCP).

- Purple or reddish areas on the skin, or growths with a raised surface on the skin usually appearing on the arms or legs, but also occurring on the mucous membranes in the mouth, throat, anus, and nose (related to Kaposi's sarcoma, KS).

- A thick, whitish coating on the tongue or inside the mouth and throat that may also cause a sore throat. This is called thrush.

Michael and Joe had been friends for ten years. Michael, a student and part-time taxi driver, had not seen his friend Joe for over two years when Joe moved from Louisiana and took an apartment in a city nearby. Michael said, "First of all he had showed up at my door from New Orleans, and he looked horrible. He looked real skinny and exhausted. I ascribed the exhaustion to his just having driven cross-country nonstop, and that he was skinny to the fact that he was getting older and his body was changing. Then a week later he called me, and he said he couldn't breathe. He came over to visit me, and he was exhausted from climbing the stairs. He said he had been over visiting some friends, and he'd smoked some

14

hashish, and it had hurt his lungs, and he thought maybe that was the reason he couldn't breathe. So I asked him when that had been, and he said three days ago. I told him that was ridiculous. That stuff doesn't last for three days. A week later I called him, and he was lying on his bed and felt horrible and couldn't do anything. So I told him he should go to the doctor."

Jack and Bruce loved to spend time outdoors; both men worked outdoors, Jack as a carpenter, and Bruce on a crew repairing city streets. They went somewhere almost every weekend, to Galveston for the beach, to East Texas camping, and even once to a hunting ranch. When they both got vacation time together that winter, they decided to go to southern Mexico for the beaches and the sightseeing.

Jack explained, "When we got back to Houston, we were both a mess. Both of us had those intestinal bugs, with diarrhea and all that. We went to the doctor who gave us these drugs. In about a week I was all right, but Bruce didn't seem to get better. The parasites went away, but then he felt weak, and he was having trouble breathing, and he was coughing all the time. I had noticed too that he had a lot of white coating on his tongue and in his mouth, but that had been going on for a while. Then one night we went out to the bars, and he said he couldn't stand the smoke, so we sat outside, although it wasn't warm, and then we went to his place. I was really worried about him, so I spent the night at his place. All night he couldn't breathe, and he was gasping for air, and I really didn't know what to do about it. I mean, I didn't have anything but cold medicine, and I could see that it was more than that.

"So that morning, early, I took Bruce to the emergency room at a hospital nearby. I called the doctor who had been treating us, and he said we were in the right hospital. He was a gay doctor who treated lots of venereal diseases. He came by around noon—we were still in the emergency room—took one look at Bruce, and told us that he was going to call in a specialist, a pulmonary specialist. He looked in Bruce's mouth and shook his head. 'Damn it,' was all he said."

Linda explains, "I must have made a hundred phone calls that night after Gary left and the next day. I called everyone in the country who could tell me anything about Gary's health. One person led me to another and that one to another. I kept hearing over and over again that no one knew for sure what would happen to him. But that, yes, it would certainly be better for him to be at home where someone could look after him all day. He was too sick to work—I could see that without anyone telling me—and probably his health would just get worse if he worked. Everyone told me the

15

same thing, too. No one will get the disease from him unless they have sex with him or exchange blood with him. The family was safe. So late that afternoon, I felt like I knew how to approach the whole problem, and I called him and told him to come down that weekend, and we would speak to our parents. He seemed so relieved that he started to cry on the phone.

"You know, before those two days I never remember Gary crying about anything. He got his tough, athletic manner from our father. Yet he was so unsure of us—his family—that he'd left his lover Bob in the car outside when he came in to see me that evening at my office. Almost like he was afraid I'd throw him out. I keep wondering where that fear came from. I had never hesitated to show him I loved him. Neither had our stepmother, Rose. Of course our father had always done his masculine thing."

RESPONDING TO YOUR FRIEND'S SYMPTOMS

If symptoms of ARC or AIDS appear, urge your friend to see a doctor who is familiar with AIDS. Go with him if that makes you both feel better. If you have had intimate contact with your friend— that is, if you have had sex with him involving the exchange of body fluids—then have your blood tested too, and make sure all this is done in the strictest confidence. Be extremely careful at this point how your own and your friend's medical bills are submitted to health insurance companies. Make sure there is no mention of AIDS or T-cell ratios. Speak to the doctor or medical lab about this. Many insurance companies will try to cancel your coverage at the first hint of AIDS. Assuming that all tests indicate that your friend has ARC, then urge him to modify his behavior to avoid irritating the condition or further weakening his body. You should remember, these symptoms need not progress to full-blown AIDS, and the condition may well be reversible at this point. This does not mean that the virus will go away—infection, as far as we know, is lifelong—but *symptoms* can lessen or disappear.

James and Earl, brothers less than a year apart in age, black men in their mid-twenties, had been close all their lives, and had even left home together after high school to make their own way in a big city. They had lived together most of that time. James first noticed Earl's problem when he woke twice in the night and found Earl tossing and turning and sweating profusely. "What's happening?" he asked one night, waking Earl. Earl shook his head. "You tell me. I have little fevers all day. Then I sweat at night. I'm not feeling good."

"I began to pay much closer attention to him after that," James

16

said, "and I realized that Earl was getting sick. He had rashes, he started losing weight, he didn't have as much going on. I mean, Earl made things happen wherever he went. Me, I made elevators run, but Earl made the streets run. Finally, I said to him, 'You know, we got to get to a doctor. You can see this ain't right.' He had a beautiful build, and it looked like his body was slowly coming apart."

Changing Behavior

The first thing you must urge your friend to do is eliminate all high-risk behavior and begin to pamper himself. The following suggestions apply to all people at risk for AIDS and should be vigorously adhered to.

Safer sex only: No high-risk sexual activity, even with a spouse or long-term lover, unless you have been monogamous for the last ten years. Follow the safer-sex guidelines printed in Appendix C. Even if you and your friend both tested positive for HIV antibodies (if you decided to do this test), and you feel you can no longer infect each other with the virus, you cannot afford to expose your friend or yourself to any other venereal disease that some sex practices can cause even among monogamous couples; they may prove someday to be a cofactor in the onset of full-blown AIDS. There is also evidence that there are many variations of HIV. The effects of being exposed to several variations is not known, but further exposure could be dangerous and perhaps hasten the onset of illness.

Watch your health: You and your friend should start taking the best possible care of your health. This includes:

- Getting enough sleep every night; no all-night parties, or drinking at the bars till they close, or going through the weekend on five hours of sleep.
- Eating properly. Eat three meals a day. At least keep food in your body at all times. Don't skip meals and force your body into the strain of running on reserves. Don't eat meals of junk food. Take vitamins, and get a nutritional supplement if either of you is losing weight. You can find these supplements in many health food stores. Ask your doctor to recommend one, if you cannot find one to your satisfaction. Some are available through pharmacies, but they are expensive.

No recreational drugs: Stop recreational drugs—no poppers, crack, cocaine, grass, or heavy drinking. All these substances, some of them toxic, simply damage the body and make it less resistant to

17

disease. If you've stopped unsafe sexual practices, you should have no need to take antibiotics or iodine medicines after sex to prevent gonorrhea or intestinal parasites.

Plan trips carefully: Don't plan trips to places where sanitary standards are different from those in the United States, such as most of Latin America, Africa, most of Asia, and parts of Europe. The reason for this is very simple: Your friend's body has little resistance to infections like intestinal parasites and diseases that might be common in other parts of the world, but are not common in the United States.

Avoid crowds: Try to stay out of crowded places, if possible, simply to lessen your friend's exposure to colds and flus and any other airborne germs that might be present.

Avoid strong sun: Stay out of strong sunlight. Do not get sunburned. There is evidence that large amounts of sun on the skin weakens the immune system for a period of time.

Avoid any elective surgery: This is not a medical opinion and is based only upon observations of case after case by the authors. It appears that when men with even the mildest symptoms of AIDS have surgical procedures of any kind, they have a very hard time recovering. In some cases the symptoms of AIDS simply get worse and worse until a major opportunistic infection occurs a month or more after the operation.

Avoid stress: Stress can weaken the immune system. If your friend's work or aspects of his life are stressful, he must begin to plan a method of lowering his stress level. Of course, covering stress reduction would take a book in itself. But a few simple rules can help.

Start by noticing what causes the stress. This is a matter of paying attention to yourself, yet it is not as simple as it sounds. You have to learn to notice. "At this moment I'm calm. I don't feel any stress." Then later, "At this moment I'm not calm. I feel a great amount of stress. What happened between that first moment and right now?" Of course, the point is to become aware of the causes of stress at the moment they occur, not to notice only when you are already full of stress and tension.

You might discover that there are a million little irritations in your life. You can't stand the way your secretary answers the telephone or your boss yells. You find your daily trip on the freeway leaves you dazed. Your roommate seems not to be doing his share of the work at home. The person you are dating is not really dependable and leaves you waiting sometimes for up to an hour.

Notice the causes of the stress. Then work against them or eliminate them. If you cannot do anything about the cause, then try to change your attitude toward it. Get a book on stress reduction and begin to use stress reduction techniques, if they help and if this is a big problem for you or your friend. It may be that you will learn to deal with your stress in your own personal ways.

What's Left?

After this list of "don'ts," you and your friend might ask, "What's left?" What's left is what's important.

- Safer sex. Get one of the new safer-sex videos, and see how much fun all this can be.
- Companionship, the love of your partner, and your friends and family.
- Dinners with friends at home and in restaurants.
- Parks, the outdoors, and weekend trips.
- Cultural events, especially if you can go at off times to avoid crowds.

The main lesson to be learned here is that your friend must begin to pay attention to his body. And so should you, since you may now be under greater pressure than you have ever known. Your body—each person's body for that matter—will let you know when you are using it too hard, when you are doing something to it that is not healthful. You just have to be watching and listening. Am I getting too tired? Does it feel good to do this activity? Help your friend to notice by noticing yourself and talking about what you see and feel.

Now you and your friend must stop and think. What are we doing to ourselves? Who made the rules that say how we should behave if our behavior is destructive to our health? In other words, you and your friend should question why you have any need to do anything that is not healthful behavior. Can anyone who is urging you to do things that are dangerous to your health really be your friend? Is that person to be taken seriously? These are times of vast changes in our lives. You may discover that what you thought was important a month ago is trivial today, and perhaps even dangerous.

"I said to Earl one day," James said, " 'You've got to slow down. You can't keep up this running, coming home in the middle of the morning, sleeping all day. You're wasting away.' He looked at me like I was stupid. 'And if I don't keep up, how'm I going to make a living? This is a tough business, little brother. 'Yeah, and you ought to get out of it,' I said. But it didn't make any difference what I said, he was a big man and he was making money."

Be a friend: Try to include your friend in all the activities that you did previously, from skiing trips to shopping trips. But, when you're with him, pamper him a little. Try to see that he eats properly, doesn't get too tired, doesn't get drunk, doesn't use drugs. Try not to irritate him about your care.

Whatever you do, don't run away. Don't avoid him. Don't make your friend think that your behavior now is just a precursor of the abandonment he is going to feel if he gets truly sick. Remember that one of the most important components of health is a desire to be healthy. In other words, motivation. Someone who feels the companionship and love of his friends will have more reason to try to remain healthy or to try to regain his health. Should he get sicker, however, he is going to need you all the more.

2
BECOMING A CAREPARTNER OR CARING FRIEND

If you find yourself becoming a carepartner or a caring friend of someone with ARC or AIDS, you should be prepared for vast changes in your life. Nothing is ever the same once AIDS enters your life, and you have to deal with it on a daily basis. (For the sake of simplicity we will refer to ARC and AIDS only as AIDS for the rest of this chapter.)

Inexorably, whether you notice it or not, your interests will change, your needs and wants will change, even your values will change. Soon you may wonder, "What is happening to me? Why do so many of my conversations seem silly to me? Why is my job less interesting? Why am I always so restless? Why do I always seem to want to leave where I am to go somewhere else, usually to where my friend with AIDS is just then?" You will have become a carepartner, a caring friend. You will have begun to live a life probably more intense and painful than anything you knew before, but a life certainly richer and more rewarding.

SHARED EXPERIENCES

There are some experiences that almost all carepartners and caring friends share, some characteristics and attitudes that you will develop. These, too, are part of the definition of a carepartner or caring friend of someone with AIDS.

You cannot wait: As a carepartner or friend of a person with AIDS, your sense of time—and urgency—will change. Often, initially, you might feel that you have put your own life in parentheses for the duration, that you are waiting for the day when you can begin to live again. Then, one day it occurs to you. "What am I doing? What am I waiting for? If I am waiting for something, then I must be waiting for my person with AIDS to die." But this is not a healthy response. It cannot be, because it turns the time spent

21

with your sick friend into something negative, destructive—an experience no longer motivated by love, but driven by anxiety and inner conflict. You cannot say, "I am doing all I can to help you live, but I will never be free until you die."

Instead, like people in a thousand other situations of grave stress, you begin to learn to live for each day. "Today I will deal with today, and I will make life as rich for me and my friend with AIDS as I can. Whatever we would have done without the disease, we will do *with* the disease—if that is possible."

Tom said, "Because Mart and I both had been so sure it was going to be a quick, dismal, dreary end, each day that we had— each good thing that happened to us—we became aware of. It was a gift. Each additional day and joyful experience was a bonus that we hadn't expected to have. Therefore, we valued it even more."

A deeper relationship: As a carepartner and a friend, you will develop over time a deep, symbiotic relationship with your friend with AIDS. Because you are sharing some of the most profound moments in human life, you will be calm together, distressed together, panicky together, nervous together. And the changes can be sudden, devastating, soul-wrenching. When your friend goes through a period of being relatively disease-free and all is well, you and he may get the sense that everything may be all right after all. Perhaps you'll feel that you will both wake up to discover that this whole thing was just a bad dream, a nightmare you somehow shared.

When some opportunistic infection strikes again, you may go through the same fear and dread as the person with AIDS. Then, one of you grabs onto reality first, and you both calm down. "Look," one of you says, "we got through this before. We'll do it again. And we'll just have to deal with whatever comes along. That we owe to each other."

Len and Evan have been through many ups and downs during Evan's illness. Len, in his forties, an editor in a large publishing company, was in Texas visiting his family when Evan called him from his parents' home in Florida and told him he was sick again. Len said, "We both flew back home immediately. I remember on the plane that my mind was in turmoil. 'How did he get sick so soon again? He'd only been out of the hospital six weeks.' I felt so depressed and angry. When I got home, Evan was there with two friends who had picked him up at the airport. He, too, was discouraged. 'How can I get sick every six weeks?' he said. 'My body's not going to be able to take that.' But we sat together for a while, sort of leaning against each other, and we began to calm down. Then Evan's friends left, and we began to get things ready for him to

22

take to the hospital. Without saying anything, we both knew that we would do what we needed to do. The panic, the depression, all of that was gone."

Giving basic care: Finally, as a carepartner or a caring friend, you will give care at the most basic level to your friend with AIDS. You will run errands, wash clothes, cook meals, deal with doctors, argue with insurance companies, change sheets, take temperatures, dress sores, sit for hours to keep him company, wake up in the night to give medicine. And usually you will do all this while you continue to cope with your own life—going to work, dealing with the boss, taking the train or the freeway—and facing the changes taking place within yourself.

Hugh and John, both in their late thirties, went through incredible changes as John became sicker and sicker with chronic diarrhea. Hugh, a contractor, described his life in these words: "The first few months that John was sick, I just didn't believe it—I mean what do you do?—it was like every conceivable problem in the world was there. . . . I got a big job renovating a kitchen, and I was trying to do all the work myself, so I could make more money. Meanwhile I got up at six and made breakfast every morning, and then went to work, ran home to make lunch, ran back to work. So naturally everything got all screwed up, and I got fired. John owed two months' rent, I owed a month's rent. I told John everything was taken care of, meanwhile nothing was taken care of."

Suzanne described her life in these words after her daughter Michelle came down with AIDS: "I don't know how much of it was that I didn't want to think. I was constantly running. Anything she wanted I ran for. Even when I was visiting her in the hospital, I was running to Sixth Avenue, Seventh Avenue. 'So you want a grape, no problem.' Somehow, I think running is also running away from what's happening. It's too large a problem to really digest. I would talk about the fact that Michelle was dying, and we made funeral plans. But it's not really real. Not when it's one of your children."

ATTITUDES TOWARD AIDS

Being a carepartner or a friend of someone with AIDS is different from being the carepartner or friend of someone with any other apparently terminal illness, such as cancer. Carepartners and friends of people with AIDS encounter many attitudes and circumstances that make this experience different and more difficult. Here are some of attitudes and problems specific to AIDS.

A disease and a stigma: AIDS is disease, transmitted sexually or with IV needles, which at this time still remains incurable, and about which there is a great deal of misunderstanding; the disease is a stigma for an individual in and of itself. Many people are so afraid of AIDS that they react in ways they would never display toward someone with any other apparently fatal disease. They also react badly to people associated with those who have AIDS.

Jeffrey, Paul's lover, relates this story. "I went to a party just for a little while because I needed to relax, and this very handsome man came over to me and started a conversation. He wanted to know why I was by myself, since he said he couldn't imagine that someone hadn't managed to tie me down. I couldn't think of anything to say except the truth, so I told him about my lover, Paul, that he had AIDS. The change in him was amazing. He disappeared in no more than a minute. It was one of the first times I realized what this disease could mean. He treated me like I had leprosy. I was really hurt."

Prejudice against the afflicted: The majority of the people afflicted with AIDS continue to be homosexual men and IV-drug users, and these are populations toward which there is already immense bigotry and prejudice. With the diagnosis of AIDS, there comes the sense that people will now categorize both the ill person and his friend into one of these populations and will reject and despise them accordingly.

Suzanne lives in a beautiful town house with her husband, Bob, and her daughter Camille. "I always wish that I could paint a really good picture of Michelle," Suzanne says. "She was unusual, but the fact that she was a drug addict paints a certain picture. You know, there's a very large support network for the gay population with AIDS, but the stigma attached to anyone who was a drug addict already—this almost makes them modern-day lepers, and not just the addict, but the entire family, me, my daughter Camille, and my husband, Bob.

"Michelle was always a difficult child. She was born with four defects in her heart. And I think the medication that she received during all those years of operations and pneumonia just grew into street drugs. I don't think that's an unusual thing, but it's something the medical profession doesn't really examine."

James talks about when his brother Earl went into the hospital the first time. "I really got pissed. Here were all these brothers and sisters treating us like we were from another planet, coming into the room in space suits to stick a thermometer in his mouth. I said to one of the women, 'What's going to happen, Sister? Those germs going to jump off his tongue onto your arm?' She just looked at me like, 'Go to hell,' but she said, 'You boys did this thing to yourself. You got to pay the price. I ain't taking no chances.' "

Fear of infection: The contagious aspects of AIDS sets it apart, especially when spouses or lovers are involved. Usually, people caring for someone with a potentially fatal disease do not have the fear that they are going to get the illness, whereas a friend or a carepartner to a person with AIDS, because of previous exposures, may indeed have great and justified fear. This applies especially to lovers and spouses who have had sex with the person with AIDS. Parents do not have to deal with this, nor do friends who have not had a sexual relationship with the person with AIDS. Homosexual friends, however, have their own fears related to AIDS, and being around a friend with the disease only increases these fears.

What is more, even the most well-meaning and loving friend or relative, not to mention uncaring strangers, may be beset with fears of contagion that have nothing to do with reality. They might be afraid to drink from a glass in your friend's home or hospital room, or even to walk into the room without a mask and plastic covering from head to foot, to use dinnerware, to use the bathroom, to touch a doorknob. They might sit as far across the room away from your friend as they can. You know all this behavior is based upon irrational fears, but it hurts nonetheless.

The disease forces revelations: The revelation of the disease often means the inadvertent exposure of other aspects of a person's life that he may not have had to reveal in the past—such as the fact that he is homosexual or has used drugs intravenously. Again, this applies to people who have not "come out" to parents, siblings, fellow workers, or even to spouses.

Hugh became frightened because his friend John was very sick and he had not told his family anything about his illness. Hugh said, "I called his family and told them I thought they should come up. I had never spoken to these people before in my life. I told the brother that he should come up, but I didn't mention anything about AIDS. Later, when they were in New York, I was talking to John's mother and brothers in the waiting room. She was this very proper southern lady, who chain-smoked constantly, tailored to a tee, very charming, and she asked me. 'What's wrong with John?' So I told her that John had no immune system left.

" 'What does that all mean?' she asked. And I told her that John had AIDS. That must have been a shock to her, because she turned to one of her sons and said, 'I didn't know that John had that style of life. I do declare.' Then she turned to another of her sons and said, 'Robert, I think that we should go eat.' Then they left for lunch."

Abandonment: In any other terminal illness, the friend or carepartner will get a great deal of support from his own family and friends, and from the sick person's family and friends. But AIDS can cause not only death but abandonment by friends and family. In many cases both the ill person and the caring friend find themselves utterly alone, ignored by family and friends, at exactly the time when they have the greatest need to be surrounded by support. Incredibly, they can find themselves alone in dealing with the disease, or they have to rely on agencies set up to help them.

Michael said, "The minute that I heard that my friend, Joe, was in the hospital, I went to see him. When the diagnosis was confirmed, Joe called his family, and his family—well, his mother anyway—initially sounded like she was going to let him come home. She said, 'I talked to the doctors in New Orleans, and I'm finding out that I can't get it from kissing you, and we can share the same glasses and plates and stuff, so everything sounds okay.' It sounded like he was going home. Then, twenty-four hours later his father had flipped out and told him, 'You can't come home.'

"Joe didn't know what he was going to do. I said, 'You can come stay with me if you want.' I said it pro forma, strictly ritualistic. I really believed his family was going to get over their temporary aberration, and he was going to go home. That's really what I thought was going to happen. Of course, you know it didn't."

Mart had a very different experience. His mother came to stay with him four days after he came out of the hospital. "I had never told her I was gay," Mart said. "She had asked me once a year ago if I was gay, and I had denied it. When she got here, she was going on about how much healthier I was, that I was going to be fine. Tom got me to the side and said, 'You've got to tell her. Right away. You can't let her think that.' You see, we hadn't told anyone what was wrong with me.

"Tom went out and left me and my mother here together. And I said to her, 'I've got to tell you something pretty bad.' And I started to cry. She said, 'Tell me. Just tell me.' So I told her I had AIDS. I think I told her first that I was gay and that Tom and I had been more than roommates all these years. And that was a difficult thing to do, but once it was over, I felt relieved. She was supportive and has been since then."

Rose, Linda and Gary's stepmother, had raised her husband's three children since the oldest, Linda, was seven, and the youngest,

26

Gary, was two. Rose tells of the Saturday afternoon Linda and Gary came to see her and their father, Charlie. "When I saw them," Rose said. "I touched Charlie's arm, and we both knew something terrible was wrong with Gary. He had that look about him that said, 'serious illness.' We hugged him and had him sit in the big, stuffed chair. Linda explained it all to us. I guess that's what makes her such a good businesswoman. She knows all the facts, she lays out the alternatives, then she makes recommendations. 'He has symptoms related to AIDS,' Linda said, 'and some of them are very serious. There's the possibility at this point that he could recover his health if he gets bed rest, nourishing food, an environment without a lot of stress.' Before she finished, we knew that he might die from this illness.

" 'Then he should come home where I can take care of him.' I said. 'He's my son and my responsibility. No mother ever loved her son more.' I looked at Charlie, and he looked at Gary, 'Yes, by all means come home. If there's any place in the world where you can get well, it's under the care of Rose.' He reached over and put his hand on mine. So it was settled that afternoon. Gary planned to move the following weekend. Not one of us brought up the fact that Gary had just told us he was gay."

Avoiding the real issue: Sometimes, when homosexual men or homosexual couples—if they have not previously revealed their sexuality to their families—tell their families that one of them has AIDS, and hence that they are a homosexual couple, the families focus on the fact that they are homosexual, and not on the fact that someone has a possibly fatal illness. The families can then reject the person or the couple because they are gay and abandon them either for a short time or permanently. Families can react the same way to the revelation that someone has been an IV-drug user.

As a matter of fact, it may be easier for a family to abandon a family member who is part of a couple, because at least they know the ill person has someone to take care of him. It is incredibly devastating when a single person with AIDS reveals his illness to his family and his family rejects him. At that point, he has only friends and agencies to depend on, and he may have great fears of suffering and dying alone.

But abandonment can actually work positively for you and your friend. If both of you are strong enough, and you are emotionally healthy people at the onset of the illness, abandonment can bring you closer together emotionally. You will turn toward each other, because there aren't other supports. The intensity, the closeness, the loving, and the sharing in the relationship are at a level that many people never find throughout their lives. If you have to, you can go it alone.

Joan said of her husband's reaction to the news of their son David's illness, "Barry, basically, was flabbergasted. 'You mean David is a homosexual? I just can't believe it. He didn't get that from me!' I wanted to say to him that it was obvious all through high school and college that David was different. David didn't date many girls, and he never seemed very interested in them. So I repeated, 'Barry, David may get AIDS, that new disease. He may get very sick and die.' But Barry couldn't focus on David's illness. It was almost like he wasn't interested in it. 'They'll figure that out,' he said, sort of dismissing the whole thing—I think because he really didn't know anything about it. 'But this stuff with other boys . . . he was in the church choir. What if our friends find out?'"

Lack of support from medical professionals: Medical professionals and hospital staffs sometimes don't provide to people with AIDS the kind of support that they provide to people who have other potentially fatal illnesses. They may isolate the person, because they are not capable of dealing with the illness, either physically or emotionally. Some of them, despite the facts about AIDS that they have been told over and over again, are not able to cope with it, out of fear of contracting the illness themselves, or out of prejudice against the life-style of the sick person. Some medical professionals also do not provide the recognition to the carepartner or friend that they would automatically give to the significant other in some other relationship, such as parent, husband, or wife of the sick person. They ignore the need for the carepartner or friend to be involved in decisions regarding the patient.

Hugh said, "I took John down every week to the doctor for blood work. And every week he was ten or fifteen pounds lighter. And the doctor would say, 'This cytomegalovirus, sometimes it takes a long time to go away. He has a very severe case.'

"I called up the doctor, and I would say, 'Tell me. Does John have AIDS or what? Is he going to die?'

"And he would say, 'John does not have AIDS, and he's not going to die.'

"I said to him, 'Well, he certainly looks like it.' "

Nor do medical professionals, across the board, keep the carepartner or friend informed of the progression of the illness from the medical perspective or the medical processes involved. So the carepartner can even be isolated from professionals, who, generally in dealing with other illnesses, would try to involve a family member or spouse in the medical process.

These attitudes about AIDS, summarized here, make huge demands on the carepartner or caring friends. They must fight not only the disease but the rest of the world as well.

SPECIAL FEARS OF CAREPARTNERS AND FRIENDS

All of our friends make demands on us, and all of them come to us with assets and liabilities. We accept and overlook the liabilities because we like the person, because to us his assets outweigh his liabilities. It is the same with persons with AIDS. The demands they can make on us may be greater than those of any other friend. At the same time, the rewards they give us can be even greater yet. Nevertheless, when someone we know comes down with AIDS, sometimes our inclination is to stay away, to try to forget that we ever knew the person. Why? A complex web of psychological issues, mainly related to some of our deepest fears, comes into play.

Fear of our mortality: Except in wartime, when the circumstances are very different, we do not have to live with the real possibility of the deaths of our friends, especially when they are young, as so many persons with AIDS are. Such a possibility is the furthest thing from our minds. When we are confronted with the relentless fact of death, we don't know what to do. We don't know how to react, so we feel awkward, distressed, and downright terrified. "This could happen to me!" we think. Being around the person reminds us that someday we'll die too. So we stay away.

This strong aversion to death is a universal condition of all peoples in all societies, and how we are taught to handle it very much determines our attitude toward death. In the United States, we tend to deny and cover up death. We pretend that it doesn't happen, and we refer to it with euphemisms.

Mark and Sam have been friends since high school. Mark, twenty-six, a computer programmer living in Los Angeles, described his feelings this way. "Sam hadn't really been sick, so when he called me to tell me he had AIDS, I was shocked. I rushed over to see him. When he answered the door, I saw that he looked like he always did, except that he had this purple spot on his arm. It hadn't been there a week earlier when he and I went out dancing together. He kissed me on the mouth, as he always did, and I suddenly found myself pulling away. I was repulsed. I thought, 'My God, this man may be dying. Tomorrow morning I could wake up with a spot just like that on my nose.' "

Fear of contagion: You may be afraid that this person will give you the disease, even though you know better. You have heard

29

reports on the news or seen them in newspapers about the presence of the virus related to AIDS in saliva and other body fluids. You have been told that it can live for various lengths of time outside the body at room temperature. Will you come in contact with the disease by kissing your friend? By using any glassware or utensils in his house? When you go to the hospital, you may see the most incredibly elaborate isolation procedures in effect. So you wonder: "These people are supposed to know about contagion. If the disease is spread only by intimate contact with highly infected body fluids, what are they afraid of? Why are they wearing masks just to deliver a food tray?"

Suzanne's first experience with hospital procedures was terrifying. "That first Sunday, when Michelle was in the hospital, I remember arriving at her room and seeing this orange 'Isolation' sign, and people running in and out of the room—you know, when they first admit you, they put you through a million tests—and they were all wearing masks and gloves, and some had these Halloween costumes on. I became terrified. There was so much publicity around that time, and I was thinking about the rest of my family, about my other daughter. My God, Michelle has been going into the refrigerator and drinking from the milk carton. She had open herpes sores. She shared the bathroom with us, even though there's two bathrooms. We had all been taking care of her. So I spent a couple of days chasing young men up and down the hall asking about the rest of us. They all assured me that AIDS was not easy to get. The procedures are for the protection of the patient. They should explain that right off. That was such a frightening experience. I mean, they would come in covered in plastic to change the garbage."

Fear of similar life-styles: If you are a homosexual male or were an IV-drug user at any time, you may recall all the similarities in your life-style with that of the person with AIDS. "Is my fate already sealed?" you wonder. Again, this may cause you deep anxiety.

Mark said, "It seems like Sam and I have always been friends. We had fooled around a little in the beginning, but sex never really worked for us, so, with that out of the way, we became really good buddies. We did so many things together, you know, out to the bars, the discos, the baths, the beach, the movies. We went to San Francisco on weekends. We bought grass from the same guy. We always discussed all our little affairs. So when he got sick, I freaked out. How long was it going to be before it happened to me? I started looking in every mirror I passed for KS lesions. I couldn't believe that I was having these really negative feelings toward Sam."

Fear of helplessness: You may feel helpless to do anything for this person. Often, persons with AIDS become depressed, anxiety-ridden. They are going through the most difficult changes possible, and you don't know what to do to help them, even though they may be your old friends, people you love. You want to help, but you feel that you can't. So you stay away.

Linda tells what happened when Gary, her brother, came home to stay with their parents. "When everyone—I mean my mother and father and brother—got over the shock of finding out that not only was Gary gay, but that he had ARC and could get AIDS, then we all settled in to help him get well. He moved back into his old room at home, and much to my surprise, Mom and Dad let Bob, his lover, come to stay with him every weekend. 'He's so sick,' my father said, as if he needed to justify giving Gary the comfort of the person he loved, 'and the room has twin beds.' You know, they knew all along what was going on with Gary, but they never wanted to admit it or think about it, much less discuss it.

"After a few weeks, though, everyone started getting so depressed, because Gary wasn't getting any better. We all felt so helpless because nothing we did seemed to make any difference. He was still losing weight, and no one could get him to eat much, and the medicines were nothing but analgesics to keep his fever down. I remember one day my mother, Rose, called me and said, 'God forgive me, Linda, for even thinking such a thing. Sometimes I want to send Gary away. I don't want to see him. I want to shut the door to his room and pretend that he's still living in Chicago. I feel so helpless; I go out and sit in the car and cry so he can't hear me.' "

Wanting to be a friend: We don't feel good about staying away from our friend with AIDS. Usually we feel guilty. After all, this is a person who needs help and companionship—someone we may have shared many good times with in the past. Now we are going to behave just the same way as those who abandoned him when he really needed them. Our reaction at this point has much to do with how we see ourselves.

Most of us think of ourselves as loyal, trustworthy, faithful friends who can be counted on when the going gets tough. We may have been through hard times with our friend in the past, like the breakup of a relationship, the loss of a job, or the death of a family member. Caring for someone with AIDS or ARC will be much harder. But we can do it if we want to.

31

In a subsequent chapter, we will discuss these fears one by one and talk about how to deal with them. In the meantime, remember that each of these fears is natural, is normal under the circumstances, and that we should not feel ashamed or guilty because we have them.

HEALTH INSURANCE

At this point in your relationship with your friend with AIDS, there is one practical matter about learning to care that you must deal with immediately. Health insurance is critical and is of such importance it must be brought to your attention now.

If you or your friend have health insurance, hang on to it. Pay the premiums faithfully, and read the policy to see if there are ways the insurance company might try to cancel the insurance at the first hint of AIDS. Usually there is no way the company can do this if you have had the insurance for some time, especially longer than two years. If you or your friend have policies at work, get a copy of the policy and read about the conversion privileges in case one of you is forced to stop work. Most employee policies have clauses in them that allow the participant to convert the policy to individual coverage if he should be terminated at work. If you or your friend has to stop work, convert the policy as soon as it is allowed. However, conversion policies are often much less generous than the group policy. Some are nearly worthless. Investigate other possibilities ahead of time if you wish, but do not let an existing policy drop.

Getting health insurance: If you or your friend do not have health insurance, go out and get it. There is usually an open hospitalization plan at Blue Cross/Blue Shield. Look this company up in the phone book. This is not the best insurance program, but it can relieve you of tremendous problems. If there is open enrollment—meaning everyone who applies is accepted under certain conditions—you should sign up immediately. Remember, the most catastrophic bills, if you or your friend becomes ill, will be hospital bills, sometimes running at the rate of a thousand dollars a day.

If you can, get group insurance, if not through your job, then perhaps through a professional organization, a church, or your union. In fact, it is so important to have this insurance you may decide to change jobs to one with a good health insurance plan.

However, no matter how you go about getting the insurance, tell the truth on the application. If you withhold important information,

32

the insurance company will discover it when you make a claim and use it as an excuse to cancel your policy. You do not have to give information the company does not ask for, such as the results of blood tests you may recently have had.

Whatever you do, don't delay. If you have no health insurance coverage, start looking for it today. Inquire at several companies, but do not apply to more than one company at a time. If they find out you've applied to more than one company—and they probably will—they might all reject you, since this type of information is computerized just like credit information. Read the policy manual carefully to make sure that the plan covers AIDS-related illnesses.

Components of health insurance: Health insurance usually has two separate elements: hospitalization insurance and medical insurance. The first will pay for your hospital bills; the second, for doctors' bills. Hospitalization usually pays for all charges while you are in the hospital, including all medicines and tests, except for private doctors' charges. You will not be charged for visits to your room by doctors who are on the hospital staff. The hospitalization component of health insurance is usually more generous than the medical component.

Some health insurance policies pay 80 percent of doctors' charges up to a certain limit. Others, like Blue Cross/Blue Shield, will pay only a small part of the doctors' charges according to a set schedule the company publishes ahead of time. Usually, health insurance policies that pay a large part of doctors' charges are expensive. Most health insurance policies do not cover dental work or correctional care of the eyes, although many will pay for dental surgery or for medical problems with the eyes.

Health maintenance organizations (HMOs) are another way to get medical care at reasonable costs, although these organizations are not available in all parts of the country and may be unwilling to accept anyone at risk for AIDS. When you join an HMO you must go to that organization for medical care, unless you want to pay for it yourself. You have to use the doctors and hospitals affiliated with the organization. Your freedom of choice is severely restricted, and if the organization is incapable of dealing with AIDS, you could be in trouble.

If you have one of these organizations available to you at work, investigate the possibility of joining it. It may be very difficult to ascertain the quality of care given to persons with AIDS, since an inquiry about this condition could lead to automatic rejection. You may have to ask your friends or do other research. Call one or more of the organizations that were set up to help persons with AIDS-related problems, listed in Appendix D. It will take some time and effort to get this problem solved, but you must make the effort.

Robert Kuttner, economics correspondent for the *New Republic*, wrote in the June 30, 1986, issue of *Business Week* about the problem in health insurance in the United States:

> In the U.S., most working-age people receive health insurance as a fringe benefit of their job. Yet more than 35 million Americans have no health insurance. Whole categories of people can't get it because they are sick. Anyone with a cured cancer is routinely turned down for health insurance. The insurance industry would like to deny health insurance to people with a high risk of contracting acquired immune deficiency syndrome, a step that would probably be unlawfully discriminatory.

Mr. Kuttner then goes on to point out how the problem of AIDS "demonstrates the illogic of the entire health insurance system." The insurance company wants to make the largest profit possible and therefore tries to deny coverage to the people who are most likely to make claims—the people at the highest risk of getting sick, the people who need the insurance coverage the most.

When someone is denied insurance, somebody will end up paying, be it the individual, who uses up all his assets to pay his bills, or society, because medical providers will get the payments from some level of government. Of course, the solution to this problem might simply be to institute universal health insurance in the United States so that everyone who needs coverage can get it.

If all else fails, you or your friend might become eligible for Medicaid (for more information, see Chapter 9). To do this, your friend will not be able to have many assets. Discuss this carefully with a social worker in a hospital or at an agency set up to help persons with AIDS.

Finally, many insurance companies have policies that pay a certain amount of money for each day you are hospitalized, perhaps $60 to $120 a day. These policies do not require medical examinations and are available by mail. You often see ads for them in magazines. Since the policies are not expensive, this too might be an added form of protection you might get.

3

WHEN YOUR FRIEND IS DIAGNOSED:
The Medical Aspects

One of the most devastating, terrifying, and saddest moments you and your friend, lover, spouse, or child will ever live through is the moment you are told that he or she has AIDS. Our reactions are as different as our personalities. We can react with anger, intense fear, denial, even a certain numbness. More than likely, whatever your reaction, it is appropriate.

Hugh and John had been to doctors who specialized in intestinal parasites, seeking to find the cause and then a cure for John's chronic diarrhea. They were told to come back the next day for the results of some cultures. "The next day I didn't go with him," Hugh said. "But he got back about eleven o'clock, and he was crying. . . . He said that the doctor told him he had a case of AIDS. I said, 'Who told you you had AIDS? You just can't tell someone they have AIDS.' I just held him, trying to get him to calm down. I mean, there I was, comforting this person, and I was freaking out . . . most of the time during this experience, I'm giving comfort, and any second I'm ready to lose just about everything."

Jack and Bruce waited for the pulmonary specialist in the small room that was part of the emergency room. "The specialist came about three in the afternoon," Jack said. "He was a young man, kind of rugged-looking, like he grew up on a ranch in West Texas. He seemed like one of us. He leaned against the wall and looked at Bruce. 'Can I talk in front of him?' he asked, indicating me. 'That's Jack,' Bruce said. 'Anything you say to me you can say in front of him.' The doctor stuck out his hand, first to me then to Bruce. 'I'm Dr. Bill. Glad to make your acquaintance. May have seen you men around.'

"Then without any more introductions, he said to Bruce, 'You've got AIDS. The problem with your lungs is pneumocystis carinii pneumonia. That's the AIDS pneumonia. We're getting a room ready for you now. You'll probably be here two to four weeks. We can treat your pneumonia. Do you know anything about AIDS?' he asked.

"Bruce and I were both too stunned to answer. 'AIDS. It can't be,' I said. Bruce was shaking his head back and forth with his eyes sort of shut. 'Shit, my yellow rose of Texas,' he kept repeating. The doctor seemed to get uncomfortable, and he said, 'Look, I'll leave you men alone awhile. I'll be back later with your doctor when they've got you in a room.' As soon as he left, Bruce and I just grabbed for each other. We held on, rocking back and forth for the longest time. Later, we heard them coming to take him to a room."

Joan and Barry flew to the West Coast after their son David called them to say he was in the hospital. "When I walked into the room and took one look at him," Joan said, "I knew what the problem was, but something inside me was holding on to a thread of hope. But then David told us that he had AIDS. I felt my heart sink. I reached out and grabbed Barry's arm. My head spun around for a minute, and tears welled up in my eyes. Through my tears, I could see that David was looking at me, and he was afraid, and I realized, 'Well, okay, I can't make him feel more scared than he must already feel. I can't cry.' So I said, 'I love you,' and I got up and went over to the bed and hugged him. Barry just sat there speechless."

James and Earl were sitting together in a hospital room when the doctor told them that Earl had AIDS. "His case is unusual, because he has both PCP and KS," the doctor said. James says of that moment, "I wanted to punch out the doctor. I was so pissed. 'What are you talking about, fool?' I wanted to say. 'Where you coming from with this shit?' I wanted to get crazy. But Earl was sitting right next to me, and he'd heard what I heard. So I turned to him, and his eyes were closed, and his face was all pulled tight, like he looked when he broke his arm. And he was hanging on to his chair like he was going to fall out. I thought, 'God almighty, that doctor just told me my brother has AIDS.'"

Marilyn and Tim, a married couple both in their late twenties, were both part of a very high-fashion scene in New York. Tim was the sales manager and top sales representative for a very popular clothes designer, and Marilyn was a model who worked steadily, although she had not made any covers yet. They had used drugs intravenously a few times but thought nothing of it. Tim had been feeling sick for two or three months, until finally, they went to the doctor, who then sent them to a specialist. Marilyn said of their visit, "It didn't register. He may as well have been from planet X. The doctor had just told me and my husband that he had PCP, 'and that means AIDS,' he added. But I was either numb or freaked out, or something, because I just said, 'How long will he have to be in the hospital?' We were planning a trip to London next month, and if we have to put it off, we have to give them a month's notice.' After I said that I thought, 'What are you saying? Have you lost your mind?' It didn't register for days. It just wasn't possible. And for days Tim just shut down. He didn't say anything."

Your reaction: If you call a friend to ask how he is doing, or if you are visiting him in the hospital, and he tells you he has AIDS, how do you react? What do you say? There is no easy or right answer, but in general, it is best to allow your friend to focus on himself. Don't start talking about your fear of getting AIDS. You will sound insensitive. Your friend may well think, "He's worried about his window getting broken while my house is burning down."

Tell your friend that you are very sorry to hear this news, and tell him how you feel. Then ask, "But how do you feel? Can you tell me? Who have you told? Tell me if there is anything I can say or do right now except to tell you that I love you and will stick by you."

DEALING WITH YOUR FRIEND'S NEEDS

At this stage you do not have to confront what the diagnosis means. You do not have to deal with where all this might lead over a period of months or years. You have to deal with *right now and the very near future.* Your friend is probably going through the same reactions you are. You should try to get both yourself and him to concentrate on what needs to be done right now. It will help you get over this period of shock. Stay busy. Get yourselves set up.

Your immediate concern is to make sure that your partner or friend has the best of everything that can be provided to him by medical professionals and hospital staffs. You need information. You need resources.

The right doctor: Are you and he satisfied with your friend's doctor? If not, speak to friends who may have had experience with or developed some expertise about AIDS. Get references from organizations dealing with AIDS patients. Talk to doctors and nurses about who is well known for treating AIDS patients in your region. If you have to, call the hospitals in the area for recommendations. Do not think you have to remain with the doctor who diagnosed the case, or the one who referred you to the doctor who made the diagnosis. But whatever you do, make sure you have confidence in your friend's doctor.

Howard and Alex had to solve this problem. Immediately after Alex was diagnosed with KS, Howard went to their regular doctor, the same internist who had been seeing Alex, to get himself checked out. But the doctor didn't seem to understand Alex's condition, even after the diagnosis by an oncologist. Howard says, "I told the internist that Alex had been diagnosed with KS, how tired he was, how he coughs, and he can't control himself when he coughs. You know, Alex had been calling his doctor practically every day about the cough, but the doctor told him it was nothing.

"So, finally, after my making an issue with the doctor—I guess I put a bug up his ass—he agreed and said he would try to get Alex into the hospital.

"The doctor who diagnosed the KS didn't say anything about going into the hospital, but he did say that Alex shouldn't go to this internist anymore, because our doctor didn't know anything about AIDS or AIDS-related diseases. He suggested to Alex that he go to see another doctor at a totally different hospital, which he eventually did . . . once the pneumonia was arrested. He was certainly right. Alex's cough turned out to be PCP."

The right hospital: Are you and he satisfied with your friend's hospital? What kind of reputation does it have? Find out. Ask friends. Ask doctors. Ask agencies dealing with AIDS. If you are not convinced that your partner will be getting the best possible care, then find a doctor who can put him into a hospital that you will feel satisfied with. If you are in a large metropolitan area, you may find hospitals that have much experience with AIDS patients, such as San Francisco General, which has a special ward, and Bellevue in New York, which has a special program. Newly opened in Houston is the Institute for Immunological Disorders, a special AIDS hospital. If you are in a small town, you must be very careful about leaving your friend in a local hospital.

Stella tells about her odyssey to find the right hospital for her husband, David. "At that time David was having a lot of trouble with his ankle joints. He saw an orthopedic surgeon in Louisville, and he suggested that David have ankle surgery. In July 1983, David had the ankle surgery. And I'm positive he had AIDS before the surgery, in my own mind. But, of course, convincing David, there was just no way. So he went ahead with the surgery, and he developed what the doctors here thought was pneumonia. They treated him here for approximately six weeks. We did go back to the doctor in Louisville, and he said pneumonia, too. And finally, I took him to the emergency room at Somerset and convinced them that there was a bad problem there. So they did admit him, but it was just for the normal pneumonia. The doctor here was very nice, and he did the best he could, but I tried to explain to him that David had AIDS, and I couldn't make him understand or believe me, especially around here where we've only had thirty-eight cases of AIDS in the state so far. So I finally called David's hemophilia nurse in Louisville, and I said, 'Either get him out of this local hospital, or I'll take him out myself.' So they decided to transfer him to the University of Kentucky. When I got up there, I told the doctor I was almost positive that David had AIDS. He said, 'No, he doesn't have AIDS. As a matter of fact, I don't think he's very sick at all.'

"So I said, 'Test him.' Five days later we got the diagnosis that David did indeed have AIDS. He had pneumocystis, and he had a hard time recovering from that because it had gone on for six weeks. He spent seven and a half weeks in the hospital that time, and he did recover with some drugs from the Centers for Disease Control."

It is extremely important to you and your friend that you both feel he is getting the best and most up-to-date care. So if you have to spend time taking care of this now, do it. It will free you for many other problems you will need to solve later.

Join a carepartners' group: If you are the primary care giver or an involved caring friend, try to join a carepartners' group, if any exist in your area. These groups can be the greatest resource you will find anywhere. Over the period of time that they exist—some for several years now—the groups accumulate, like oral histories, the experiences of all the people who have ever been in the group. You can bring up any problem to these groups, be it medical, emotional, or mental, and someone will have been there before or know someone who has.

In large cities, there are special groups for partners, parents, and friends. Each one of these groups will have a slightly different perspective on the situation and problems unique to the partici-pants. Parents have to deal with the possibility of the loss of a child, but they should not have to deal with fear of infection, as would a spouse, lover, or friend who has had sex with the person with AIDS.

Tom explains one important understanding he got from joining his carepartners' group: "I began to realize that Mart's illness wasn't going to be all doom and gloom when I got into my carepartners' group and began meeting men who had much longer experiences than mine and many ups and downs. And most of all, Mart has been doing very well."

After Tim's diagnosis of PCP and his later diagnosis of KS in the hospital, he and Marilyn did not know how to relate to each other. They fought. They were like two children lost. Marilyn said, "I had to do something, because I didn't know anything about what was going on, or what was going to happen. So I joined a group of women whose husbands or sons had AIDS. I just couldn't believe my ears. I mean the stories those women told kept me up all night from one week to the next. And Tim and I were not getting along at all. All of a sudden he had some need to tell me all. He was telling me stories about other women, and even some men he had had sex with. I don't know why he thought I wanted to hear that stuff. Probably he didn't care if I wanted to hear it or not, he just wanted to talk about it. I started thinking, 'I don't want to go through this. Nothing says I have to deal with this or with Tim.' And it was then that I started thinking about leaving. I brought up how I felt in group. Most of the women seemed to understand, but one thought I was being a selfish bitch, planning to run out on my husband when he needed me."

Linda and Rose drove seventy miles in one direction to attend a meeting of women involved with persons with AIDS. Rose explains her reaction. "I'm in my sixties now, and it's hard to surprise me. But that group of women amazed me. I felt immediately that I had found kindred spirits. We are all faced with this terrible thing. My son, that woman's husband, that woman's daughter, they all had this disease. I'm not one who cries a lot, but I cried when I talked about Gary. So did Linda. We love him so much, but we were just watching him waste away before our eyes. They all understood. They held our hands. They made all kinds of suggestions of ways to help Gary. Then, when the meeting was over, each woman hugged all the others. We didn't go every week after that, but we went as often as we could, and everyone understood."

RECOGNITION FROM MEDICAL PROFESSIONALS

Sometimes the medical professionals that you and your friend have to deal with may not treat you as an important person or significant friend in the life of the person with AIDS. They do not take your relationship seriously. You will be surprised at the number of doctors—specialists of different kinds—who can become involved in your friend's case, so that means that you will encounter this problem over and over again. You and your friend should establish in the beginning the following: Does your friend want you present, when possible, for medical examinations? For medical consultations? Does he want you informed about any and all medical procedures? Later, you will both have to decide if he wants you to have the power to sign consent forms for treatments or procedures. (We will cover this matter in Chapter 8.)

If the answer is yes, then you should tell the doctor together.

You can simply say, "I am the primary care giver to the person, and I want to be present when possible at all examinations and consultations. I want to be kept informed of any and all medical procedures used on him, and I want the right to consult with him before any procedure is performed."

If the doctor asks, "Who are you?" then tell him or her that you are the 'significant other' or the 'caring friend,' in this person's life, and that you expect to have the same rights and privileges as a spouse, sibling, or parent. If the doctor seems hesitant, then have your friend repeat the message. Have your friend tell you not to leave the room if the doctor or nurse so orders, and have your friend inform all medical professionals that whatever they have to say to him, they should say in front of you. Other people before you have had to handle this situation.

"For a long time, when the doctors came in to see David, " Stella said, "I was polite and left the room, because they wanted me to. Then one time, David was trying to tell me something, but you know, with the cytomegalovirus he wasn't speaking too clear, and then finally, I realized what he was telling the doctor. 'She doesn't have to leave anymore. She wipes my butt, and she can stay.' So after that I stayed in the room when the doctors were there. I was sure glad he said that. He had a great sense of humor, all the way through." Stella laughed.

Tom and Mart also had to confront the problem of recognition from medical professionals. "I was at work. Mart called me and said, 'They just told me they're moving me into a private room, because of the possibility that it's AIDS. Can you come and help me?' He sounded very upset. I said. 'Sure, right away.' So I left work, went over there, and we got all his stuff together. After a while they moved us to a new room.

"Then we waited and waited, and I was fussing around with the plants. Finally Dr. K. came in. He said, 'Hi. Can I speak to you?' Mart said, 'Sure.' Dr. K. looked at me and said, 'I mean alone.' Like that.

"After I left, he told Mart that he had a confirmed diagnosis of pneumocystis and that it was AIDS. So Mart told him that anything he had to tell him he should tell me at the same time. Dr. K. came out and called me into the room and apologized for excluding me, but said that he always handles these things privately with the patient first."

"Somehow, because of Dr. Bill," Jack says, "Bruce and I knew not to take any crap from the other doctors and nurses and the cleaning people in the hospital. Right from the beginning, I think we scared everybody anyway. I mean we're both big men, and we

41

don't always act friendly. So they gave me some kind of a pass, so that I could come and go when I wanted to, and I used to stay there with him a lot and sleep on a cot in the room. You know, his family was way up in the Panhandle and he didn't want to tell them anything. And my family? Well, they live in a small town in East Texas, and I sure as hell wasn't going to tell them anything. So we stuck together in that hospital. I didn't care what anybody who worked there thought about us."

You must remember that medical professionals in most cases are not accustomed to dealing with homosexual couples, IV-drug users, or people with AIDS, and they do not know how to react. It is up to you and your friend to educate them about how you expect to be treated. They will learn to respect you.

If you find doctors who are impossible to deal with, who are disrespectful, then get rid of them if you can. If they are part of the hospital staff, tell them first that you are going to report them to the administration, and if the behavior continues, do so. If that fails, speak to your local medical association. Finally, make a complaint about your friend's treatment to the state agency that regulates hospitals. They will investigate your complaint.

LEARNING ABOUT THE DISEASE

Carepartners, parents, friends, spouses, and many persons with AIDS become practical experts on the disease, the opportunistic infections associated with it, and the drugs used to combat both the disease and these infections. They read extensively, go to lectures and conferences, and do research in medical libraries. This, too, is a worthwhile activity, since it helps both you and your friend make better and more informed decisions in dealing with the doctors and the treatments they prescribe. Remember, AIDS is new to medical professionals too, and in some situations they might not be aware of some treatment that you have read about or heard of in support groups which is being tried at another hospital. They might also be doing endless testing on your friend for their own information, to learn more about the disease and how it affects the body. You and your friend might decide that some of the tests cause him too much discomfort; you can demand that they be discontinued.

Participate: You and your friend should take an active part in your friend's therapy. The more you and he know about what is going on, the more you will feel part of the fight. This is very important not just physically but emotionally and psychologically as well. If your friend feels that he is the helpless victim not just of the disease but of medical professionals and of the hospital and its staff as well, then it will be much more difficult for him to fight. His will to fight on is probably the most critical element in all the therapy.

There are several publications that can help you learn more about the disease. You will find them listed in the bibliography at the end of this book. Each publication is accompanied by a brief description, which should help you choose which might be most helpful to you.

Opportunistic infections: AIDS is a very complex disease that manifests itself in myriad different ways, so generalizations about it are difficult and, of course, do not apply in all cases. But the vast majority of all AIDS cases are diagnosed with the manifestation of certain opportunistic infections. *Pneumocystis carinii pneumonia* (PCP) is the most common, followed by *Kaposi's sarcoma* (KS). In descending order of occurrence, the following infections appear in AIDS patients: candida esophagitis, cytomegalovirus, cryptococcosis, chronic herpes simplex, cryptosporidiosis, and toxoplasmosis. You will probably want to know more about these infections; they are covered in Chapter 5, where each is described and the drugs used in each case are named. Some of these drugs are very toxic and have many undesirable side effects. The more you know, the more you will be able to participate in your friend's treatment. Always discuss everything you know about your friend's condition with him, if you sense that he is willing. And always be ready to talk to the doctor.

Stella more than once correctly diagnosed her husband David's condition. "I was the one who told the doctors David had Addison's disease. I said to the doctor, 'He's turning black. There's a problem here.' I got out the medical books and found out what was going on. The nurses told the doctors that they better listen to me, 'She's never been wrong yet.' Whenever he had a disease, I told him, 'He's got this, so let's do this.'"

Tom feels that his intervention may have saved Mart's life, or at least spared him much greater suffering. "They started treating Mart with Bactrim, and he didn't respond. He started to degenerate, deteriorate. The pneumonia progressed for three days. By the end of the three days, he was on oxygen and could hardly breathe. The next step was the respirator. I was on the phone to the doctor several times, telling him that the treatment wasn't working and something was going wrong, because Mart wasn't getting any better. I was getting frantic. Finally, the doctor came in—and that's when they changed to pentamidine. As soon as they did that, he

43

started to respond. He had twenty-one days of pentamidine. He just gradually got better. By then we were starting to get educated as to what AIDS is."

If your friend is diagnosed with KS, no immediate medical treatment may be necessary. Talk to the doctors about this. Chemotherapies used for KS are very toxic and should be used only when they become necessary. There are also experimental programs using various drugs that you might want to try, if you and your friend should have the opportunity and decide it could be helpful. We discuss experimental drugs later in this chapter, as well as alternative therapies. But remember, in most cases of KS, you have time to decide what to do. Don't feel rushed into anything.

Marilyn and Tim had a very positive experience with the oncologist who diagnosed Tim's KS. "The first thing he told us was that, if we wanted to, we could do nothing," Marilyn said. "Tim's lesions were just on the skin, and there wasn't any danger to his life from them now. They were on his legs. 'Also an advantage,' the doctor said, 'because he can hide them for cosmetic reasons, if he wants to.' The doctor told us that radiation was very effective against KS on the arms and legs, but really wasn't necessary now. If the lesions spread, we could try chemotherapy, if it became necessary, but that the chemotherapies were very toxic. We could try interferon later if we wanted to, but Tim couldn't get in an experimental program because he'd had the pneumocystis before. As it was, we didn't do anything until much later, when we had to."

Jerry, a real estate salesman in his late thirties, was never sick a day and showed no symptoms of AIDS when he noticed red "spots" on his legs. After three months of avoiding the issue, his lover, Arnold, made an appointment for him, and he went to the doctor, who did a biopsy of the "spots." A week later the doctor told Jerry he had KS. "After a few days, when Arnold and I got over the shock, I started looking at all the alternative treatments. One looked worse than the other. Finally, I talked to some guys who were on a macrobiotic diet. A couple of them had been healthy for more than three years after diagnosis with KS. So I decided to try that. For about six months the spots got worse, then they started to fade and flatten out. It's been a year and a half now, and I've still never been sick, not even with a cold. Arnold and I live an almost normal life."

Other opportunistic infections must be treated immediately, PCP especially. Read about these in Chapter 5.

In the United States all drugs sold by drug companies must be approved by the Food and Drug Administration, an agency of the executive branch of the federal government. Before a drug is sold to the public, the Food and Drug Administration tries to make sure that the drug is effective against the condition it is prescribed for—at least that it does what the drug company claims—and that it does not have side effects that outweigh the possible good results from using the drug. To assure that at least these minimum standards exist, the agency requires that drugs be put through a series of tests and trials. Early trials of a drug are "dose escalation" studies that involve small numbers of people who are given different doses of the same drug to determine the most effective and safe dosages. Once dosage is established, clinical trials are begun. These are usually "double-blind" studies, because half the people in the trial are getting the drug and half the people are getting a placebo—perhaps sugar or salt—and neither the patient nor the doctor conducting the trial knows until the results of the study are in who was getting what. The same procedures are being followed in the development of drugs for use with AIDS patients.

Some drugs are antivirals, which in some way might interfere with the virus itself. Others are immune-system enhancers, intended to boost the damaged immune system. Among the antivirals being studied during 1986 were azidothymidine (AZT), foscarnet, HPA-23, ribavirin, and dideoxycytidine. Immune-system enhancers included interferon alpha, ABPP (biopirimene), and isoprinosine.

AZT: One drug has begun to show some promise in prolonging the lives of some people with AIDS. Toward the end of September 1986, the federal government and the drug company Burroughs Wellcome announced that azidothymidine, called AZT, had been used in double-blind studies on 282 patients at twelve research centers. The result had been so promising that it was decided to give the drug to all the people in the study. Of the 145 patients receiving AZT for periods ranging from three to six months, only 1 had died, while 16 of those in the other group receiving placebos had died. The announcement of this success also said that those taking the drug had fewer infections and other AIDS-related problems. The drug acts in a way that interferes with the replication of the virus within the cell.

Officials of the government and the drug company were quick to point out that AZT was not a cure for AIDS, that no one knew the long-term effects of the drug, and that it apparently was already showing some bad side effects, such as interfering with the bone marrow's ability to make blood cells, thus causing anemia. Nevertheless this drug has shown more promise than any produced so far. There is a toll-free hot line set up by the National Institutes of Health and Burroughs Wellcome, the company producing AZT, for physicians and AIDS patients seeking information about this drug: 1–(800) 843-9388.

Getting into a program: At any one time there are openings in these clinical trials for approximately a quarter to a third of all persons with AIDS in the United States. This means that all the rest are left out, and they probably would gladly participate—even though they know they might be getting a placebo or that the drug or procedure might be dangerous.

Many experts have questioned the morality of limiting the access of persons with AIDS to drugs that might help them. Dr. Martin S. Hirsch of Harvard University, at congressional hearings in 1986, called these restrictions a "national tragedy," and said that the trials should be open to everyone. Dr. Mathilde Krim, cochairperson of the American Foundation for AIDS Research, has questioned whether researchers have the right to refuse people "a small measure of hope or the dignity to fight to the end." Nevertheless, for the foreseeable future there will not be openings in the trials for all those wishing to participate.

If you and your friend wish to learn about, and perhaps participate in, the experimental drugs currently being tested, first ask your doctor what programs are available. Often, if doctors are involved in AIDS treatment, they are involved in research or drug trials also. If your doctor is not helpful, then contact the hospital where your friend is treated. Doctors associated with the hospital may be running trials or may be willing to place your friend in a program. You can ask other people with AIDS, other friends or carepartners, and organizations involved in helping people with AIDS. You can also contact the National Institute of Allergy and Infectious Diseases, Office of Research Reporting and Public Response in Bethesda, Maryland: (301) 496-5717; or the Centers for Disease Control in Atlanta, Hot line: 1-(800) 342-AIDS. If you call these organizations, ask for the person in charge of setting up, or reporting on, AIDS drug testing.

The federal government has also designated fourteen institutions as research centers for AIDS drug trials. These are Memorial Sloan-Kettering Cancer Center and New York University Hospital in New York City; Harvard University in Cambridge, Massachusetts; Johns Hopkins University in Baltimore, Maryland; Stanford

University in Stanford, California; the University of Miami, in Coral Gables, Florida; the University of Pittsburgh, in Pittsburgh, Pennsylvania; the University of Rochester in upstate New York; the University of Southern California in Los Angeles; the University of Texas at Austin; the University of Washington in Seattle; and the University of California, Los Angeles, San Diego, and San Francisco campuses. It will take effort and persistence to get into these trials, but it may be worth the effort, if not medically at least psychologically.

Federally unapproved therapies: Many persons with AIDS are willing to try almost anything that may help them, especially since there seems to be so little they can do to fight the disease. As a consequence people are using drugs that sound promising if they can obtain them anywhere in the world.

One of the most common unapproved therapies is a combination of the drugs ribavirin and isoprinosine. These drugs can be bought in Mexico over the counter in drugstores. Much has been said and written about this combined therapy, which has given some people great hope. However, people do not claim to have been cured by taking these drugs; they say only that their health has improved.

If you and your friend decide to try any unapproved drugs follow at least minimal precautions:

- Discuss the therapy with your friend's doctor. Try to arrange with the doctor to have periodic blood tests, so that you really know what the drug is doing, if anything. You should make sure that, even if it does no good, at least it will not do harm and not perhaps worsen your friend's health.

- Get the drug from a reliable source. If you buy the drug on the street, you have no way of knowing what you're buying or what you're giving to your friend.

- Get the dosage right. If two are good, four are not twice as good and could be poison.

- If your friend's health starts to change for the worse, stop the drug immediately.

There are risks, sometimes serious risks, in taking any unapproved drugs, and we are in no way advocating that people do this. But if they choose to try this route, it is understandable under the circumstances. It gives people hope.

Nonmedical therapies: There are many nonmedical therapies that people have found helpful to them in one way or another. Whenever anyone tells you about one of these therapies, find out

47

what results are expected, the benefits of these results, and the risks your friend is taking. Among these therapies are vitamins, nutrition programs, special diets, acupuncture, meditation, yoga visualization, and stress reduction techniques. Your medical doctor will not be encouraging when you mention many of these therapies but will probably tell you that most won't do your friend any harm. Some of these therapies are listed here.

- Macrobiotic diet: Many of those who have KS and no other opportunistic infection have tried the macrobiotic diet proposed by Michio Kushi, who has founded the Kushi Institute in Massachusetts. Proponents of the diet claim that it purifies the body, brings it into balance, and slows, if not stops, the progress of the disease. There is considerable evidence that this diet works in some persons with KS and prolongs life. See the *New York Native*, No. 170, July 21, 1986. You can find out more about this diet by calling the Macrobiotic Center of New York at (212) 877-1110. We will discuss this diet further in Chapter 5.

- Vitamin therapy: People have tried megadoses of vitamins, especially vitamin C, and some claim results from this therapy, but the results seem to be temporary. You can write to Health Action, 704 S.E. 16 Street, Portland, OR 97214, for more information about this therapy.

- Holistic approaches: The following description of holistic medicine appears in the literature of the Holistic Medical Association. "Holistic medicine is considered to be a system of medical care which emphasizes personal responsibility and fosters a cooperative relationship among all those involved, leading toward optimal attunement of body, mind, emotions, and spirit."

  Apparently, holistic medicine does not exclude conventional medications, but includes them in a broader program that looks at the whole person. A holistic medical program will include medication, and perhaps even surgery, but it will analyze the person's whole life. What are his values? What does he eat? What does he think of himself? Is self-hate part of his sickness? Does he rely on the spiritual side of life for any nourishment, or is this something he ignores? You can get the *Holistic Health Care Directory for AIDS* by writing to NY AIDS Action, 263A West 19 Street, New York, NY 10011.

- Louise Hay is popular among persons with AIDS. Her emphasis is on self-healing, self-nurturing, and wellness. She has produced a tape, "AIDS, A Positive Approach," which many persons with AIDS have found helpful and which can be obtained at bookstores selling largely gay materials. Her book *You Can Cure Yourself* (Hay House, 1984) can be obtained by writing Hay House, 1242 Berkley Street, Santa Monica, CA 90404.

Midwest Research, Inc., has produced a tape entitled "Psycho-neuroimmunology: The Beneficial Effect of the Mind on Health" (tape 64). This is a subliminal tape, designed to be played while the listener does other activities, even talking on the telephone, watching TV, or eating. Concentration is unnecessary since the subconscious mind picks up the messages, even if the conscious mind is ignoring them. Subliminal tapes should not be used during sleep, as they could interfere with the natural process of sleep. To find out more about this tape call Midwest Research at 1–(800) 221-7295.

Whether you or your friend have any interest in these different therapies is entirely a personal preference. They are listed here for your information only, and no claims are made that any of these are effective or ineffective.

4

COPING WITH THE DIAGNOSIS:
The Emotional Aspects

Sometimes, almost at the moment that they learn that their friend has ARC or AIDS, carepartners or caring friends undergo a profound emotional experience. In a single moment the carepartner or friend draws incredibly close to this ill person. They bond. This powerful emotion serves as a sustaining force throughout the whole arduous journey that is AIDS.

Tom describes his feeling after he and Mart had been told that Mart had AIDS: "One of the things that happened instantly, within minutes after I found out Mart had AIDS, was that I said to myself, 'I am going to do everything I can to help Mart through this.' There wasn't any question. I didn't even consider any other alternative. There wasn't any other alternative. It was simple—'If this is true, then it's as if I've got it, too.' We're in this together. I took a vow, without consciously doing it, that I was going to be a rock for Mart to the best of my ability."

Jack tells of his experience that day after Bruce was diagnosed in the emergency room. "When they got us up to his room, for the first time ever, I saw tears run down Bruce's cheeks. You know, we don't cry down here. We don't hug either, but who gives a shit anymore. We'd been hugging down in emergency. I said to him, 'I don't want you to be afraid. I'm going to be here, night and day if you want me to. We're both strong, and we're both tough, and we're going to make it through this thing. I'll cover your back, and you can depend on me. God knows, you're the first man I ever really loved, and I'm not letting you go anywhere without a fight. And you can bet your ass I never lost a fight in my life.' He smiled when I said that and pulled me to sit on the bed. 'We're a tough team,' he said, 'and I never lost a fight either.' Then we both cried a little and sort of calmed down."

At the beginning of John's illness, Hugh and John were having great difficulty because Hugh had to work to pay the rents on both their apartments and John needed twenty-four-hour care. So for a while, John went to stay with a friend, Armando. But John wasn't getting the care he needed there either, so Hugh decided John needed to be in his own apartment for Christmas. Hugh describes what happened: "I went out and got a Christmas tree. I took it to John's apartment and decorated it. John had a beautiful apartment. Then I went to Armando's to get John and take him home. It was really hard to get a cab, and John was looking horrible. I remember sitting in the back of the cab, holding John, and I had such feelings. I mean, I think I bonded with him at that moment. I don't know if the feelings come when you know somebody is dying, or if you've always loved them. To this day I don't understand these feelings, and I still have them."

Mark describes what happened to him about a week after his friend Sam told him he had AIDS. "I took off work early that day to take Sam to the hospital because they were going to run some tests on him, and when I drove up to his apartment building, he was sitting there on the steps outside all by himself. He looked so lost, like this little guy waiting to get swallowed up by the big world. I felt so much love for him. I wanted to protect him. It was like all the good feelings that I'd ever had for him, in all the years I'd known him, came back at once. I knew then that I'd always be his friend. No matter what happened."

Joan was shocked when her husband, Barry, finally spoke that day in David's hospital room when they learned their son had AIDS. "Barry sat there speechless for a while, then his face changed, and I thought he was going to cry. He got up and put his hand on David's shoulder. 'I'd give anything if I could stop this from happening,' he said. 'But I can't. I just want you to know that your mother and I love you. We'll take care of you. We want you to come home as soon as you can travel.'"

Joan continued, "I knew what it was costing him to say those things. I had never heard him say, 'I love you,' to one of our children, and I was thinking of all our friends—church, the bridge club, the country club. What were they going to think? It scared me to think of his golf buddies—their jokes about queers, and how God was teaching those perverts a lesson. I thought to myself, 'All these years of marriage and he's a lot braver than I thought.'"

But along with that bonding, or sometimes in place of it, some people experience an almost overwhelming sense of fear, dread, and revulsion; they may not be able to overcome these feelings. If they can't cope, they will disappear from the life of the person with AIDS—and they might also break off contact with his caring friend or carepartner. But after the initial shock, most caring people will do all they can to handle their fears; the bonds they feel will carry them through.

Jerry's lover, Arnold, initially had an argument with his sister Sofia when he told her that Jerry had AIDS. She was horrified. She had been friends with them for years, since Jerry and Arnold had been together, and they visited her and her husband many times. Now she was pregnant and terrified. "She told Arnold that he and I couldn't come to dinner that Thanksgiving," Jerry said. " 'I'm finally pregnant,' she explained, 'after all these years of trying, and I'm not going to take any chances with it.' Arnold laughed at her. He said, 'You can't get AIDS from having dinner with someone or having them in your house.' She said, 'Well, tell that to Bob. That's not what I've been hearing.'

"I only heard one end of the conversation," Jerry continued, "but they started yelling at each other, and then Arnold hung up. About a month later, before Christmas, Sofia called and asked us to come to her house for Christmas. She didn't explain to Arnold why she wasn't afraid anymore."

CONFRONTING FEAR

When your friend is diagnosed with AIDS, you will probably be terrified, both for your friend and for yourself. At this early stage, fear is an utterly natural response. You are facing an intense and difficult situation of the kind that few people will have to confront. No one can predict for you at this time what the outcome will be, so right off you will have great fear of the unknown. At first neither you nor your friend has any idea what is under your control and what is not. But once you've started working toward getting your friend the best of everything in medical care, then you have at least started to establish areas of control for both of you—areas of control that will make you both more comfortable, less afraid, and more loving. But your terror will not swiftly abate. Your fear may be so great you may wonder if you will be able to function at all.

Hugh tells of his reaction. "I tell you, I used to leave the hospital at night, and it was like my body was running on electricity. I had such pain and I was really feeling it. I use to cry . . . crying just to make it to the corner. 'Please God, don't let me drop dead here on the street. What do I do?' "

Fear begets fear: *Don't be afraid of your fear. Your fear is often more threatening than any reality, or any possible reality, behind it.* "I'm afraid to talk to him about this," you say. "I'm afraid to do this or that because this or that might happen." Usually, you are not afraid of what is happening at this very moment. You are afraid of the future. This fear is more paralyzing and frightening than any fear of present happenings, because you can do something about present happenings, even if it's just to run away. But you can't do anything right now to change future events, because you don't even really know what these events will be, and you can't run away from them because they are not real.

"It took me a long time," Len said, "to figure out what was causing me such constant feelings of dread and fear—what was keeping me on edge all day, no matter what I was doing, and up all night. I started paying close attention to the thoughts that rolled through my mind all day, especially when I found myself sighing or groaning under my breath. I began to see that my mind was filled with pictures—almost like subliminal flashes—of all these horrible events that might happen: Evan wasted away, suffering helplessly in a hospital bed; me in agony, alone and desperate, perhaps sick, in an empty, silent house. After a while it occurred to me: 'I'm afraid of my own thoughts.' I wasn't afraid of the situation I was presently in; somehow I was handling it—for better or for worse. It was things that might happen somewhere down the road that terrified me. It didn't occur to me that, when I got down the road, I might be in the same situation I am right now, somehow handling it—for better or for worse."

Recognize this fear as simply fear, as an emotion, not as a fear of real events. Ask yourself, "What is the worst possible consequence of this action if I take it? What is the worst thing that can happen if I say this to him right now?" Suppose you are afraid to go visit your friend in the hospital for the first time. What is the worst thing that can happen to you when you go? Will you feel afraid? Will you cry? Will you feel awkward? How likely is it that you will lose control of yourself and run in a panic from the building? How likely is it that you will be grabbed by the first doctor who passes by and told that you have AIDS, too?

In almost every circumstance, you will discover that the worst possible consequence of taking some action in no way justifies the amount of fear you feel. In most cases you will discover that the worst possible consequence is also the most unlikely outcome of any of your actions. Suppose your fears come true. When you go to the hospital that first time to see your friend, perhaps you find yourself tongue-tied, embarrassed, unable to look at your friend, getting sick from the smells of the place? What happens then? You won't die. Your friend won't die. You will simply make the best of it. And no matter how your visit turns out, you made it.

You must try, now, to understand your fears. Isolate them,

53

analyze them, take them apart, and look at them piece by piece. You are not aiming to overcome fear completely—that's probably not possible—only to live with it more comfortably.

Confront your fears: Ask yourself a series of questions about each thing you fear. Begin with the most obvious.

"What am I afraid of? Can I put a name on it? Can I describe it as an event or a thing?"

"Is this fear real? Is the event imminent? Is it possible? Is it probable that this will happen?"

"Is this fear rational? Can I do anything about it? If I can do nothing about it, can I live with it?"

"What is really at risk here if I do this or that?"

If you have a friend or therapist or go to a group, discuss your fears with this person or group.

Neil, a man in his thirties whose lover of six years, Ron, had recently been diagnosed, said, "I can't tell him how I feel. I can't tell him that I'm terrified of this whole thing." Yet Neil was so distressed that he would burst into tears periodically during the day and felt he was being driven crazy with fear and dread. His friend, Melba, who was also his therapist, told him, "You must tell him how you feel. He knows that you're afraid. He's as afraid as you are. Is he going to leave you if he discovers you're afraid? Is he going to fall apart and be unable to cope any longer? Is he going to die if he knows you're afraid? Is he going to love you less or reject you?" In each case Neil answered, "No, of course not." He knew that the consequences he feared most were not real, yet the fear had paralyzed him.

You will find that discussing your fears with your friend with AIDS will open many new avenues of communication between you. You can explore places together that you would never have dreamed of even entering before. Discussion will make it possible for both of you to make room for your fears in the relationship. Rather than the fears destroying the relationship, they become part of it.

Peter, a person with AIDS in his late twenties, had been a teacher in a private school. As soon as his boss learned what was wrong, she fired him immediately. Peter exaggerates her proper New England accent. "We love you, Peter. We wish the world were different. But we wouldn't have one pupil next year if anyone discovered that one of our teachers had AIDS." Peter just left.

Peter never had a lover, but he had many friends. Alone in his apartment, he described his friends' reactions. "They're all busier than I am denying that I have this illness. It's discouraging. They come in here, and they can hardly look at me. And when I mention that I see my health, and probably my life, slipping away, they act like they want to slip away too. There's a woman who comes to see me, Diane. She's a social worker connected to the hospital in some way. She's really nice and we've become friends. One day I said to her, 'You know, Diane, I'm in this situation. No one has gotten out of it alive yet.' I thought she would look away or leave or something. Instead she said, 'Yes, that must be very hard for you to look at. I'm sorry that you have this illness, but your perception of it seems accurate to me.' For some reason I wanted to get up and hug her. She was the first person who seemed willing to help me to see what I knew was there."

Fear of contagion: You flinch when you kiss your friend hello. You feel that your hands are contaminated when you touch anything in his hospital room or apartment. You feel uneasy about drinking from a glass he may have used, even though it has been washed. You are afraid to eat or drink in his presence. What are you afraid of? You are afraid of coming into contact with the virus associated with AIDS and of becoming infected. Yet you know that you will not get AIDS from being around your friend who has the disease. You will not get the disease from glasses, forks, air, toilet seats, or even if he coughs on you. Documented cases of transmission of the disease by casual contact *do not exist*.

To help you overcome this fear, try this. Take that glass in your hand. Examine it closely. Ask yourself what evidence you have that the virus could be on this object. Ask yourself with evidence you have that even if the virus is on this object there is sufficient quantity to cause infection. Ask yourself how you think the virus is going to make its way into your bloodstream from this object. Ask yourself what evidence you have that the virus associated with AIDS alone is sufficient to cause disease. Broken down into smaller pieces, this fear may not appear real.

If you are the partner of the person with AIDS, or even if you had sex with him at some time in the past, you may be afraid that your friend is going to accuse you of giving him the disease. You may be afraid that you did give him the disease or that he has infected you.

In most cases, who gave the virus associated with AIDS to whom is hard, if not impossible, to determine, and even thinking about that issue is just a distraction for both you and your friend. Just as you can't fear the future so that you are paralyzed in the present, you cannot become preoccupied with the past, about which you can do nothing. All this will get you nowhere.

Once both of you have been open with each other, you will feel more comfortable. You won't be trying to hide your little defensive actions against contagion, and your friend won't be trying to ignore them.

Len said, "After Evan got sick, I was never afraid of getting anything from him. Worry about that seemed silly to me. After all, whatever had gone on between us was already done and was over. We had only been together about a year and a half when he started getting sick, and who could tell who gave what to whom? My biggest worry was that he'd catch something from me."

Fear of your friend's new condition: You will become more comfortable and less fearful as you become familiar with the disease and how your friend is affected by it. It is natural for you to fear what you do not know, to be uneasy around the unfamiliar. The deserted street that seemed terrifying and threatening the first time you saw it no longer threatens you so much the tenth time you've walked it. Observe how animals are cautious and fearful around unfamiliar people or other animals.

You will read more about AIDS. You will be around other people in the same situation as you are. You will have conversations about your feelings. Also, as time passes, you will begin to see that your friend is the same person he always was.

Linda said, "Somehow, I wasn't afraid for myself around my brother, Gary. But I found myself going crazy when he was around my children. I couldn't stand to watch them kiss him or sit on his bed. And if he coughed or touched his mouth around them, it was all I could do to stop myself from running over and pulling them away. I was so ashamed because I knew better. But I couldn't help myself.

"Then my feelings began to change. I read everything I could find. I watched those parents on TV who seemed so irrational and crazy about children with AIDS going to school. And it began to sink in. There is not one case of someone getting AIDS from being around a person with the disease. I noticed, too, that the more I was around him, the more I saw my brother there. After a while he was just my sick brother, not at threat to any of us."

Fear of mortality: No one gets out of this world alive, and death is the natural end of every life. Everyone knows that fact. Yet, as Dr. Elisabeth Kübler-Ross writes at the start of her book, *On Death and Dying*, "Death is still a fearful, frightening happening, and the fear of death is a universal fear, even if we think we have mastered it on many levels."

The intricate psychological structure that people have created in their minds, both consciously and unconsciously, to help them deal with the fact of death is much too complex to examine completely in this book. A rich discussion of it can be found in Dr. Kübler-Ross's book. For our purposes here, we need only remember two facts from that book that will help us understand our reaction to our friend with AIDS. First, when we are young, we believe that we are immortal. Death can only happen to other people and not to us. Second, psychiatrists believe that our unconscious mind cannot conceive of our death, and as Dr. Kübler-Ross says, "In our unconscious mind we can only be killed. . . . Therefore death itself is associated with a bad act, a frightening happening, something that in itself calls for retribution and punishment."

So when our friend becomes sick with a life-threatening illness, it is part of our natural makeup to become fearful. One of our most cherished beliefs is being challenged: that we will never die. Further, our unconscious mind sees our friend's possible death as an act of violence, an act that provokes us to anger, forces us to feel guilty, makes us seek to even the score, or even to punish ourselves and other people around us for letting it happen. So it is natural for us to feel anger, confusion, guilt, and depression under these circumstances. As time passes, you will begin to sort through these confused and confusing thoughts. This book will help you do that. Just understand now that it is okay to feel as you do.

Being a friend of someone with AIDS will teach us more about our mortality, and how to make peace with it, than most other experiences. After all, your friend is probably more afraid of death than you are. Someday he may want to talk to you about this. Later, we will see how other people have handled this difficult aspect of their friendship with a person with AIDS.

Fear of identification: The past is the past. You can't change it, you can't erase it, you can only try to forget it.

In the past you and your friend may have participated in many similar activities. Your life-styles may have been very much alike. So you are wondering why he is sick and you are not. You are wondering when this might happen to you.

First of all, if your fear is great, find out if it has any basis in reality. Have your blood tested for any abnormalities. Have antigen skin tests done. Discuss your T-cell ratio with the doctor. Discuss any symptoms you feel you have. If you need more assurance, and if you think it is wise, you can find out if you have antibodies to HIV. But before you do this, read Appendix B. If all this testing leads to the conclusion that you have not been infected, practice the safer-sex guidelines printed in Appendix C and take it easy.

If you have been infected, the situation is more grave, but it is not dire. The best estimates now available are that 20 to 30 percent of those infected will come down with the disease within ten years of infection. Others, another 10 to 20 percent, will present some symptoms and develop ARC. So the odds are in your favor that you will not get sick. Nevertheless you may feel as though you are walking around with a loaded gun pointed to your head. You may be constantly checking in the mirror for KS lesions. *This fear is not going to go away, but the intensity of it will lessen with time.* That the fear abates has been the consistent experience of men who have known of their infection for years. If you are infected, but show no symptoms, you absolutely must follow the safer-sex guidelines (Appendix C) and life-style changes recommended for people with ARC earlier in this book (pages 17–19). You do not want to endanger your health, and you do not want to spread this virus to anyone else.

Whether or not you know you are infected, it will help you to talk to your friend about how you identify with him or her. Bring your fear out into the open and discuss all the activities you shared that cause you fear. Tell your friend that you are bringing up these things because you want and need to be comfortable around him, but you cannot be as long as you are hiding what you fear.

Mark and Sam solved this problem with a painful discussion. Marks says, "It got to the point that I couldn't look Sam in the face. If he caught my eyes, I got uneasy and looked away. One day he said to me, 'Something's wrong here. You and I have got to talk.' I looked at him, and I wanted to cry. 'I'm making myself crazy,' I said. My feelings started to pour out. 'Every time I'm around you, I think about going to the baths with you. I think about all the things that we did together. All those things that put us both in danger of getting this disease. Not just you, me too. We did the same things, and you're sick and I'm not. I may be next. Being around you reminds me of that and scares me. Sometimes I feel guilty. Why did this happen to you and not me?'

"Sam said, 'I haven't thought of that? Why I'm sick and you're not? Do you know how mad I am? I'm mad at you. Did God or somebody throw some dice, and I came up a loser and you didn't?' Then he started shaking his head. 'Goddamn it, Mark, I hate my feelings, too. I don't want you to get sick, I'm just jealous. I want to be healthy too.'

"Then we had the longest cry. We weren't usually very affectionate together, but that day we lay on his sofa and just held each other."

Fear of helplessness: If you stay away from your friend with AIDS because you feel helpless to do anything for him, you are probably trying to do the wrong things. You know you can do something for your friend with ARC by helping him to monitor his life and remain as healthy as possible. If your friend has AIDS, you can do little, medically, to influence the course of the disease or to change your friend's health. Beyond caring for him and helping him understand his situation and choose his treatments, you may feel helpless.

What you can greatly influence, however, is the quality of your friend's life. You can help your friend to have a better life, a life full of those things, big and small, that make each day worthwhile. You can help your friend create a life that is worth living, that helps him continue to fight with dignity and courage. This is the area on which you should concentrate. Many persons with AIDS attribute the fact that they are alive and happy today to the caring friends and carepartners who stepped in and helped them make life worth the struggle. We will come back to this time and time again as we progress through this book.

In summary, you have a right to have fears when you approach your friend with AIDS. These fears, both rational and irrational, can become part of the relationship and help it to grow, especially if you can share them with your friend with AIDS. You can say, "I'm telling you this because it's important to me that I be comfortable around you. And this fear—or at least my trying to hide it—is making me uncomfortable. These are extraordinary times, extraordinary circumstances, and I think that we should be able to talk and share things that we never even thought of before."

DEALING WITH DENIAL

You and your friend will probably react to the diagnosis of ARC or AIDS with disbelief and denial. "No," you might say, "this can't be happening." Your friend might say, "There's some mistake. This can't be happening to me." You saw these reactions at the beginning of Chapter 3.

Denial is a way your mind protects you from realities that could overwhelm you with anxiety, realities that you are not yet ready to deal with head on. It provides you with the time you may need to get used to the situation and to devise means of dealing with it. Denial gives you and your friend time to work through your feelings.

Denial is useful: You should not think something is wrong with you if you cannot accept the reality of the situation that your mind knows is happening. Denial under the circumstances is perfectly normal and appropriate behavior. You and your friend will probably use denial not just immediately after the diagnosis but from time to time throughout your friend's illness and your relationship. When the situation becomes too painful or too filled with anxiety, you may find yourself talking as if your friend is not sick, acting as if the whole thing never happened, or making plans you know you will probably never carry out—in effect, indulging yourself in a not-quite-real world. You are using denial to cope.

Your friend is no doubt experiencing the same denial that you are. Be very careful and sensitive to how your friend is feeling at any given moment. He may be able to talk about his illness only now and then, and then only for a brief time, or he might overcome his denial of his illness early on. You have to be careful and to listen.

James relates this story about his brother Earl. "For weeks while he was in the hospital and then when he came home, he never said anything about being sick. It scared me. He acted sick. I mean, he didn't go out drinking or dancing. He didn't try to go back and move the streets. He needed twelve to fourteen hours sleep a day just to be able to be up the other twelve. But he didn't talk about being sick. Then one day we were watching a ball game on TV, and the commercial came on. He clicked off the sound with the remote, and said, 'I can count on you, can't I? You know, I mean, when this thing gets really bad.' I was off guard, and it took me a minute. But I realized he was looking at the thing. I said, 'You can count on me no matter what happens.' Then he clicked the sound back on and that was that."

Sometimes people cannot get past denial. This is a matter that you may or may not need to confront. There have been many people who have died still denying that they were sick. This applies to people with any illness, not just persons with AIDS. We will return to this subject later in Chapter 10.

Denial can be dangerous: Sometimes people's denial influences their behavior in ways that could be perilous to themselves and to others. Here are some manifestations that you might watch for.

- Your friend may not take his medicine because he doesn't believe he needs it, because he insists he is not sick.

- Your friend may continue his life just as if nothing had changed, indulging in behaviors that hurt his health, like getting drunk, taking drugs, staying up all night.

- Your friend may attempt to practice unsafe sex, because he does not believe he is doing any harm.

60

If you see any of this behavior, you will have to confront your friend. You will especially have to confront your friend if his behavior endangers anyone other than himself.

Denial and anger: Occasionally now, early in your friend's illness, you will experience moments of profound anger. Actually, anger is almost like water in your body. It is present in every cell; it is part of every emotion and action. You have a thousand reasons to be angry, and you may find some of these reasons flashing through your mind at any time. "This isn't fair," you think. "How can this be happening to us?"

You have a right to be angry, as does your friend. From nowhere, your lives have been interrupted, your plans dashed, your future made uncertain. And there is no focus for this anger. Are you angry at the virus? At God? At your lover? Your parents? At the world? At the doctors and the nurses? What is the object of the anger? The danger here is that both of you will project this anger into your environment and strike out unreasonably at whomever is there.

"One evening right after work, I went to see Bruce," Jack said, "and he was surly. 'Why the hell didn't you bring me something to eat?' he said to me as soon as I stepped into the room. 'I just got here.' I said. 'You didn't say anything about food when I called you today.' He snarled and yelled at me, 'Asshole, I have to tell you everything.'

"I was tired. I was hot. I'd been framing a roof all day. I felt like punching him in the face, so I stepped out into the hall. The nurse came up to me. She had heard him yell. 'He's been acting up all day,' she said. 'He even called the doctor a stupid bastard. I won't mention what he called me.'

"I went back into the room and sat down. 'Back off from me,' I said. 'I'm here. I love you. You want something, I'll go out and get it.' He just ignored me and turned on the TV. I sat and watched TV for about an hour, then I left. He was still mad when I left. The next morning he called me at home like nothing had ever happened."

At this time, early in your friend's illness, you have many things to do, and you do not want anger to interfere with getting things done. Express your anger when it is appropriate, but be very careful. You can easily hurt people who are trying to help. Remember also, your denial can act as a buffer between you and this enormous anger, because it allows you not to confront the situation. Later, when you and you friend are set up, when many of these preliminary issues are settled, you will have to deal with your anger, just as you have had to deal with your fear.

61

There is always reason for hope.

Almost half the people who have been diagnosed with AIDS are still alive today.

People who have been diagnosed are living on the average much longer than they did at the beginning of the epidemic.

Federal, state, and local governments have become alarmed by the AIDS problem and are finally finding the funds for AIDS research, education, and support services.

Medical institutes, universities, and drug companies are doing relentless research looking at a variety of drugs to treat:

- the opportunistic infections related to AIDS,

- people now infected, with or without symptoms, to stop the progression of the illness,

- people with AIDS itself, to restore the immune system.

Although the problem is always described as "extremely medically difficult," almost weekly there are indications of progress, both through more conventional means of research and through genetic and molecular studies.

Some people claim to have slowed or stopped the progression of the disease through holistic medicine. These methods have always been ignored by people in conventional medicine, yet they may provide help and sustenance.

You and your friend have good reason to maintain hope that a solution will be found to this problem, and that it will be found in time to help both of you.

5

OPPORTUNISTIC INFECTIONS IN AIDS:
Their Symptoms and Treatments

When your friend is diagnosed with AIDS, you will begin your own crash course in infectious diseases and treatments, in drugs and procedures that are all new to you. Gradually, you will start to understand what specific symptoms mean, what to expect when your friend's treatment starts, how your friend may react to a drug, and what questions to ask the doctor along the way.

Also, remember to keep your partner or friend informed, and help him to be as much a participant in understanding the illnesses and treatments as he wishes to be. Some persons with AIDS want to know everything about everything being done to them. Others want to know nothing; they leave all the questions about treatment up to you or to the doctor.

You must ask your friend early on in the illness—and continue to ask throughout—how informed he wishes to be at that specific time. He does not need to know everything. *He needs to know what he wants to know.* He may want to know only the name of the condition or the infection, how it's treated, and what discomfort he can expect. He probably does not want to know the percentage of patients who recover from this particular illness and the percentage who do not, how bad the side effects from the drug will be, or what permanent damage the treatments may do to his system. You have to judge from what he says each time something happens how much your friend with AIDS wants to know. Always, of course, he has the option to ask the doctor.

As you read this chapter, keep in mind that people with AIDS do not get diseases from organisms that are exotic to our part of the world. They do not get leprosy, for example, or malaria, or sleeping sickness, or elephantiasis, because the germs causing those diseases are not present in our environment. Nor do they get diseases against which their bodies already carry antibodies, such as polio or smallpox. Most of the diseases common among AIDS patients are caused by common germs that may be present in everyone, but are

63

easily controlled by our bodies as long as our immune system is intact.

There also seem to be three degrees of illness among persons with AIDS. Those with only KS seem to be the least sick; those with PCP and other opportunistic infections, but no KS, are sicker; those with PCP, KS, and other opportunistic infections are by far the sickest.

There's one simple and important rule to follow when you care for a friend with AIDS: Pay attention. Always try to notice any changes in your friend's condition. If your friend starts to run a fever, record it every four hours or so. If your friend gets a new rash or develops a cough, if he stops eating for a day or two, if he becomes very pale—then tell your friend to call the doctor, or contact the doctor yourself if your friend wants you to. Your early vigilance can be very helpful, and it will save your friend discomfort, pain, and often needless anxiety. Most infections are less severe if they are treated early, when symptoms first appear.

Be careful as you read through this chapter. The sheer number of infections that people with AIDS are prey to may overwhelm you. Remember that your friend may not develop all or even most of the diseases listed here. And remember—as you always must with AIDS—to take one day at a time and one problem at a time.

COMMON OPPORTUNISTIC DISEASES

Earlier in this book we listed symptoms that often indicate the possibility of the onset of AIDS. Chapter 3 also discusses the experimental drugs that are being tested to help treat the underlying causes of AIDS. This chapter, however, deals with the most common opportunistic infections associated with AIDS, together with their symptoms, the drugs used to treat them, and some of the side effects of these drugs. An important note about side effects: Some are unavoidable and nothing can be done to alleviate them. Others, such as nausea and vomiting, can be controlled to some degree by such drugs as Compazine. So when your friend is taking a drug that is causing him difficulty, ask the doctor what, if anything, can be done to spare your friend this additional discomfort and trauma.

Remember also that many of the drugs the doctors are using are new to them, too. They might know about the drug from a medical journal, or from a conference on AIDS, or from a telephone call from a colleague on the coast. So sometimes you have to understand that a treatment may be new not only to you, but to your doctor, too, and he may not know immediately what to do or what to expect. Be patient. The doctors treating AIDS-related infections today have had the benefit of several years' experience now, and generally they do know much better what they are dealing with and how to treat some of the infections. There are, of course, some diseases that are not treatable.

The two most common infections in persons with AIDS are PCP and thrush.

Pneumocystis carinii pneumonia (PCP): PCP is the most common life-threatening infection in persons with AIDS. About half of the people with AIDS first manifest the syndrome by getting this disease; and almost all will develop it during the course of their illness. Along with KS and many other conditions, it is one of the criteria used by the Centers for Disease Control to define the presence of AIDS itself.

PCP is a parasitic (protozoan) infection of the lungs with symptoms similar to any other penumonia: high fevers, shortness of breath, and, in this case, a dry cough. It seldom affects people who do not have AIDS, although the Pneumocystis carinii protozoan is a very common organism that is present in most people. It just does not cause disease in those with normal health.

Some people who have developed AIDS-related PCP in areas of the world where little is known of AIDS have been treated by doctors as if PCP were ordinary pneumonia. However, drugs to treat more common pneumonias are ineffective against PCP. If your friend has any of the symptoms of pneumonia and has been showing some of the symptoms of AIDS, you should insist that he be tested specifically for PCP. You should insist that his blood work also include a T-4 and T-8 cell ratio test (a reversal of the normal ratio can be an indicator of AIDS) and other tests for signs of an impaired immune system. PCP usually recurs after a period of time, since it is never completely eradicated from the person's system.

PCP is usually diagnosed by a procedure called a bronchoscopy, in which the doctors insert a long tube into the lungs to perform both a visual examination and a biopsy. To get samples of the tissue, doctors use a brush, not a knife, which could create a hole in the lung and deflate it. The doctors also perform a bronchoalveolar lavage in which they wash the lungs and then pump out the liquid for analysis.

There are three drugs in the first line of defense against PCP. These are trimethoprim-sulfamethoxazole, pentamidine, and dapsone. Trimethoprim is the drug with which doctors usually begin treatment for PCP, because it is the most familiar to them and is not expensive. It is called Bactrim by one drug company and Septra by another; a doctor may use either term and mean the same thing. Trimethoprim is administered intravenously for twenty-one days. Sometimes treatment can begin in the hospital and be completed at home by a visiting nurse. However, after seven to ten days of treatment, a large percentage of AIDS patients have a toxic reaction to it, developing rashes, a low white-blood count, a low platelet count, and fevers. Some persons with PCP do not respond to trimethoprim at all.

If your friend with AIDS has a toxic reaction, your doctors must wait a few days for the blood counts to recover and the rash to subside. Then they will probably begin treatment with pentamidine, which is also administered intravenously, and after a week or ten days can be administered at home. Total days on this drug may number up to twenty-one. Pentamidine, which used to be supplied directly by the Centers for Disease Control because it was rarely used in the United States before the AIDS epidemic, is now being sold through a drug company, and it is very expensive.

If you see a doctor begin to administer pentamidine directly into the muscle of the buttocks, do not allow it. Such injections can cause huge swellings, which can become sterile abscesses and may take many very painful days to disappear. If the doctor does not know how to administer this drug intravenously, have him call one of the medical centers specializing in AIDS in New York or San Francisco.

Dapsone is an antileprosy drug which is also effective against PCP. It is taken orally and is becoming increasingly common. In mild, recurrent cases of PCP some doctors have successfully prescribed dapsone and trimethoprim to be taken orally at home.

Both trimethoprim and pentamidine have undesirable side effects, ranging from loss of appetite, which is very common, to inflammation of the mouth, nausea, vomiting, and anemia. Pentamidine can also cause rashes and short- or long-term diabetes.

Sometimes during treatment for PCP, or at some other point during the illness, the texture of the hair of the person with AIDS will change. If thick and curly, it may become soft and straight. The cause of this is not completely known. It could be due to the disease itself, or it could be a fungal infection that invades the skin and the hair follicles.

Candida: Candida, commonly called "thrush," is a fungal infection found in almost all AIDS patients. It is seen as a whitish coating on the tongue and in the mouth. It is usually not a life-threatening condition, but it can spread to the esophagus and make eating or even swallowing very uncomfortable or nearly impossible. Thrush is, however, not difficult to control, and the use of clotrimazole troches four or five times a day will usually get rid of it. The troche, a large tablet that is dissolved in the mouth, simply kills the fungus. However, as soon as treatment ends, thrush usually recurs, so the use of a troche daily keeps it in check. Side effects of this drug are extremely rare.

Nystatin, another antifungal drug used for thrush, is commonly called "swish and swallow." It's a liquid, taken four times a day, that is used like a mouthwash and then swallowed. Nystatin, which is very effective, has few side effects, and these rarely occur.

Common Viral Infections

There are several viruses that cause infections in persons with AIDS. There are also viruses, for example, Epstein-Barr virus (the cause of mononucleosis), that are present in people with AIDS—and indeed in many other people—and whose connection with the disease is not clear. These viruses of themselves may not have been pinpointed as the cause of a specific condition, but they are present in various organs that can be diseased.

Here, we will discuss the viruses that cause specific diseases.

Cytomegalovirus (CMV): This virus is a common infection in persons with AIDS. It is actually a virus commonly found in homosexual men, but it is usually harmless. Its exact role in the development of AIDS is not well understood, and it could be one of the factors influencing the onset of the syndrome, as could the Epstein-Barr virus.

In persons with AIDS, cytomegalovirus can appear in the eyes (CMV retinitis), lungs (CMV pneumonitis), brain (CMV cerebritis), or colon (CMV colitis), or it may attack other bodily organs, including the trachea or the liver. If left untreated in the eyes, it can cause loss of vision. In the colon or intestines, it can cause chronic diarrhea, wasting, and very painful cramps. Until recently there was no treatment for CMV. Early in the AIDS epidemic, persons with CMV usually died slow, painful and wasting deaths. Often they went blind. Today, however, an experimental drug called by various names, among them DHPG, has been used successfully to prevent the virus from replicating. Not all doctors will know of this drug, but it is available to AIDS patients on a compassionate basis. It has shown good results in many cases, but the drug must be continued in maintenance doses after the initial infection is brought under control.

Herpes simplex: Herpes simplex virus is found in nearly all persons with AIDS, and it can cause them many problems. This

67

virus is very common in the United States and is found in nearly 90 percent of the adult population, although it does not cause symptoms in nearly that many people. Herpes manifests itself as sores around the mouth and lips and in the genital areas. It can cause fevers and a great deal of pain. In AIDS patients, infections with this virus are common, persistent, and often severe. The treatment for herpes simplex is the same as for herpes zoster, which follows.

Herpes simplex is as contagious in an AIDS patient as it would be with anyone else who had it. It is not advisable to kiss a person with AIDS on the mouth when he has herpes sores on the lips—just as you would not kiss anyone else on the lips under the same circumstances.

Herpes zoster: Herpes zoster, commonly called shingles, is a form of chicken pox caused by the zoster varicella virus. This virus is present in nerve cells and expresses itself by traveling down a nerve root. Infections can appear as patches of raised, red bumps on the skin of the legs and buttocks, or the arms and back, following the path of a large nerve root. Like herpes simplex, these bumps can turn into painful sores that can itch at the same time. Often, these outbreaks are accompanied by fevers and malaise.

Herpes simplex and herpes zoster are treated with acyclovir, which is very effective. It can be taken either intravenously or orally, usually for a period of five to ten days. Thereafter, a daily dose may be prescribed to keep it under control. Herpes sores can also be treated topically with Zovirax, the trade name for a cream containing acyclovir. It is very expensive. Acyclovir is a well-tolerated drug, with side effects that are few and rare.

Brain and Central Nervous System Problems

Persons with AIDS can develop three main problems that affect the central nervous system and which can cause behavioral and mental problems. A person with AIDS may begin to lose muscular coordination, withdraw socially, or show other signs of physical and mental impairment.

Cryptococcal meningitis: Cryptococcus neoformans, a yeast infection, most commonly appears in persons with AIDS as meningitis, an inflammation of the brain. It can also cause lymphadenopathy (swollen lymph glands), endocarditis (inflammation around the heart), and even skin ulcers. The symptoms of cryptococcal meningitis are high fevers and terrible headaches.

Cryptococcal meningitis is treated with the drug amphotericin B, usually in conjunction with another drug, flucytosine, over a six-week course. Amphotericin B is so toxic that it must be slowly dripped into the body intravenously for eight-hour periods each day. Usually, after the second week of treatment, the doctors will examine the spinal fluid for antibodies to cryptococcus. If the antibody level falls, the doctors know the disease is being brought under control.

The side effects of amphotericin B can be powerful and numerous. It can cause nausea, vomiting, loss of appetite and consequent loss of weight, fever, severe chills, and cramps. It can cause the hands to shake, or result in blurred or double vision and other clinical problems.

No drug can totally suppress cryptococcal meningitis. Relapse is common, so continuing treatment with some drug, probably amphotericin B, will be necessary.

Toxoplasmosis: Toxoplasma gondii, or "toxo" as it is called, is another parasitic infection that attacks persons with AIDS. It is found all over the world and lives in many people in a latent state causing no symptoms. In AIDS patients, it usually invades the nervous system, especially the brain, resulting in seizures, high fevers, and a decreasing level of consciousness. Toxo used to be one of the more life-threatening and frightening infections that occurred in persons with AIDS, since continued infection can lead to immobility and the inability to speak. However today, thanks to new treatments, it is less threatening, though still dangerous. It is usually diagnosed after a brain scan that may reveal cerebral lesions. Early symptoms of toxo can include inattentiveness, fevers, loss of feeling in one or more limbs, or even a sudden seizure.

Toxo is very treatable and the drugs against it effective. It responds to sulfadiazine and pyrimethamine administered orally for six weeks. Sometimes this disease is treated at home, and hospitalization may not be necessary. However, infection has a tendency to reappear as soon as the therapy stops. Many doctors will keep the person with AIDS on the drugs at a low dosage as a prophylaxis (a protection against recurrence).

Both sulfadiazine and pyrimethamine are extremely toxic with severe side effects. But since toxo is life-threatening, there is no choice except to continue medication, while attempting to treat whatever disorders result. Among the most common side effects are loss of appetite and weight loss, nausea and vomiting, mouth and tongue pain, and anemia. Either drug may cause loss of hair, decreased hearing, diarrhea, sensitivity to light, and even kidney damage. These drugs are also very hard on the bone marrow, which manufactures blood cells, and hence can further depress the immune system by lowering the body's ability to make blood cells.

Sometimes, when the patient does not respond to treatment for toxo, the doctor may be doubtful of the diagnosis. Few doctors these days will do a brain biopsy, since this is a complicated procedure that can lead to other complications, but it may become necessary. The problem also might be leukoencephalopathy.

Leukoencephalopathy: Some AIDS patients may develop a slowly progressive dementia, leukoencephalopathy, that may eventually become so severe that they are immobilized and totally incapacitated. This disease is usually fatal. Not a great deal is known about this condition, called progressive multifocal leukoencephalopathy. It often begins with fevers, headaches, malaise, then loss of memory and motor control, clumsiness, loss of logical reasoning, delusions, and hallucinations.

This can be an extremely difficult condition for you, the carepartner or caring friend, to face. After a while, you feel you are no longer in the company of your friend, but with a child, or with someone becoming rapidly senile. It takes great love, compassion, and patience to deal with someone in this condition.

The causes of leukoencephalopathy are not well known, but they appear to be extremely complex, possibly involving several viruses including human immunosuppressive virus (formerly called HTLV-III), cytomegalovirus, Epstein-Barr virus, and other viruses not usually found in the brain. Leukoencephalopathy is not generally a treatable condition, and doctors usually can do little more than make the patient comfortable.

Diarrhea

Persons with AIDS often suffer from diarrhea, which can have one or more of many causes. Giardia lamblia and Entamoeba histolytica—two parasites that had been prevalent among homosexual men for about ten years—are still around, but are much less prevalent today. These parasitic diseases seldom appear in persons with AIDS, and have been nearly eradicated among homosexual men. But there are other infections that can cause diarrhea. Some are listed below.

Salmonella and shigella: These bacteria can infect the intestines and colon of a person with AIDS. Both salmonella and shigella can cause severe diarrhea; both can be treated with ampicillin and trimethoprim-sulfamethoxazole. Salmonella can also be treated with amoxicillin. Both bacteria usually respond to treatment, but the treatment is very difficult and hard on the person with AIDS. The drugs have various side effects, especially trimeth-

70

oprim, which can cause rashes, fever, nausea, vomiting, and consequently loss of weight. These bacteria can also be treated with milk, which has a high level of antibodies against these infections. This treatment is sometimes successful.

Cryptosporidiosis: When your friend with AIDS is suffering from a severe watery diarrhea that does not respond to any of the treatments noted above, the problem may be cryptosporidiosis.

Cryptosporidium difficile, or "crypto," is a small parasite that causes chronic, watery diarrhea in persons with AIDS, resulting in rapid dehydration and wasting. Anything that a patient tries to eat or drink, when he has this infection, simply passes through his body as painful diarrhea.

There is no established treatment against this parasite, and many times the medical people can only keep the infected patient hydrated by intravenous infusion of liquids and give him morphine to keep him comfortable. A feeding tube will also prolong the person's life.

Researchers are working with three drugs, spiramyucin, alpha difluoromethlornithine, and amproium, to combat this infection, but their efficacy is still under debate. Soon perhaps a drug will be found that is effective against this parasite, just as in the last few years, since the beginning of the AIDS epidemic, a drug has been found that is effective against CMV.

If your friend gets crypto, you should use special precautions when dealing with his excretions, since you can be infected by this organism. In a person with a normal immune system, crypto can cause severe diarrhea for about a week, then clear up by itself. It has been known to do this in a very few cases of AIDS.

There can be other causes of diarrhea in persons with AIDS, such as CMV, as noted earlier. It is a common and difficult problem, but one that must be investigated and dealt with promptly.

Bacteria

Although many kinds of bacteria invade persons with AIDS, and as noted earlier can cause diarrhea, the two following are most serious. They cause a variety of disorders.

Mycobacterium avium complex: MAI, mycobacterium avium-intracelluare infections, can appear in various organs of the body or in the blood. These bacteria are found in almost half of all persons with AIDS, although they do not cause symptoms or disease in everyone. However, in some people with AIDS, MAI can cause diarrhea and intestinal pain, persistent high fevers, and weight loss. It can also be found in the lymph nodes and in the liver, where it causes dysfunctions. Any of the symptoms mentioned above can alert you to the possibility of MAI, but, unlike PCP, it is not ordinarily a disease that you specifically notice. The doctor may suspect the presence of MAI because of elevated liver functions or through biopsy of a swollen lymph node. It can be detected through blood and tissue cultures. If necessary, cultures can be done using bone marrow.

There are two effective drugs against MAI: ansamycin and clofazimine, which is an antileprosy drug. Leprosy is similar to MAI and is caused by mycobacterium leprae. Both drugs are experimental and do not in every case reduce the symptoms. They also are very toxic and can cause nausea, skin problems, and possibly bone marrow problems.

Mycobacterium tuberculosis: Tuberculosis (TB), another bacterium found in persons with AIDS, can cause lung disease and diseases in other organs. It is more commonly found in IV-drug users with AIDS than in homosexual men. Historically, tuberculosis has been found in AIDS patients who are not from the United States, but this disease in on the increase here also. If tuberculosis occurs in the lungs, this disease causes coughing and high fevers.

Several drugs can be used to combat TB effectively. Isoniazid is the drug of first choice, although it can result in anemia, fevers, rash, swollen glands, and temporary memory impairment. Usually isoniazid is used in combination with rifampin and/or ethambutal. But all these drugs are very toxic, and they can cause hepatitis, nausea, vomiting, visual disturbances, loss of appetite, and loss of weight. Other drugs mentioned in treating TB include cycloserine, ethionamide, and streptomycin. Ask the doctors what drugs they are planning to use to combat the TB. Then ask to know all the side effects. Many times when drugs are used in various combinations, no one really knows how they interact with each other.

CANCERS

Persons with AIDS can suffer from various cancers. Early in the epidemic many persons with AIDS were diagnosed as having a particular cancer, such as lung cancer, when in fact the disease was AIDS, and the cancer was KS in the lungs. These cases, apparently numerous, are not counted as AIDS cases by the Centers for Disease Control and are still not in the published totals.

Two cancers appear most often in persons with AIDS and both are unusual.

Kaposi's sarcoma: KS, as this disease is called, is a cancer of the small blood vessels of the body, and usually first appears as red blotches on the skin, which in time turn into purplish-red lesions, hard to the touch and raised above the level of the surrounding skin. They often show up first on the arms or legs, but can spread to the chest, back, face, and neck. They also appear in the mouth and throat, where they become more dangerous, and eventually they can appear in internal organs such as the intestines, colon, or the lungs. KS of itself is not a leading cause of death among AIDS patients, although it is the second most common opportunistic infection leading to diagnosis of AIDS. KS is not a cancer that spreads from one place to another as do most cancers—each lesion appears without connection to the others—so, for example, removing the first lesion, or several lesions, is not a useful therapy to prevent the spread of the disease over the body.

If the KS is limited to the skin, you and your friend may want to try one of the holistic methods of bringing it under control, especially if it is the first and only manifestation of AIDS. The macrobiotic diet has seemed most effective in keeping KS patients healthy for long periods of time, although we are not recommending this course of action here. A macrobiotic diet is a Japanese approach to diet that reduces protein intake, especially red meat, reduces fat, eliminates sugar, and increases the intake of complex carbohydrates, which are found in grains. The diet tries to find the optimal balance of natural foods to eliminate the cumulative effects of bad nutrition over a lifetime. It may also work because people on this diet are usually taking extremely good care of themselves.

You can find out more about this diet and who to contact in your area by writing or calling the Macrobiotic Center of New York, 32 West 89 Street, New York, NY 10024, (212) 877-1110. Or, if you live in a large metropolitan area, look in your phone book or call information; there are many centers in other cities.

If KS appears after your friend has been treated for some other opportunistic infection, then you may need do nothing at first, until there is facial, mouth, nose, or throat involvement or the KS is advancing to such a degree that it is itself becoming life-threatening, especially if it is compromising the lungs. At that point, chemotherapy or radiation therapy may be necessary, although these treatments are never really desirable, but at best, just necessary evils.

Radiation therapy can reduce the lesions in a particular area, such as the throat or mouth where they are making it difficult or impossible to eat or swallow, or on the face where they are causing particular discomfort because they are highly visible or disfiguring. KS is very sensitive to radiation therapy, and sometimes a single large dose will prove effective on lesions on the arms, legs, and some parts of the torso. But large doses of radiation are not ordinarily used when the eyes, throat, or mouth are involved, because of the enormous damage they can do to other organs in their path. If radiation is needed in these areas it may be done in smaller doses over a period of a week or two or a month. Radiation therapy causes soreness, swelling, and injury to the body. It cannot be used to combat lesions in the intestines, on the lungs, or on the trunk of the body.

Chemotherapies are difficult also. These drugs are going to make your friend sick each time they are administered, so be prepared. He will often experience nausea, vomiting, and extreme fatigue. In some cases his skin will take on a brownish tint. Chemotherapies are immunosuppressive, since they interfere with the production of blood cells in the bone marrow, and therefore other opportunistic infections occur more frequently in patients who have been pre-scribed chemotherapeutic drugs. Actually, some doctors recom-mend that no chemotherapies be used unless the lungs become compromised and breathing becomes difficult, because chemother-apies hasten the onset of other infections and weaken the body further. There is very little evidence that AIDS patients with KS taking chemotherapies live longer than people in the same circum-stances who have no chemotherapies.

Vinblastine and vincristine are the two drugs most often used in treating KS, because they seem to cause the fewest side effects and are the easiest to administer. Vinblastine is given intravenously once a week, and it produces some relief in almost a third of the patients, while another third seem to stabilize. Vincristine, which is given intravenously every week or sometimes biweekly, gets about the same results. Sometimes doctors alternate these drugs, one one week, the other the next week.

When KS is more advanced, begins to invade internal organs, or the drugs mentioned above have failed, then some doctors use the drug etoposide on a twenty-one-day cycle. Etoposide (VP-16) usu-ally causes the patient to lose his hair. When the doctors begin to use combinations of drugs, such as vinblastine, doxorubicin, and bleomycin, you will know the situation is very serious. These com-binations can suppress the immune system to such a degree that other opportunistic infections are very likely.

One experimental therapy for KS is alpha-interferon, which is being studied in various locations around the U.S. In some cases it seems to stop the spread of KS and at the same time act as an antiviral. Certain studies demonstrate 30 to 40 percent of the patients showed some response to the drug.

However, alpha-interferon is very toxic, causing high fevers,

74

nausea, vomiting and consequent weight loss, headaches, pains in the muscles, and great fatigue. But people may want to use it because of its promise not only as treatment for KS, but as an antiviral. Gamma interferon, called interleukin-2, also is being studied, but there is not much positive evidence available about it at this time.

Lymphomas: Lymphomas are cancers of the lymph nodes. In many persons with AIDS, this disease spreads quickly to sites outside the lymph nodes, such as the marrow of the bone and the central nervous system. The type of lymphoma most often found in persons with AIDS is called high-grade, B-cell non-Hodgkin's lymphoma.

The response rate to chemotherapy treatment of lymphomas in AIDS patients has been low, from about a third to a half of all patients. Furthermore, the relapse rate is high, and many people on chemotherapy develop other opportunistic infections.

Many of the drugs used against lymphomas are used in combinations, including cyclophosphamide, bleomycin, doxorubicin, vincristine sulfate, and prednisone or bleomycin sulfate, vincristine sulfate, prednisone, doxorubicin, dexamethosone, and procarbazine. Sometimes methotrexate is mentioned. All these drugs are highly toxic, causing nausea, vomiting, weight loss, hair loss, fatigue, low white-blood count, mouth ulcers, kidney problems, and sensitivity to light. This is only a partial list. It is often best not to treat lymphomas at all, and some doctors recommend this course of action, since the chemotherapies hasten the onset of other opportunistic infections and cause the person with AIDS great discomfort and suffering. At some point, however, you will both have to make this decision.

You and your friend with AIDS should discuss whether or not to use aggressive chemotherapy when presented with this disease. Discuss with the doctor all the alternatives and as many of the possible results of each alternative as are known. You may have to contact one of the cancer institutes to find out if there is a less toxic chemotherapeutic treatment being developed for AIDS patients that is not so devastating to their immune systems.

OTHER PHYSICAL CONDITIONS

In addition to the infections and cancers we have mentioned, which is only a list of the primary opportunistic infections you might encounter, there are certain conditions that are prevalent among persons with AIDS which, although they are annoying and can cause some discomfort, are generally not life-threatening. They can often be treated at home.

Fevers: Many persons with AIDS run almost constant low-grade fevers that sometimes shoot up, or spike, to 102, 103, or even 104 degrees. Fevers are, of course, an indication that something is wrong, and you and your friend should have these fevers checked out. But you may be told by the doctors that they can find no cause for them, that the fevers are simply part of having AIDS. In this case the doctors prescribe analgesics, such as acetaminophen (Tylenol), ibuprofen (Advil), Indocin, Naprosyn, or one of several others, but almost never aspirin, because it upsets the stomach. Some of these, such as acetaminophen and ibuprofen, have few side effects, but must be taken often, while others such as Indocin are very effective, not only in controlling fevers, but also in reducing body aches and pains. Indocin needs to be taken only twice a day, but it can have numerous and serious side effects, although they are not common. Naprosyn, a newer drug, seems to have all the positive attributes of Indocin without the same danger of side effects.

Analgesics are used to control the fevers and keep them down. Many times when your friend is having fevers, the night sweats will return. Night sweats are the body's way of releasing excess heat. Very often, when fevers break, the heat that has built up in the body is taken from the body in the form of sweat. However, if these drugs keep the fever at or below normal, the night sweats also tend to disappear. This is not always the case.

Fevers are a fact of life in AIDS, and if the doctor knows about them and has prescribed an analgesic that is working, then don't worry. If, however, the analgesic is no longer working or there is a change in the pattern of the fevers, make sure the doctor knows. Something is going on. It may be that your doctor can do no more than change the analgesic, but you will know that only after you have asked.

Rashes: Your friend with AIDS will probably suffer from many different rashes off and on while he is ill. Rashes can be caused by reactions to some of the very toxic drugs used to control various opportunistic infections; they can abate when the drug is discontinued or through treatments in the hospital. Some rashes, such as herpes zoster, are easily recognizable, and the treatment is standard. However, if herpes zoster involves the eyes or the face, it should be treated in the hospital.

Some rashes, such as psoriasis or seborrea, have causes which the doctor can diagnose and treat. Other rashes have no cause that any doctor can pinpoint, and treatment for them is mostly hit or miss.

76

Some prescription drugs that you might encounter are Lotrimin (clotrimazole cream), miconazole, and Eurax (crotamiton USP lotion). There are, no doubt, dozens of other creams and lotions that persons with AIDS have found effective. They should use whatever works.

For general skin discomfort, due to itching or soreness, some doctors recommend soaking in Aveeno Bath, an oatmeal treatment. If your friend has dry skin, get the Aveeno that is oilated for dry skin. This seems to be an effective and relaxing treatment.

Another nonprescription possibility is triple-antibiotic ointment and over-the-counter antifungal creams. But check with the doctor before using hydrocortisone, since even as a cream some of it will get into the bloodstream, and there is some indication that it is immunosuppressive. For foot fungi, you can use foot sprays, such as Tinactin, which are effective.

Sometimes, a virus or fungus gets into the fingernails or toenails of the person with AIDS and causes these to become disfigured in some way or another, either in shape or color, or both. For example, the nails can turn white. This condition is often best left alone, since removing the nails could open the body to infection, and some of the treatments are toxic and pose unnecessary risk to the person with AIDS. Discuss this with the doctor.

Although it is difficult to resist, the person with AIDS must try not to scratch these rashes. They are caused by some organism, and scratching may simply spread the rash or create sores which can become sites of infection.

Be alert to the sites of infection. Tell the doctor immediately. Infections in persons with AIDS can be extremely dangerous and can spread quickly.

Bedsores: Many times persons with AIDS spend long periods of time in bed. One of the possible consequences of this is the development of bedsores, or decubitus ulcers. These can develop at pressure points, spots where the weight of the body puts pressure on the skin in contact with the bed and limits the supply of blood to the skin for prolonged periods of time. Areas where bedsores usually occur are the buttocks, shoulder blades, heels, arms, hips, chest, or knees—whatever part of the body the person lies on most. They can also form on the ears or elbows. Watch for red sore areas on the skin. The first thing to check is the hardness of the mattress. A hard mattress will be more likely to cause bedsores.

If your friend is in the hospital, and you see that he is developing bedsores, tell him that he must move his position more often, even if it is difficult with IV tubes and all the other hospital apparatus. If he cannot move himself or will not, tell the nurses that they must turn him more often. Ask them to move him every two hours. Massage the red areas to get the blood circulating again. Bedsores should be prevented rather than cured. Once developed, they are difficult to get rid of and are a constant source of infection for your friend. They can become quite large and terrifying—large, open, raw sores surrounded by decaying flesh and infections.

If you can do it, turn your friend yourself. Get the nurses to show you how to do it. Your friend with AIDS must not be allowed to lie in the same position, or on the same side of the body, all day or even for more than a few hours. When he is at home, you will have to help him turn himself.

There are also pads that you can use to help prevent bedsores. Some of these are made of sheepskin, or a material like sheepskin; others are made of foam rubber that is perforated or shaped in such a way as to distribute the weight of the body over a larger area. There is also an egg-crate mattress cover that is very helpful in preventing these sores. You may have to put pads on your friend's heels, elbows, and even his ears.

Molluscum: Molluscum contagiosum appears as small skin-colored, dome-shaped growths on the skin, usually on the face or the chest and sometimes on other areas, such as the back of the hands, of persons with AIDS. These growths, or cutaneous papules as they are called in medical parlance, are caused by a proxvirus and are actually lesions that grow down into the skin. They are not life-threatening and can be removed, sometimes by freezing, but with some discomfort. Many doctors just leave these alone unless they become too numerous, too large, too conspicuous, or are making the person with AIDS very uncomfortable. Removal opens the body to possible infections.

There is a great temptation for the person with AIDS to pick at these mollusca, but since they are caused by a virus, they can be spread in this manner.

Aches, pains, and malaise: Many persons with AIDS suffer from various aches and pains, and from a general malaise that leaves them virtually incapable of doing anything, even though they may be physically able. You should speak to the doctor about this. If your friend with AIDS is immobilized with fear, anger, or malaise, and all your efforts cannot get him out of it, then you may have to talk to the doctor about an antidepressant, while you and other people you have helping you try to get your friend to look forward to some positive experiences in his life again. We will begin a discussion of this aspect of caring for someone with AIDS in Chapter 7.

6

GETTING YOUR HOUSE IN ORDER: Dealing with Legal and Financial Matters

When the person with AIDS is healthy early in the illness after diagnosis, it is a good time to deal with many practical issues that could cause big problems later for himself and for those who care for him. These issues have to do with the law, with living accommodations, with places of employment, with medical insurance, and with arrangements should you or your friend die.

Even though you and your ill friend may want to put off dealing with the hard facts of the outside world and with the practical preparations for future illness and possible death, neither of you will want to be dealing with these problems in a crisis. You do not want your friend to be fighting off an infection of toxoplasmosis, and then to discover that his parents are going to inherit the apartment the two of you have lived in and paid for together for ten years, because the deed to the apartment is in his name and you never got around to changing it.

LEGAL ISSUES

Lawyers have been telling us for years that we all need wills, and yet many of us—especially many homosexual people—do not have wills of any kind.

The current AIDS crisis has shown us how totally unprotected under the law the people are with whom we have formed relationships and with whom we may have shared our lives for many years. If a man dies without a wife or children, under the laws of intestate succession (which vary from state to state), his property passes to his closest relatives by blood: his parents first if they are alive, his brothers and sisters if they are alive, and his brothers' and sisters' children if they are alive. In some cases, very obscure and distantly related people can inherit the man's property.

Furthermore, a property will is only one of the legal issues people with AIDS and their friends should deal with. Other issues include a living will, power of attorney, and property that can pass outside the will.

The will: Homosexual men and women, and people living together who are not married, as is sometimes the case with those using drugs intravenously, have a special need to have wills drawn up. If you or your friend should die without a will, it is extremely likely that the most important person in your life, your friend, or significant other, will get none of the property that you may have accumulated together. The law makes no provisions for lovers, friends, or any other people not related by blood or marriage to the person who died. So if you and your friend want to protect each other, then you must have wills. It is best in most close relationships that both the person with AIDS and his friend or significant other draw up wills. This gives the persons a sense of being bound together legally; no matter what happens, you have both taken care of each other. The law must now treat your property almost the same as if you two were a married couple. Your wills have made you an entity that the law will not destroy if one of you should die.

In a will, you and your friend can do as you please with your property. You can leave it to your friend, your significant other, or your favorite charity. You can distribute it in any amounts you wish. You can give instructions about how you want your debts paid, and you can even name the people to whom you want to leave nothing.

In a will, you and your friend can also express many of your wishes. He can say what he wants done with his body. Does he want to be buried or cremated? Does he want a funeral or a memorial service? Where does he wish to be buried, and what provisions has he made to be buried there? Because many of these provisions must be acted upon as soon as a person dies, your friend with AIDS should show his will to significant persons in his life while he is still healthy.

Finally, you and your friend should name someone to carry out the provisions of the will. This person is called the executor and is responsible for probating the will in surrogate's court. All this means is that the executor must take the will to the surrogate's court that has jurisdiction and file it. The court will oversee the proper execution of the will if there are challenges. The executor will also have to deal with hospitals, doctors, insurance companies, property, and whatever else is involved.

A lawyer should draw up a will. There are standard-form wills that can be purchased in better stationery and office supply stores, filled out, and made legal by signature before a notary public and witnesses. But only a lawyer will know the special circumstances of leaving property to a nonrelative in your and your friend's particular state. He alone can make sure that the will can't be easily challenged by the family. A will might cost about $300 to have drawn up.

If you cannot afford a lawyer, call an agency set up to help persons with AIDS in your area. More than likely they can refer you to lawyers who will perform this service for you. See Appendix D for a list of these agencies.

If your person with AIDS is in deep denial and does not want to have a will drawn up, then talk to him occasionally about what the provisions would be if he were to draw up a will. At the right time, you can tell him that you want to have wills drawn up for both of you, but that he doesn't have to deal with his will right now. Perhaps, he will allow you to have the will done for him, to be signed sometime later. Otherwise, if it is proper for you to do so, see what your friend will allow you to do in arranging property to transfer outside a will. That is covered later in this chapter.

Living wills: Both you and your person with AIDS may want to draw up living wills. These documents describe what you want to happen in many different medical situations; they can relieve your friend or significant other of the anguish of not knowing what you want done, at a time when he may not be able to ask you.

If you or your friend becomes so sick that no medical treatment can help and you cannot sustain life on your own, then a living will states whether or not you want your life prolonged by artificial means. In most states, a living will is not a legally binding document that loved ones or doctors must follow, but you will have at least made clear your wishes to the people closest to you and those who are responsible for your care. This document will remove any doubt from the minds of people who love you and who may have to make the most profound decisions about your treatment. You do not want them tortured later by the thought that they did not do the right thing in a crisis.

It may be difficult for you even to initiate such a discussion with your ill friend, but such decisions may be on his mind as well. Give him time and the choice of professional counseling, if he wants it, to decide how much extraordinary treatment he wishes to undergo in the later stages of his illness, should he ever need such treatment. If he is conscious at some point when he is very ill, and in need of artificial means to stay alive, he will be asked again about treatment, regardless of whether he has a living will or not. If your friend is wary of such a document, or won't draw one up, make sure you and he and anyone else who would have a say in the matter, his parents for example, have talked about it and all agree about what should be done. A living will should also be drawn up by an attorney, but you can do it between yourselves, if necessary.

Making funeral arrangements: Many persons with AIDS have very definite ideas about what they want to happen should they die, including whether they want to be buried or cremated, where they want to be buried, who they want present, or where they want their ashes scattered. If your person with AIDS wants to discuss these matters, do so, gently. It is, of course, better to discuss them when he is healthy. Also, be sure to check with people who have already had to deal with the situation or with local AIDS organizations.

Perhaps most important of all is to know ahead of time which funeral homes will handle AIDS patients and which will not. Whether or not what they are doing is ethical or moral is not at issue. You do not want to be dealing with uncooperative funeral directors at a time of crisis.

Many people with AIDS want to plan their own memorial service with their carepartner or friends. It may be their last chance to share with friends and family the poems, writings, and music that they particularly loved and which they want remembered in association with them. They may want a memorial service to be a reflection of what they had in their love relationship or of what they had achieved in their lives.

"I didn't have to go to the funeral home for arrangements," Stella said. "Those had been made before David died. We picked out our burial plot. We didn't have to worry about that. Most of the things that people have to take care of after somebody dies, we took care of before David died."

You may have a great deal of difficulty discussing these issues with your friend with AIDS, but you must do it if you both can. It's a topic you can bring up gently and drop if the reaction you get is not cooperative. But you can at least plant the seed that you want to know your friend's wishes in this matter.

You should also try to find out the wishes of other significant people in your friend's life, such as his parents or siblings. They may have definite ideas about what they want done, such as burial in the family plot, and you may want to honor these, even if they are contrary to your friend's wishes. If you sense that it is possible, without causing a big breakdown in relationships among all the people involved, bring up the differences with your friend and discuss them. But be careful. You don't want a raging controversy swirling around you and your friend when he is very ill. And this can happen. Remember, the living have needs, and sometimes the family of a deceased person will need a funeral so that they can say good-bye, even though the sick person said he did not want a funeral.

Power of attorney: Power-of-attorney papers authorize one person to act in the name of another. You or your friend can appoint someone to deal with all your financial or medical affairs. The person so designated can deal not only with everyday matters, but also make more significant decisions. So a person with power of attorney in *financial* matters could write checks on your account, pay your bills, in effect do almost anything you as the authorizing person could ordinarily do yourself. The person with power of attorney holds that power when you are sick, in a coma, or in some other way incapacitated and cannot act for yourself.

The person with power of attorney in *medical* matters is authorized by the person with AIDS to make decisions regarding medical treatment. If your friend should reach a point where his life can only be sustained by artificial means, or if further medical treatment offers no hope for relief or better health but will only prolong suffering and pain, then the person with medical power of attorney can make the decision, which may already have been expressed in a living will, to withhold further medical treatment or not to use artificial-breathing or other devices to prolong life. Further, this document can state the signer's wish that the person with power of attorney should be able to visit him at any time of the day or night, especially during times of crisis, when the hospital might restrict visits to family members only and exclude carepartners or caring friends.

Having power of attorney can become particularly important when family members become involved, especially if serious decisions need to be made when the sick person is not able to participate in making them. Under these circumstances, you should always try to consult the family if they have shown interest and want to be involved, especially since it may take time for them to recognize the reality of your relationship with your friend or partner.

Property outside the will: You and your friend with AIDS may not want to deal with property you own jointly, like an apartment or house, joint bank accounts, and certain insurance policies outside the will, all of which you may choose not to mention in the will. Thus you can be sure the property will pass smoothly to the person you want to receive it. If you and your friend or significant other own a house, apartment, or loft together, make sure that the deed describes you as joint tenants with a right of survivorship.

Make sure that your bank accounts are joint accounts, or change them to trust accounts that the ill person holds for you. You or your friend can name each other on your insurance policies as the beneficiary without mentioning this fact in the will.

These precautions are necessary in many cases because the family of your friend may not recognize your relationship and hence may challenge the will. Even if the will is executed properly, they could cause you months of distress, challenging your right to keep the apartment, house, or bank account. Outside-the-will property can be passed from one person to the other according to the law, so the passage is less likely to be challenged.

LANDLORDS AND RENTING AN APARTMENT

One of the most tangled webs that persons with AIDS, their carepartners, and friends have to deal with is maintaining rental apartments in areas where the market is tight, where rents are controlled, and where it is to the landlord's advantage to turn the apartment over. Of course, if you and your friend with AIDS have lived together for many years, there should be no problem. But if you have recently moved in with a friend with AIDS, there can be some difficulty. You should probably not expect to keep the apartment if your friend dies, unless you can persuade the landlord when you first move in to put your name on the lease. Sometimes, landlords will do this in exchange for a rent increase. But in cities like New York, expect nothing. In cities with high vacancy rates, you will have many more options. Check these matters out with your local AIDS organization or the agency dealing with rental-housing advocacy in your area, if there is one.

In every state, you have some rights, and in some states, such as New York, a person renting an apartment is allowed to share it with one other person, but the landlord must be notified. This does not mean that the landlord is required to put your name on the lease.

No matter where you live, if you receive correspondence from the landlord, especially legal documents, deal with them immediately. You may not know what can happen next according to local law, and you might find your possessions and your friend on the sidewalk when you return home from work. Fear throughout the country is fierce and your legal rights—and the interpretation made of these rights—may vary from place to place. Speak to the landlord, if you can, about what the legal papers mean and what his intentions are. Call your AIDS organization immediately.

Furthermore, do not tell the landlord or any other tenants in the building that you know only casually that your friend has AIDS.

This is taking an unnecessary risk that could leave you open to harassment of one kind or another. When it comes to the reality of AIDS, many people become almost totally irrational.

DEALING WITH PLACES OF EMPLOYMENT

Only you and your friend with AIDS can judge your situation at work; you have to decide what you can tell people. Many react in bizarre ways to the mention of AIDS, and you may become the victim of AIDS discrimination at your job if the wrong people find out there is AIDS somewhere in your life.

The Carepartner's Job Is Probably Safe

Since you are not sick, it will probably be easier for you to hide what is going on in your life, if you feel you must. It will make your life more difficult, but you can do it. If your employer is sympathetic and close to you, and if you have had a long relationship with him or her, it may be possible to reveal what's preoccupying you. If so, this will be a great relief. A sympathetic boss may make it easier for you to be absent from work to take your friend to the doctor or to do all those many things only possible during business hours, like dealing with insurance companies or questioning hospital billing. Friends at work may also be sympathetic and helpful and may help you deal with the stress you are under. Many fellow workers have proven themselves valuable friends when they became aware of this epidemic on a personal level.

"I've been lucky at work," Jeffrey, Paul's lover, said, "because my boss has been very understanding. He's let me do a lot of things that are unusual. He's covered for me and let me arrange days in strange ways."

Caution: In highly competitive work situations, people may use your personal life against you. You may find that someone you thought you could trust is now using the information he has against you. He may begin by letting people know that you are a homosexual or involved with someone who used drugs intravenously. He might start trying to instill fear into fellow workers that you can infect them. If this happens, you will find it very difficult to defend yourself. The irony is that most people know better but will be afraid to come forward..

Further, you have to be especially careful if you work in a job that deals with the public or has to do with food. You and the medical establishment may know that you are no danger to anyone, but most people don't believe it.

Large corporations: You will probably find less sympathy in a large public corporation than you would in a small company where people become more involved in one another's lives. A good way to judge the situation is to notice whether employees in various minority groups—homosexual men, lesbians, blacks—socialize with each other openly. If they recognize each other, but covertly, and apparently do not have many friends among their fellow workers or bosses outside their group, then you should recognize that the atmosphere is too repressive for openness. If your friend or spouse is an IV-drug user, you are in much the same position, perhaps an even worse one. You will get little understanding by explaining that drug abuse is an illness. People may stay away from you even if your spouse is a hemophiliac.

Less interest in your work: You may discover, as you deal with problems of life and death, that office politics seem silly to you. You may find yourself distracted, thinking about your friend with AIDS, and then begin to worry about your performance on the job. This can become a threat to your employment.

These feelings toward work are entirely natural. Huge changes are going on in your personal life. You should expect the same things to happen in your work life. Many carepartners and friends change jobs in the middle of this experience, a time when common sense would tell you to hang on to what you have.

Len describes an experience he had one day at work. "I was sitting there in my office, and I was in a state of turmoil. So many things seemed to be pressing in on me. Then, I thought of St. Malachy's Church, only a few blocks away, and a feeling of warmth came over me. In my mind, I saw myself in that church sitting beneath the soaring arches with the statues of the saints and the stations of the cross on the walls all around me. I saw this feeling of peace sort of descending from the dimness overhead like a blanket over me. So I put on my coat and went over there.

"But peace was an elusive thing that day. Instead, when I sat down in the church, I started to cry, and my crying just went out of control, and I couldn't do anything to stop it. Soon my sobs were so convulsive that my body trembled and shook. I felt that inside me a trapdoor had fallen open, and out of the darkness below came an icy wind carrying months of uncertainty, chaos, anger, frustration, and pain.

"I was thinking, 'Everything is in such a state of flux and change, that I don't know what I'm doing anymore. Why am I doing these things?' So much of what I do every day seems silly and meaningless to me.

"I can't go to those business meetings anymore. I don't want to hear about market penetration, market share, information platforms, medium-range plans, and short-term objectives. All the antics of business seem like so many stupid games adults play with tin soldiers. And they play with such deadly seriousness, willing to destroy each other insofar as they can to gain some advantage. What has any of this got to do with life and death? What has any of this got to do with the things that are important to me?"

If you have different feelings toward your work, that is all right. Many carepartners and friends of persons with AIDS make important career and life changes along the way.

Having AIDS May Mean Your Job Is in Danger

Persons with ARC may begin to get sick while they are working and have to spend time away from their jobs. People with AIDS may have to spend long periods of time in hospitals and recuperating afterward. Many times, if they work for governments, nonprofit organizations, in their own businesses, or in a profession where work is easy to find, this is not a big problem. In most other situations the person with AIDS must be very careful.

Jeffrey tells how Paul had to deal with rumors at work when he returned after his first hospitalization. "Some people didn't think he should have gone back at all, and there was all kinds of talk behind his back. Some were saying that he had come back because before he had been sleeping with his boss."

Paul relates this story. "I had seen this before in L.A. This guy I was working with had AIDS and died. It was ridiculous. Everyone had a can of Lysol on his desk, and you were supposed to spray the phone and spray the room whenever Al left. Even then it seemed awfully stupid to me. I didn't want to see that sort of nonsense going on in my office. My boss said to me, 'People who treated you like shit before you were sick are going to treat you like shit after.'"

Jeffrey said of Paul's employer, "His boss was wonderful. I met her twice. I went up once to get some things from her, and I sat and talked awhile. She was very supportive, very concerned. She said, 'If you need anything, or any help, just let me know.' She was willing to help out in one way or another.'"

Marilyn tells of Tim's reception when he tried to return to his former employment. "Tim represented the lines of three designers in cities in New England. He made a lot of money because he really worked hard. He got those clothes in stores that no one ever heard of. But they sold. He really had a knack. But some reception he got when he went back to those showrooms! They took one look at him—he was very skinny, but he looked pretty healthy—and they knew all the rumors were true, and told him where to find the door and how long it should take him to get down the elevator. No one even asked if he could do the work. Of course, 'dear ole Dad' was out of town for weeks on end. Finally, Daddy's secretary said to Tim, 'I think it's a disgrace what they're doing to you, and I'm even ashamed to be working for your father. I won't be much longer. If he'll do what he's doing to you—his son—what would he do to me if I ever needed anything, even after fifteen years with him?"

Peter, who was fired from his teaching job in a private school when it was learned he had AIDS, ran into very unsympathetic people when he made a complaint to the Justice Department about discrimination based on a handicap. "It sounds to me like you were fired because they were afraid you would infect the children," the person said, "not because you have a handicap." Peter did not have the energy to fight the case, so he settled for disability payments and a job as substitute teacher in a public system where no one knew him, except for the old friend who hired him.

People can be cruel: Sometimes at work, outside work, in public and private places, people can do cruel and inconsiderate things to people who are sick with AIDS. Mostly, people act out of fear and ignorance, but their actions hurt no less.

Stella tells about the paranoia she felt. "David was a deacon in the church down there, and he was a Sunday school teacher, and he was very, very active in the church. But I was so paranoid about the disease. I was so afraid that people would think I was going to give them a disease that I was afraid to fix food for dinners, because I was scared to death that nobody would eat it. It just got so that I was so paranoid about the disease that I never took food anywhere, and if I went to someone's house, besides my family's, I would never drink out of a glass or cup unless it was a Styrofoam cup that I could throw away. And up until recently, I had Styrofoam cups here, so if people came, I gave them coffee out of a Styrofoam cup, because I was so afraid they would think they were going to catch something."

Joan explained what Barry had been told by his closest friends about AIDS and their dry-cleaning business. "Insane as it sounds, our friends warned us not to let the word get out that David had AIDS. 'People are going to stop coming to your stores. They're going to think, "Why take even the smallest chance? AIDS has been in that store and that house. Why have to think about that when you take in your dry cleaning?" There are lots of other places to take it where you don't have to think about that.' I don't suppose they thought that we had made friends with any of our customers. But it was a risk, so we didn't take it."

Legal Protection Against Discrimination in the Workplace

Both you and your friend with ARC or AIDS can be subject to discrimination in places of employment and can be fired. According to the Justice Department's interpretation of the relevant law, if your boss or potential employer fears that you might spread the disease to fellow workers or customers—even though there is absolutely no medical evidence to support the fear that AIDS can be spread by casual contact in the workplace, and not one documented case of AIDS spread in this manner—then he can discriminate against you by not hiring you, or by firing you.

AIDS is a handicap according to federal law, just as is blindness or being crippled. ARC is not. Persons with AIDS are protected just as are other disabled people from discrimination in employment, housing, and public accommodations, based on their handicap. If a disabled person is discriminated against, he can complain to the Justice Department and, ordinarily, the Justice Department will follow up on the complaint. Employers dread these cases, because they are time-consuming and can result in bad publicity and expensive settlements.

Now, with its insensitive and illogical interpretation of Section 504 of the Rehabilitation Act of 1973, made public on June 22, 1986, the Justice Department has, in effect, stated that people with AIDS, and even people who are antibody-positive to HIV (HTLV-III), can be discriminated against if the employer claims he did it to stop the spread of the disease.

However, a majority of the states reject the approach of the Justice Department regarding persons with AIDS and have laws that protect these people from discrimination. According to the *New York Times* on September 17, 1986, New York, New Jersey, Connecticut, Florida, Illinois, Maine, Massachusetts, Michigan, Minnesota, Missouri, New Mexico, Oregon, Washington, and Wisconsin have such laws. In some of these states, you are protected if you are "perceived" to have a disability. Check with your local AIDS organization or legal defense agency if you feel you are being discriminated against because of someone's perception that you could spread AIDS. Check with your state Attorney General's office for information about the correct agency to contact for protection against discrimination based on a handicap.

89

Several states have filed a brief with the Supreme Court challenging the Justice Department view that federal law does not protect against discrimination based on fear of contagion.

If your friend with AIDS is working and he feels that his performance could lead to his dismissal, or he feels that he may be fired because he has AIDS, he should immediately check into any disability programs the company may have and apply for benefits before anything is said to him.

DISABILITY PAYMENTS AND OTHER BENEFITS

When your person with AIDS stops working, either because he has been fired or his sick leave has run out, he will usually qualify for disability payments from some level of government. Do not hesitate to apply for this money. It is his by law. A social worker is usually called in by the hospital who can take care of this for you, or there are associations set up to help people with AIDS, which can do this paperwork. Find out all about the payments due to your partner. Also find out if he is eligible for disability payments from work. Many companies have disability insurance plans that supplement the government disability payments to bring the disabled person's income up to 75 percent of what it had been before the disability. However, approach this issue with extreme care. Companies do not like any employee going on permanent disability, since it may raise the premium they pay to their insurance company.

If you have no social worker to do this work for you, or you and your friend prefer to do it yourself, here are the sources of disability income.

Sources of Disability Income

There are at least four sources of disability income open to people in all parts of the country. These are your state's disability program, the federal Social Security Disability, the federal Supplementary Security Income programs, and welfare, which is usually run by your county or city.

Your state: Each state has a program, usually part of its unemployment insurance program, that pays benefits in cash to workers who are temporarily disabled. These programs have various criteria for eligibility, but they usually include the following:

• The applicant must have worked a certain number of weeks in the previous year, or a certain number of weeks in the previous several months.

90

- His income had to have been at a certain level when he worked; this is usually a very low level that can easily be met.

- There will usually be no restrictions about income from other sources, outside working, no quibbling about assets, and no age requirements.

Benefits from your state will have a limited duration, however, usually twenty-six weeks, because this is the length of time that you must wait to get Social Security Disability. Check the listing in the state government section of your phone book for Unemployment Insurance or Disability to find the place to go. You will have to produce a birth certificate, and probably various other papers will be required.

Social Security Disability (SSD): These are payments made by the Social Security Administration, a department of the federal government, to provide an income to people who have worked and have paid Social Security and who are disabled before they are sixty-five years old, or who were disabled when they were eighteen or older and continue to be disabled. The program provides monthly cash payments, based upon how much the person earned in the past. These payments continue until the person returns to work, and can continue even then if the person's income is very low. Most persons with AIDS are eligible for these payments if they had some work history.

- There is no income test from sources other than work.

- There is no question about assets.

- The size of the payments is based on the person's income while he worked.

- After two years on disability, your friend becomes eligible for Medicare coverage. Check immediately to see if he is eligible for food stamps.

To begin the process of obtaining these payments either talk with the social worker who comes to your hospital or is connected with the agency in your area set up to help people with AIDS, or call the Social Security Administration office in your area, listed in the phone book in the U.S. Government section.

Supplementary Security Income (SSI): If your friend with AIDS has not worked, or does not qualify for state or Social Security Disability payments because he had not worked long enough, apply for Supplementary Security Income. This is a program for needy people who are sixty-five or older or those who are

91

disabled or blind. SSI is the source to turn to when you do not qualify for other payments.

There are various requirements for those payments. Before the government gives anyone SSI, it wants to make sure the person is poor and in great need. It wants to know the applicant's income, which the government defines as "anything received that can be used to meet the needs of food, clothing, or shelter. It includes cash, checks, items received 'in kind' such as food and shelter, and many items that would not be considered income for federal and other tax purposes." When the applicant lives with his parents, and he is of age, if they give him free food and rent, that would be considered income from a gift. In other words, the government wants to know everything about any money that might come into the applicant's possession, including Social Security, veterans' benefits, and disability insurance. The income limit for a single person is $409 a month, but is subject to various modifications. You should talk to your case worker about this.

To qualify for SSI, your friend with AIDS cannot have assets greater than $1,700. Excluded from these assets would be a car, if used by the household to perform essential daily activities (he must have a way to get around). If the car is not used this way, only its market value over $4,500 is counted as assets. Also excluded from his assets would be furniture, clothes, and other household goods up to $2,000 (he must have a bed and he can't run around naked), a burial fund of $1,500 (which once put aside can't be touched), and his house and the land around it, no matter what its value. Included in his assets are everything else he has, for instance bank accounts, cash, savings accounts, stocks and bonds, antiques, a second house, and so on. If he transferred any assets to anyone else in the two years before he applied for SSI, he can be disqualified; the law would presume that he did it in order to collect SSI. If your friend qualifies for SSI, he will usually qualify for food stamps since the requirements are much the same.

Food stamps: To qualify for food stamps, your friend cannot have assets of more than $1,700. The government doesn't count the car of a disabled person (or even one car in the household of a disabled person) or the family home of a disabled person, no matter what their value. It also doesn't count his burial plot, household and personal belongings, tools he needs to earn a living, and the licensed vehicle he uses half the time to produce income.

The recipient of food stamps must go each month to a designated site to exchange his monthly Authorization to Participate for stamps. Food stamps can be used to buy food, but cannot be used to buy alcohol, cleaning products, toilet paper, tobacco, or pet food.

If your friend qualifies for SSI and food stamps, he will also qualify for Medicaid, which will pay hospital costs, long-term care, hospice care, medical costs, and prescription medicines. We will look at Medicaid in a moment.

Welfare: If your friend with AIDS is truly needy, and is waiting for either SSD or SSI payments to begin, he may qualify for Home Relief, which is public assistance or welfare. This program exists in every county in the United States, but the payment size, eligibility requirements, income restrictions, asset restrictions, and a host of other conditions vary from place to place. Thrown into the equation are such things as family size, whether his heat is included in his rent, whether he has a kitchen and cooks for himself, or whether he lives with someone who buys food and cooks.

There is a very strict limit on all the resources a person can have, whether cash, savings accounts, or anything else counted as assets. In this program, your friend may have an automobile, but it can have a very limited value.

Although payments may vary from county to county, the recipient will be paid about $100 a month for all basic needs, such as food, clothing, electricity, telephone, soap, nonprescription drugs, and everything else a person needs to live, and then about $200 a month for rent. Your friend automatically becomes eligible for food stamps and Medicaid when he qualifies for Home Relief. If he is an IV-drug user, he must register with a drug-addiction rehabilitation program in order to qualify.

If a social worker will do all the applications for you, take advantage of the help. She will know the way through the maze of regulations to collect these benefits. If you or your friend must make the application on your own, carefully check with the county welfare offices for everything you will need to do. The process of getting these benefits will be unpleasant at best. Even after the benefits for your friend are obtained, the problems will continue. Your friend will have to be recertified every three months, and this can be a hassle. Home Relief payments will end, more than likely, when SSI or SSD benefits begin; unless, of course, those payments are lower than the Home Relief payments were to start with.

Medicaid: Medicaid payments can be a great blessing, since Medicaid is a very comprehensive health program. The requirements for obtaining this coverage are very strict. If your friend qualified for Home Relief or SSI, he qualifies for Medicaid. Under some circumstances people getting SSD payments can get Medicaid also.

To qualify for Medicaid, your friend can have an income of only $409 per month from any and every source, including all government programs and gifts from friends. If his income is too high, he can spend all the money over $409 on medical expenses every month, and Medicaid will begin paying immediately after his income falls to the required level.

Your friend's assets are limited to $2,950, and that includes all cash, stocks, bonds, and other types of property that could be turned into cash. Excluded are the home he lives in, his car, his furniture, his clothes, and possessions like refrigerators, stoves, and other appliances. Again, if your friend transferred assets within eighteen months of application, he could be disqualified. If your friend owns a business, or has an equity in one, he may still qualify for Medicaid. You'll have to check with your local office.

Every month your friend with AIDS will get a sort of book of coupons that is good for all kinds of medical care, including doctors, hospitals, sickroom supplies, most drugs, home care, and most other medical services. Medicaid, while a very comprehensive medical program, will not cover anything outside conventional medical treatment, such as a microbiotic diet, chiropractic treatment, acupuncture, herbology, and most other holistic approaches to medicine.

Other sources of financial help: Depending on where you live, you may be able to get financial aid, at least on a one-time basis, from a local organization set up to help persons with AIDS or from a local church with an AIDS program. You should also check at the hospital where your friend was hospitalized for any services they can provide if your situation becomes desperate. Also, if the person with AIDS is a veteran, be sure to look into Veterans Administration Benefits. You can find the number of the Veterans Administration in the U.S. Government section of your telephone book.

Just keep in mind that there is hassle associated with all of these programs. You and your friend have to be persistent, patient, and prepared for much frustration. These programs may seem to be run by huge indifferent bureaucracies that apparently feel that everyone is trying to get something they are not eligible for under the law.

MEDICAL INSURANCE

In Chapter 2 we talked about some of the problems of American medical insurance. Because medical insurers try to show as large a

94

profit as possible, they are reluctant to pay claims. When a claim is filed, especially a large one, they will go through the claimant's medical records searching for any excuse to deny it, knowing full well that in most cases people will not contest their decision, because fighting an insurance company is like fighting city hall.

What can you do to keep your friend insured and to make sure he gets the kind of medical reimbursement that he'll need? Here are some ways the two of you can make sure you get everything you deserve.

Check medical records: Even if you and your friend have health insurance, the insurance companies may try to cancel it once they learn that one of you has AIDS. Speak to your doctor about your own and your friend's medical records, since if you file a claim, the insurance company will want to obtain them. Ask the doctor never to put into your records that you are a "homosexual male," "IV-drug user," or "possible AIDS patient." Any of these statements can cause you problems. Ask your doctor to use no such statements anywhere in your medical records, and if possible to keep them out of your friend's records.

Pay the premiums: Sometimes, when a person is sick with AIDS, he has so much on his mind, or he becomes so disoriented, he does not pay attention to the mail or to when bills are due. As a consequence, people with AIDS have lost medical insurance because they did not pay the premiums when they came due. Be very careful of this with your friend with AIDS. Make sure, as tactfully as you can, that the premium is paid when due. If he has not paid the premium, see that it gets done, tactfully or not.

Insurance at work: If your friend with AIDS is covered by health insurance at work and he is on indefinite leave of absence, or if he may be terminated when his sick leave is up, find out immediately what happens to his insurance. Many policies have conversion options that the insured may exercise with the insurance company within thirty days after the group policy ceases. Within this period, the insurance company must convert the policy from group coverage to individual coverage if the insured person applies for this coverage. If your friend is sick in the hospital or at home, you must make sure you know the facts of his medical insurance.

It is not unusual for a person with AIDS to be terminated from his job when he is in the hospital. He may not even think of his insurance until he gets a notice from his insurance company—probably a Denial of Claim form in response to bills submitted by the hospital or a doctor. This may indicate that his previous em-

95

ployer cancelled his insurance coverage thirty or sixty days ago when it terminated him, leaving him with huge hospital bills that he thought were being paid by the insurance company. Don't allow this to happen to your friend. Make sure both you and he know the terms of his employment, the terms of his insurance coverage, and the dates when his status at work changes.

Many times this whole cancellation procedure is illegal from the point of view of both the employer and the insurance company. In many states, by law, the employer must inform the employee of any conversion clause in the group policy, so that when the employee is terminated or becomes disabled, he can convert the group policy to an individual policy. However, many employers ignore the law and say nothing about this conversion privilege when the person is sick, assuming that the ill person will not read the policy or insist on his rights. Since the insurance company may have been paying huge bills, it is, of course, happy to cancel this particular person's coverage. Not only are the ill person's claims expensive, but the policy may have a clause in it that allows the premiums to be waived when the person is sick or becomes permanently disabled. So the insurance company sees itself as a double loser in this conversion.

You should not trust the regular mail service to deliver your conversion application on time, nor can you trust the insurance company to open the mail before the expiration date on your conversion privilege. If the conversion application and payment are due on a certain date, make sure not only that they get to the company before that date, but that you have proof that they did. Pay the little extra for a return receipt or for Express Mail. If they deny the conversion, go to the state agency that regulates insurance companies operating in your state.

When a claim is denied: When you file a claim either for yourself or your friend, if it comes back, "Claim Denied" or "Payment Refused," carefully read the reasons given. If the reasons are vague, call the insurance company and ask for a fuller explanation. They may cite the "exclusion clause" (all the illnesses or conditions that are excluded from coverage by the policy) or the "contestability clause" (their right to contest a claim that they say is based on misrepresentations made by the insured) as applying in this case. They may claim that your friend misrepresented his health on the application, which you have no way of answering, since you do not have the application. Nevertheless, most states do not allow companies to contest claims based on "preexisting conditions" more than two years after the policy has been in force.

If the reasons the claim is denied do not seem reasonable to you—and even if they do—protest the decision in writing. If you are dealing with group insurance sponsored by a corporation and you do not get satisfaction from the person you are dealing with, go up the corporate ladder, asking each person you speak to for the name of his or her supervisor and then speak to that person. Document each step you make with letters, if possible. Gather together all the documents you need, such as the policy, the bills being contested, the claim denial form, and all your correspondence.

If you are getting nowhere, then contact your state insurance department. Some states will require the company to respond to you within a certain time. If you still get no satisfaction, in most places you can take a claim under $1,500 to small-claims court. For larger claims, get a lawyer.

Many lawyers will evaluate your case without charge. If they think your claim is strong, they will accept the case on a contingency basis, usually suing for many times the original claim. When they win, they take part of the award, sometimes up to half. If they lose, they get nothing.

Sometimes the insurance company will be reasonable. You or your friend may not have filled out the paperwork properly, and the claim may have been denied for that reason. Or the company may want more detailed information from your doctor. In these cases the problem can be handled easily. However, do not expect easy resolution in disputes involving large sums.

Fight back: Your relationship with a health insurance company is adversarial. They want to take your money and pay out nothing. They want to exclude people who are sick, at risk of getting a serious illness, or whose family shows a history of serious illness. If they could, insurance companies would deny coverage to everyone at risk for AIDS, cancer, heart disease, diabetes, and any other disease that can be long, debilitating, and involve large hospital costs. In other words, they would like to deny coverage to all the people who need it most. Remember, the situation is not going to get better in the near future. Insurance companies may begin to try to require HIV (HTLV-III) antibody tests before they will insure someone. They may already be denying insurance to unmarried men or to people living in zip-code areas with high concentrations of gay men or IV-drug users.

But you do not have to accept their decisions. The harder you fight them—the more persistent you are—the more likely you won't have to take them to court, and the easier you'll make it for others who have to wage the battle after you.

❖　❖　❖

If you are involved with a person with AIDS, no one needs to tell you that, in general, people are hysterical, misinformed, prejudiced, and inclined to irrationality when the subject of AIDS is brought up, or when they know someone with AIDS has touched their lives in some way. Whether you're dealing with the law, the medical profession, the government, a funeral director, or an insurance company, be prepared for people to discriminate against you. Just remember, each person who discriminates against you is taking a gamble that you won't stand up for your rights. He may figure, "This person has so many problems as it is, I can get away with this. He won't have the energy to fight me on it." Don't let him get away with it. Call your local AIDS organization, Lambda Legal Defense, legal aid, and any and every agency on a local, state and federal level that might in some way be involved in defending your civil rights. People have to be taught that they cannot get away with discriminating against someone who has AIDS. It will take precious energy from you to fight it, but you must do it. In the National Directory at the end of the book (Appendix D), you will find listed legal agencies to help you.

7

LIVING WITH AIDS:
Your Relationship Changes

AIDS is usually a progressive, debilitating disease, and the longer a person has it, the more likely he will become sicker and sicker. The time after the diagnosis and the first hospitalization, if there was one, is an extremely difficult period for a carepartner or friend of a person with AIDS and for the person with AIDS himself, because a great number of things are happening to both of them—all new, with each one demanding a response.

This is when the relationship between the two people begins to undergo vast changes. This evolution of the relationship will lead in one of two directions: Either the relationship will grow deeper, more sharing, and more loving; or it will become very tense, filled with anger and resentment, and it will end. What are the things that make the difference? That is the subject of the following two chapters.

RETURNING HOME

After the diagnosis and the initial treatment for some opportunistic infection, the person with AIDS often returns home from the hospital feeling better than he has in many months. He may feel weak, get tired easily, and need a few weeks or more to rest and regain his strength, but after a while, he may feel well enough to continue his life where he feels it was interrupted by AIDS.

Going back to work: This is a time when many persons with AIDS, in effect, deny the illness. They go back to work. They try to resume their lives as if nothing had happened. They drive themselves as hard as they did before they became ill. They get up early, exercise, take the train or car to their job, work till six, eat dinner, then go out to a movie.

But there is a real difference now. Quite often the person with AIDS no longer has the strength to do all this. He gets tired faster. He begins to run fevers in the afternoons and at night. Sometimes the night sweats return. He may get strange, itching rashes. If he pushes enough, he may even get sick again very quickly.

Mart talked about his return to the business he owned: "I tried to go back to work earlier than I was ready to, and it took another month before I really could go back. My office is only five blocks away, but I found that I got tired walking just five blocks. There are times even now when I get tired, and it upsets me that I may never have enough energy to do all the things that I've done in the past." Mart finally decided to sell his business.

Jeffrey remembers Paul's return to work. "He told his doctor he was feeling better, and he wanted to go back to work. He asked his boss to reduce his work load. He was still being paid his regular salary. The company seemed very generous at the time.

"He was there exactly two weeks. At the end of the first week, he started getting these horrible, horrible headaches. They would start at two o'clock in the afternoon, and by five o'clock he couldn't sit up. He had to get out and lie down somewhere. Then, the headaches would go away at night. He'd wake up and feel fine. But then the headaches started earlier each day. He went to the doctor, who thought it was just nerves. On a Friday, he got these prescriptions, but by Sunday he couldn't stand it anymore. So he went to the hospital. He had cryptococcal meningitis. They put him on amphotericin B, and a stomach tranquilizer to go with it."

Howard said, "When Alex came out of the hospital the first time, he went right back to work. I was shocked. I didn't think he'd be able to work. He was undaunted by the whole thing. He worked in Brooklyn, and he had to be at work at eight o'clock in the morning. To get there, he had to take this crummy RR train that is a local at that hour in that direction. It was a horrible trip, and he had lost so much weight that his lower spine rubbed against his skin, and it hurt to sit on the subway. So I bought him a stadium cushion. He worked until the middle of July, and then they terminated him. I don't know why they did it. It could have been that they were cutting some people, or it could have been because he was taking too much time to go to doctors and that sort of thing. But I think it was a real cutback, because they liked him."

If you find your friend is pushing himself too hard, speak to him gently, although this may be hard to do. He may, after all, be trying to cram as much as he can into the time he feels he has left. He may feel the need to accomplish something, to leave his mark. While he is feeling good, his denial may be too strong even to allow him to hear anything about his illness. The safest thing to do, if you are monitoring his daily activities, is to slow him down as much as you can. You can do this by finding activities for the two of you that are relaxing, that require a minimum of physical effort on his part. Search for particularly interesting shows on TV, or get favorite movies for the VCR. Invite a friend or two over for a simple dinner. Go to movies on off nights when there will be small crowds. Plan weekends that are not tiring.

"Of course," Jack said, "Bruce didn't tell anyone at work why he was out, except that he was sick. So when he came out of the hospital and went back to work, people were really surprised when they saw him. He had lost about twenty-five pounds. He needed a strong back and strong arms to do the work he did.

"He was staying with me at the time, and the first two days he came home, he just fell into bed and didn't get up till the next morning. He didn't even eat dinner. I was going crazy. It took his boss about two days to figure out how weak Bruce was, and then he had him driving the truck or had him acting as flagman. But it was pretty clear, real soon, that Bruce wasn't going to be able to do that kind of work anymore. That was a big crisis for him and for me."

Staying home: Sometimes people with AIDS can't return to work. If the work they did was very demanding physically or mentally, they simply may not have the strength to do it anymore. Nor do they feel that they want to try some new, less-demanding kind of work. Others never feel quite well enough to work again.

This can be a particularly vexing problem for a caring friend or carepartner. Some persons with AIDS are very good at taking care of themselves and keeping themselves busy at home during the day while you work. They may do volunteer work, have friends they can visit, go to yoga classes, take guitar lessons, shop, and cook a nice dinner. But others may not know what to do with themselves. They may sit in front of the TV all day, bored, depressed, and angry. Whatever the person with AIDS does, his daily routine is going to be part of your relationship. And you will have to help him if his behavior begins to affect your relationship.

BEING AN IMPORTANT FRIEND TO A PERSON WITH AIDS

There are as many degrees of involvement in the life of your friend with AIDS as there are degrees of friendship. You may decide to make an occasional phone call—perhaps once a week—to inquire about your friend's health, especially of you live far away. Or you might decide to become part of your friend's support system or even his carepartner.

If you decide to become part of your friends support system, you will find yourself becoming more and more involved in your friend's life. You will be one of the people your friend counts on to be there when he needs you. You will have moments of great pain and sorrow; you will probably experience emotions that you only saw before in movies or on television. But your life will be infinitely richer. You will feel better about yourself and know yourself better. You will know more about people, about their feeling and emotions, and you will learn about relationships and the many different elements that make them work. Most of all you will learn more about love and what it means to love someone through good times and bad.

Mark and Sam had been friends for years. They had done many things together. But Mark had this to say as he became involved in Sam's illness: "I had this feeling that I was getting in over my head when I started taking Sam to the doctor and things like that. Then, when he got PCP and was in the hospital and I was the only person who was there every day, I started getting scared. What's going to happen to me? This is a big responsibility. How am I going to deal with this? This is a lot to deal with.

"But there were two other men at the hospital who visited friends—actually lovers—with AIDS, so I worked at getting friendly with them. . . . I went out to eat with them after visiting hours a few times, and once one of them told me I was a very fine person to be taking care of my friend, and he was proud to know me. I hadn't thought of it that way, but it made me feel good. I could see how happy it made Sam to see me every day. After a while I began to realize how much he was going to need me and that I wanted to be there for him."

Be consistent: Whatever you decide, be consistent. Don't call the person and say you'll be over Saturday, then call Saturday morning and say you can't make it. Don't disappoint the person by making promises and then not coming through. Don't knock him off balance by making him unsure of your support. No one with AIDS or ARC needs people around who cannot be counted on.

Often, people do not mean to be cruel or to hurt a person with AIDS. They simply do not know what they are capable of doing, and they make promises they can't keep. Before you make a commitment to a person with AIDS, be sure yourself that you are willing to stick with it, that you will make the time, that you are willing to give up other activities, that you understand the implications of your decision, and that you are willing to live with the consequences. Otherwise, cruelty and disappointment can result.

Joan and Barry had very mixed feelings toward their son David. Joan explained, "Barry had to go back home to take care of the business, do the payroll, that sort of thing. But I stayed to take care of David. I thought, as soon as he was well, I would take him home with me. But two days after he was home, Barry called me at David's apartment where I was staying. 'We can't bring David here,' he said. 'We'll have to make some other arrangements.' I said, 'What are you talking about? You told him that you wanted to bring him home.' Barry sounded so angry. 'It's impossible. I got carried away when I was there. We won't be able to live in this town. We won't have a friend. I wouldn't be surprised if we got put out of business.' I said, 'What are you talking about?' Barry said 'I told Charlie [his best friend and confidant], and he told me, if we brought David here, we might as well move. AIDS is worse than leprosy. No one would come to our house, or even sit by us in church. They'd be afraid we'd give them the disease. Can't you see the word spreading that you can get AIDS from getting your clothes cleaned at Barry and Joan's?'

"I became almost hysterical and started to cry. 'Then you tell him,' I said. I was screaming. 'You call him during the day, and you tell him. I won't do it. This wouldn't be nearly as bad if you hadn't opened your big stupid mouth in the first place.' Somehow I had known from the beginning that we weren't going to be able to take David home."

Len says, "Once, when Evan was in the hospital for the first time, a girl he had known since grammar school, Claire, had come by the hospital with a friend and brought a little plant. I wanted Evan and Claire to have time to visit alone, so I left and went to the gym, which was close by. When I got back, Evan was all excited. He told me that Claire was coming back Sunday with all the people from their hometown who lived nearby, and they were going to have a little reunion there in his room. I think five or six people were going to come. So on Sunday morning Evan got up and showered and shaved, and I came to make his room neat and stay with him till Claire and their friends arrived. To make a long story short, I went to the gym, and when I came back, it was about five in the afternoon and no one had arrived. No one did. She didn't even bother to call him and tell him she wasn't coming. I felt so bad for him I could hardly contain myself. He just lay there sort of stunned and very hurt. Fortunately neither of us has ever seen that woman again. Nor has she ever called."

How to Help

The way you can help a person with AIDS the most is to set aside time on a regular basis to spend with him, whether he is at home or in the hospital. Visit as often as you can. But let the person count on you. Sometimes, people with AIDS develop deep fulfilling relationships with friends they can count on. They love them more deeply than they have ever loved a friend. And the love, the feelings of self-worth, this gives the friend are very precious. Standing by your friend with AIDS can be the most rewarding experience you have ever had. Here are some suggestions of ways to help.

Your role in your friend's life: Call up and go by. Let your friend know that you'd like to be a part of his life, and that you want to help in any way you can. You can assure your friend that this is true if you discuss your fears with him, when it is appropriate, as mentioned earlier in this book. Show him some signs of affection, such as a hug or a kiss. Be warm around him. Try to notice good signs, how he looks, if he has changed anything around him. In short, create a feeling of warmth when you visit.

Also remember, your friend is still the same person he always was, only now he is undergoing a great change. You can figure out the subjects you can talk about and those you can't. If you blunder into something sensitive, the best thing to do is clear it up at that moment. Don't let it hang in the air, and don't let it make you feel bad later. Often, your blunder can be an occasion for closeness or even humor. "You know," you might say, "I don't mean to say things like that. I seem to stumble into them. Forgive me if I'm a witless wonder sometimes."

Mark said, "Sam had a friend, Zak, who came by to see him about twice a week. They had had a little fling about a year before Sam got sick. I was there a few times when Zak arrived, and it struck me how well he knew how to deal with Sam. He'd come in and hug him and take a long look at him, and whatever was going on he'd notice, no matter what it was, even if it was just that Sam seemed more animated or to have more energy that day. He'd say something like, "Your mustache looks good trimmed that way." Sam used to look forward to his visits, and I knew when Zak was coming, I should leave. Sam always made sure he looked his best when Zak was coming."

Reactions do vary, however. Joan describes her son David's reaction to her husband's phone call telling him he couldn't come home. "Barry waited two days to call, and I was in the room when he called. I watched David's face, and it turned to a sort of shocked

104

disbelief. 'Business reasons,' David repeated. 'People aren't as understanding in small towns. Yes, yes, I understand. I understand.' Finally, he hung up and looked at me. 'You knew that call was coming?' he asked. I admitted that I did. I told him we would see to it that he got the finest care, and he didn't have to worry about anything.

"David said that's what his father had just told him. He just lay back on his bed and didn't say anything for a while. 'Would you mind leaving and maybe coming back this evening? I have some things to do.' I said, 'Are you angry?' He answered, 'I don't know. I don't know what I expected from you and Dad. Disappointed, I guess.'

"When I got back that evening, there was a man in David's room, fortyish, very trim like an athlete. David said, 'This is a friend of mine, Don. He came down from San Francisco today. I'm going to go stay in his house up there. I can get the help I need in San Francisco. Right now I'm going to need money to close my apartment down and move.' I said. 'Anything, anything you need.' He just looked at me, 'Sure, anything.' "

Help your friend feel secure: At the end of one visit, plan your next. This gives your friend a sense of continuity. But be sure to call before you arrive. You never know how your friend might feel that day, and he may not be able to see you. If both of you decide to skip a visit, try to plan a time for your next visit right away, or promise to call back the next day. In this way, the person with AIDS feels secure that you will be around soon.

Jeffrey tells how he reacted when Paul told him he had AIDS, and how he behaved afterward. "I kept thinking that it was fate in a way. The whole thing, the way we met, the way everything went. We'd only known each other a few months. So I just figured, why deny this relationship? I felt that probably, if this had happened to me six years ago, I would have run away, not able to face up to it. Now I couldn't see leaving him that way. So I went to the hospital every day, and when he got out, he stayed here with me a week, then went back to his apartment. I went over there every other day practically and made sure everything was fine—that he had food and that he was eating. But it was really wearing me out."

Plan activities: If you can, and if he is able, go out with your friend. Take him on walks, to church, to restaurants, movies, plays, concerts, anywhere he wants to go. People with AIDS need diversions just as anyone else does, especially if they are not working and are home alone during the day. If you can take a day off, you might plan a drive out into the country to have lunch. You could drive to the coast, a lake, or some famous monument. The idea is, of course, to create a pleasant experience for your friend, to help him get his mind off things.

When you plan an activity, try to judge how much energy your friend has. Don't use up all his energy getting to wherever you're going, and then have a terrible time there because he ends up exhausted and sleepy. Plan the transportation to and from where you're going so that it is not too tiring.

If your friend is feeling good, let him make the decisions about what you will be doing and where you will be going. People with AIDS need every opportunity to make decisions.

"After Bruce had to stop work, he moved into my house with me," Jack said. "Being a carpenter, I had bought an old house that I was always working on. Lots of things changed. We still used to take our trips down to Galveston, but he'd just sit on the blanket on the beach and watch the waves. We went camping a couple of times, and I had to do most of the work setting up the tent and all, and we'd hike a little, but he wasn't very interested. I didn't know what to do. You know, he wasn't very good at keeping himself busy, and he was so angry inside it scared me. When he'd drive that Chevy of his, I was sure he was going to kill us and forty other people. But he got so loving with me. We hugged a lot. We kissed. We'd lie on the sofa together holding each other for hours watching TV. Once in a while, we'd go to the bars and have a beer or two. After a while I think he didn't like that either, because he didn't get the attention like he used to. And then he started sleeping most of the day when I was away at work."

Sit quietly: Be willing to sit with him in the evening when that's what he wants. You can be silent. You can quietly read a magazine. Or you can watch television, discuss politics and people, dish your other friends, or discuss the latest goings-on about town. You do not have to be doing anything exciting. Just realize that your being there is most important.

Linda described Bob's visits to her brother Gary, his lover. "Gary looked forward all week to Bob's visits. On Friday he was all excited, and then on Monday he was glum. It always amazed me when I was around those two. They were so much like any other couple I knew. Sometimes when Gary felt good, they'd go out to dinner or a movie, and sometimes they'd just sit and watch TV or read, or Bob would tell Gary about his job or how things were going in the city. But Bob came faithfully every weekend, even when Gary had to go into the hospital. I think Bob's visits helped Gary to fight. My mother didn't understand the way those two got along."

Rose, Gary and Linda's stepmother, observed, "All my life I had seen men together: my father and his friends, my brothers, my sons and my husband, and their friends. I thought I had seen men as close as they could be to each other. I remember how they were together during the war when they didn't know if they'd ever see each other again. But this was different. Gary and Bob were closer than any men I had ever seen. At first I didn't know what to make of it, and I asked Linda. She said, 'Ma, look at them. They're a couple.' So I started looking at them as a couple, and I saw that they were just like any other very close couple. They loved each other. They looked out for each other. They were so strongly tied together that it amazed me. They never let anything interfere with the time they had together. Once I understood that, I was more comfortable around them. I thought, 'This man makes my son happy. So what else matters to me?'"

When he's angry: You may arrive and find your friend greatly distressed, crying, angry, close to despair. Don't run away. Have a good cry together. Hold each other. Try to talk about how you feel when you want to cry. Try to talk about how you feel after your cry. Tell him that crying with him makes you feel close to him. If you can't cry, hold him and be as comforting as you can. If there is an organization in your area that will send a crisis counselor to help your friend, and you feel he needs that sort of assistance—and he agrees, of course—then call for help. Your friend may need more help than you are capable of supplying. Even if you love him, he may need someone who can provide the kind of counseling you don't have the training to provide. Stick with him under any circumstances.

If he is angry that he is sick, allow him his anger. Simply say, "You have a right to be angry. There is no logic or reason for why this happens." At the same time, do not let him blame himself. "If only I hadn't done this or that! I was such a fool to do that and that!" Your answer to this line of reasoning could be, "You did what you knew to do at the time. Lots of people did. You did nothing more or less than anyone else did. Having this disease has nothing to do with your being gay or living in a big city. It has to do with a very dangerous virus finding its way into your body."

If your friend is angry with you and seems to be picking on you one day when you are visiting, try to stay calm. He would not be doing this to you if he did not feel comfortable enough with you to share his anger.

Don't allow yourself to get angry. If he attacks you personally and you feel you may lose control, simply leave for a while. You might say, "I don't love you any less because you're angry with me, but I have to leave now for a while. I'll come back in a little while, after I've taken a walk and cleared my head." Be sure to come back, no matter how you feel about it.

"I was always there for him," Jack said, "but Bruce had this need to pick at me. I'd come home and he'd start on me. 'You're late tonight. Don't tell me traffic again. Did you bring me the beer I wanted?' It wasn't like he couldn't have done most of the things he told me to do for himself. He just needed somebody to beat up on, and I was there. A couple of times our friend Sal was there, and he said that Bruce would be laughing and having a great time right up until I'd walk into the house. Then he'd turn surly. I guess he knew for sure I wasn't walking out on him. So why not beat up on the one you know'll be back?"

Mark got rough treatment more than once from Sam. "I remember one day, I came over to his apartment after work, and he was really in a mood. 'Why do you keep coming to see me?' he asked. 'You think you're some sort of Florence Nightingale, taking pity on the poor AIDS victim. Then what do you do? Go home and dislocate your shoulder patting yourself on the back. Go around bragging about what a good guy you are?' I was so surprised I didn't know what to say, but I remembered those men from the hospital. They told me he would do this to me. I said, 'I do it because I love you and you need me. I want you to love me and be willing to do the same thing for me when I need you.' That sort of got to him, because his face softened, and he said, 'I know you love me. I'm just so frustrated sometimes I think I'm going crazy.' "

Help out with chores: If your friend lives alone, or has a carepartner who works, you may be able to help by maintaining the home and just keeping their routine together. Be sure not to interfere without asking—people have more pride about this sort of thing than you might expect. Here are some ways you might help:

- Clean the apartment some weekend; help with the wash, the dishes, the pets. Whatever you do, though, don't just charge in and take over. Ask how you can help.
- Go grocery shopping for your friend with a list he prepared.
- Help decorate the home for the holidays.
- Take your friend to the doctor or for treatments.
- Cook a favorite meal and bring it over to give your friend or his carepartner a break.

Howard said, "Other people couldn't have been more helpful. I had one friend who didn't know Alex well. He'd spend the day with

108

Alex, and he'd do amazing things. One day he helped Alex take a shower. And he's a busy man. Some people, though, don't even return a phone call."

Hugh describes how Ron, John's friend, helped at one point when they were barely coping. "One day I came home to make lunch. There was this guy there, named Ron. He was John's buddy and he was there to make lunch. He just took over the place. I got over my resentment real quick. I thought, 'Okay, somebody has to make lunch.' Another time Ron arranged for a bunch of people to come to clean. Five men came."

Help your friend's carepartner: If your friend has a carepartner, tell him or her that you are coming over on such and such evening. Perhaps he needs to take some time for himself. Sometimes you could spend time with the carepartner. He may very well need someone to talk to, and you will learn much about the couple from these little talks. People in these situations live lives with a high emotional charge. They need places to express these emotions. When carepartners see you spending time with their partner with AIDS, they are extremely grateful, and many times they develop a deep affection and love for you.

Len talks about Roger, Evan's buddy. "Roger is such a special person. He comes to see Evan on the average twice a week, and he always spends two or more hours at the house. When Evan is well, Roger and he go out to dinner and then to one of the popular discos or to the theater. These are always times for me to go off and see friends or do whatever I want. I appreciate that I get some time to myself.

"Roger always takes the opportunity to talk to me when he can and to ask me how I'm doing. After a while, I realized how much Evan and Roger love each other. I, too, feel a deep love for Roger. One time Roger went to Europe for two months, and he called us one day, from France I believe. I answered the phone and spoke to him for a moment, then called to Evan who was in the backyard. I will always have in my mind the picture of Evan running across the yard to get to the phone. Evan never ran anywhere."

Listen and talk: Be willing to talk about the illness with both your friend and the carepartner. If your friend has recently gotten sick again, or lets you know that he is feeling something new, ask him to tell you about it if he wants to. He may have a need to express his fear of what is happening. He may have a sense that he is weaker now than he has ever been before, and he may be interpreting this condition to himself. Listen. Listen carefully. Don't try to change the subject. Ask questions that will help your friend clarify what he is thinking. "This sense of weakness, what do you think it means?"

If your friend begins to talk of his fear of death, of the possibility of his own death, of his sense that his death is approaching, be very careful. Try to help him maintain both his sense of realism and his sense of hope.

Don't confuse him with denial of his condition. Don't make statements like, "Things aren't that bad. You're just down today. You'll be up and around in no time."

Nor should you depress him with doom and gloom. Don't say to him, "Yes, people in your condition seldom recover. The end can come rapidly."

Instead, acknowledge his condition. "Yes, you do seem weaker today, and you do seem to have a very clear picture of your condition and what that means." This helps him maintain his reality.

But point out all the uncertainty of the prognosis, the unpredictability of the disease, and the possibility of a medical breakthrough. "This disease is very unpredictable. You really don't know how you'll feel tomorrow, and you could easily feel much better. It has happened before. Besides, you never know what might come along suddenly that could help you."

Always take your cues from your friend. He will let you know what he wants to talk about and how far he is willing to go. Often, these discussions occur late at night, when the world outside is quiet; you may both feel alone and vulnerable at that hour, which can exacerbate your mutual fears, but can also allow you the time and clarity you need to talk.

Remember, too, your friend with AIDS has probably seen and known other people with AIDS. He may have known people who have died. Often, with his experience, he judges where he is in the progression of the disease. When he gets more than one opportunistic infection at the same time, when he cannot stop his weight loss, when his herpes won't go away—any one or all of these events may be signs to him that the disease is progressing, that he is simply on the same path as those other men who have died. Your role here is to let him know you love him, and to listen, and to assure him that you will be there. Offer him all the hope that you can, by helping him keep open the possibility of some cure, however remote. This does not mean that we lie to our friend; it means we share with him our hope that something we can't foresee might happen or that the disease could go into remission.

These are just a few of the thousands of things you might do to improve the quality of life of your friend with AIDS. Surely you can

110

think of hundreds more ways. It just takes imagination, good intentions, and good sense.

LIVING ACCOMMODATIONS

Some carepartners and caring friends already lived with the person with AIDS when the diagnosis came. However, many friends do not live with the person with AIDS, and this presents a particular set of problems. It may become obvious very quickly that your ill friend is not going to be able to maintain himself and an apartment at the same time. It might be that he simply does not have the strength, that sickness may return more quickly than expected, or that working takes all the energy he has. To commute to help someone in this situation may be very difficult for the carepartner or friend. He may find himself trying to run his own life and at the same time help his friend with AIDS run his life: cleaning for him, cooking for him, doing his laundry, going with him to doctors or for treatments. The strain on the carepartner can become great, because he may, in effect, be trying to run two lives.

Many caring friends of persons with AIDS decide either to move in with the sick person or to move the sick person into their apartment or home. Decisions like these are very brave; it means living with the illness day in and day out, with all the accompanying traumas and responsibilities. But to move in together can vastly simplify the job of getting things done, of providing care for the person with AIDS. When the caring friend becomes a carepartner, the two people have the opportunity to deepen their relationship—a relationship which will, if they are to get through this thing together, grow more intense, caring, and loving. Here are some experiences.

Michael described his reaction right before his friend Joe moved in with him. "All of a sudden it dawned on me that I had someone seriously sick moving into my house, and what I envisioned was that he was going to be an invalid and need to be taken care of, that he'd really be weak and would have to be waited on and attended to. That seemed like an awful lot, and the place was a wreck, and I'd better get it squared away." Michael laughed. "This person's got AIDS, so we'd better be more hygenic around here than we usually are. So I just sort of got manic and tore the whole place apart and put it back together. Twenty-four hours later he moved in and we began."

Jeffrey and Paul decided that Paul should move to Jeffrey's apartment because life became too complicated for them, and Paul couldn't quite take care of himself. Jeffrey said, "There were a couple of times when I'd be getting ready to do something, and he'd call and say he wasn't feeling well, and could I come out? I'd drop everything and run out there. It's not like it's around the corner. Or he would tell me the food he was making, and I'd realize that he wasn't really eating anything good for him. So we both sort of decided together that he should live here. We lived together during the month of December to see if we could stand each other, then decided after the New Year that it was okay."

"When Bruce came out of the hospital the first time, he came to stay at my house," Jack said. "We didn't really have a good sense about what the disease meant. We thought that, when he went back to work, he would start staying at his place. But when he did go back to work, we knew he couldn't live alone. He sure couldn't work and take care of a place. We had only been going together for a little over a year and a half when he got sick, and I wasn't used to having anyone around all the time, but I didn't see any other choice. I loved him. That was a cinch. I just hoped that the love was strong enough to survive living with him. He was such a slob. Whatever he had in his hand stayed wherever he put it down. Before he got sick, when we spent the night together, we always stayed in my place. I tried staying in his place once. Don't get me wrong. He took great care of himself. He always kept himself and his clothes clean. To look at him you'd think he was real neat."

Joan and her husband, Barry, had made a different choice. "After David moved to San Francisco, he seemed much happier," Joan said. "I'd call him, and he sounded so, I guess, content. Once he said to me, 'Don has been wonderful to me. I mean, I've only known him for three years, and he came through like that for me. People accept me here. I have a person who comes to see me every day. They don't make me feel crummy or like I did something really awful to get sick.'

"I wasn't sure if he was trying to hurt me or what. But I thought about what he said. Suppose we had brought him home. Not a person would have come to the house to see him. The whole family would have been outcasts. What sense would that have made for him or for us?"

DOING MORE IN THE RELATIONSHIP

As a carepartner or a caring friend, you will find that the longer you are with your friend with AIDS, the more effort you'll be making in the relationship. Because your friend is often not feeling well, is tired easily and less physically active, he may be unable to

112

do many of the duties he had in the relationship, and suddenly it's only you who cooks, washes dishes, cleans, shops, takes care of the car, mows the lawn, even pays the bills. He simply doesn't have the physical energy to do the things he did before.

Neil was very angry when he found himself picking up after Ron, who was in the house all day. "At first I thought he was just depressed or just taking advantage. We were always neat people. I mean, we didn't just take off our clothes and leave them there on the floor. And we never expected one of us to clean up after the other. But he started to leave glasses and dishes on the counter and his clothes on the floor. He didn't clean up after himself. So that led to some pretty serious arguments. I didn't feel like having to remove his stuff from the bathroom sink when I wanted to shave, and the bedroom looked like a hamper. So I griped and griped about it. One day he started to shake, and his face got all twisted up like he wanted to cry, and he said to me, 'I can't do it anymore. I hardly have the energy to get up to go to the bathroom. It tires me out just to get my lunch out of the refrigerator. Please do those things for me.' Once he said that, I started paying more attention to him. He really was exhausted all the time. Actually, it took me about five minutes to stick his dishes in the dishwasher and pick up his clothes. It wasn't any trouble once I stopped resenting having to do it."

CHANGING SEX HABITS

Few people with AIDS, once they have been sick, have much interest in sex. If your relationship was sexually active, the sexual element may begin to disappear even before the person is diagnosed. That can be a cause of tension, since neither he nor you may know what is going on.

Jack's adjustment to Bruce's loss of interest in sex was painful. "At first, before he really got sick, he used to say he didn't feel like it or he was too tired, or he had a headache, just like you see in the movies. I couldn't understand why he was losing interest. We're both athletic, and that's what our lovemaking was like. So I never had any sense that he wasn't happy with it.

"When he got sick, Dr. Bill told us that losing interest in sex was a common problem. Sounds terrible, but it was a relief. Somehow it was easier to know that he lost interest because of the disease and not because he didn't find me appealing anymore."

Paul and Jeffrey spoke about their sexual relationship in the months after Paul became ill. Paul said, "My sex drive is zilch. That would have been a real big concern a few years ago. But frankly, sex is not that important anymore. It doesn't bother me. What bothers me is, am I making Jeffrey satisfied? Are the things we're able to do satisfying to him?"

Discuss sexual problems: You must discuss this aspect of your relationship with your friend. You may have no idea how much you resent the disappearance of sex unless you talk about it, and your partner may have no idea how guilty he feels about it unless he, too, can talk about it. Sex has been an important part in most relationships, so when it disappears, big adjustments are necessary. Make these adjustments together, not separately. Keep the communication open about this problem. As you go along, you may discover that you and your friend make love in different ways, without sex; you become much more affectionate, loving, considerate. You touch more, you cuddle more, you like to spend more time together.

Practice safer sex: If your partner or spouse has AIDS and your sex life continues, you must practice safer sex. Safer-sex guidelines for both heterosexual and homosexual relationships are printed in Appendix C. You are doing this as much for your friend's protection as for your own. Even if you are completely monogamous, you can never know when some germ you are carrying—which is harmless to you—can turn into a deadly disease for your friend or spouse.

Sex outside the relationship: You may find yourself sexually frustrated with no outlet for your sexual energy if sex ceases to be part of your relationship. This is a common and difficult problem for carepartners and some friends, and one that is solved differently by each person. On the one hand, you may need a sex partner, especially in these very tense times. On the other hand, you feel your friend with AIDS will be hurt if you should find one. Further, what kind of complications might arise if you were to find a sex partner and then begin to fall in love with that person? This issue is very complex, and some carepartners find that the increased intimacy of the relationship, without sex, somehow keeps these needs under control.

PICKING UP THE FINANCIAL BURDEN

At some point, your friend with AIDS may have to quit work. Unless he has considerable savings, more of the financial burden of the relationship will now be on you. Not only will you have to do more work in the relationship, but now you will also have to pay the bills, make the rent or mortgage payment, buy all the groceries, and perhaps even pay doctors' and other medical bills and buy medicines. This can be a heavy financial burden, especially if you and your friend do not have many resources. Be sure you and your friend look into all the payments due a person with a permanent disability under local, state, and federal programs, such as Social Security Disability and Medicaid. These programs can supply badly needed help, but probably won't replace the lost income. Each of these programs is discussed in Chapter 6.

This, too, is a matter you should discuss with your friend. More than likely he feels very guilty about not doing his part financially in the relationship. You may feel resentful, also. So you have to talk about it. You should also discuss your feelings about this matter with your friends, therapist, or in your group.

SPECIAL SOURCES OF TENSION

There are many problems that cause tension in the relationship between a person with AIDS and his friend or carepartner. Some of these we have discussed earlier in this book. But there are two problems, not unique to AIDS, that every person who has dealt with a person with AIDS talks about as special areas of strain: the eating habits of the sick person and the hospital stays.

Changes in Eating Habits of Persons with AIDS

Many times people with AIDS have very little appetite. Further, the drugs they are given in the hospital or at home often destroy what little appetite they had in the first place. So you may go to the hospital day after day to find that your friend has not eaten again that day, will not eat the food you brought although he asked you to bring it, and, as a consequence, is losing weight fast.

Yet you feel, "I have no control over this disease, and the only way I can help him fight it is to get him to eat. Otherwise I am helpless." So you may get obsessive about your friend's eating habits and find it hard to understand why someone so ill just won't force the food down. Your concern can cause problems between the two of you.

As difficult as this might be to you, you must accept the fact that your friend's loss of appetite is part of the disease. He has stopped eating not because he doesn't want to but because he can't, because food may be repulsive to him.

There are several remedies you can try. At home, prepare all his favorite foods. Experiment with new things. Try foods that he liked when he was a child. Often this works. Always have the food available for him to eat, whether he eats it or not. You need to do this for yourself, so that you feel you are doing all you can. Insist that he eat. But at the point where he begins to get prickly, stop insisting. He is not going to feel better, and neither are you, if he tries to eat because you are yelling at him. The tension may be a bigger problem than the eating.

When he's in the hospital, bring him the food he asks for, if you can afford to do it. If you feel you are wasting food this way, or your resources, you might try saying, "All right, I'll get a big roast beef sandwich, so that we can share it. We'll eat together." Have the sandwich cut in quarters, and eat part of it as your own lunch or dinner. You can do this with many foods, and and it will make you less apprehensive about wasting food or money.

"Bruce never paid much attention to what he was eating before he got sick," Jack said. "Put a steak and a baked potato in front of him, or french fries, and he was a happy man. But after he got sick, all that changed. He started looking at food and smelling it. He got to be a real picky eater. In the hospital he'd complain that the food wasn't fit for the hogs, and then I'd bring him good stuff, like a hot roast beef sandwich, and he'd say how great it looked. He'd smell it, but he wouldn't eat it. I used to say to him, 'Bruce, eat man. That's what we can do to beat this thing.' But he'd just look away and tell me he'd get to it later. But he never did."

Howard had the same problem. "Alex chokes all the time when we get him to eat. He gags when he has to take capsules, so we have to crush them. He takes about fifteen things a day. He never says no, except to food sometimes. I'm really following what the doctors say in making him eat. I keep telling him that about the only thing I can do to help him fight is to give him food. That's all I can do to make him better."

Hospital Stays

Your friend's stays in hospitals can strain you to the breaking point. Not only do you have to go on with your life—get up, go to work, keep the home decent, pay the bills—but now you have to make trips to the hospital, watch over your friend's treatment, see to his comfort, bring him food if he cannot tolerate hospital meals day after day, and sit with him to keep company. You may find your life to be one continuous activity, a mad rush just to get done all the things that need to be done every single day.

What if you have to work late, or you have other commitments that you can't ignore? Then you might find your day stretching

116

from six in the morning till eleven at night. And you have not had a moment of your own. All you have done is run like crazy to keep your own life together, so that you can can continue to keep your life with your friend together. You may discover that you can and should arrange to sleep in the hospital, because this will allow you more time with your friend or spouse, and at the same time slow you down somewhat by eliminating some trips you were making from home to the hospital.

And if, sometimes, you decide you can't do it today, then you may need a rest, a break. If you can, leave work early. Go by the hospital to see your friend. Then leave early and go out to dinner. Remember that one of the greatest gifts you can give your ill friend is your continued good health and sanity.

WATCHING OUT FOR YOURSELF

You may also do many things out of love while your friend is in the hospital. Stop to get him a little gift, a plant or flowers to make his room more cheerful. Bring his favorite blanket or pillow from home, his favorite dessert from the bakery. You may call friends to tell them that your friend is in the hospital and remind them that he would appreciate a word from them.

Although you want to do all these things, you may find that this is taking a toll on you. You are beginning to run down, beginning to feel the stress and the strain. You must expect this and watch out for it. It is the signal your body and mind are sending you to begin making changes in your behavior.

Without any doubt, you and your friend or partner must now deal with your emotions, if you are to get through this experience with any measure of contentment or peace. And those emotions are increasingly intense for your friend, because his self-image and level of self-esteem have vastly changed, and for you, because you are carrying heavy responsibilities, many of which are new to you. We will examine all this in the next chapter.

8

HELPING TWO PEOPLE TO COPE:
Dealing with Your Emotions

As you look after your friend or partner, visit the hospital, do more at home, pick up the financial end of the relationship, manage your job, and cope with your own fears and pain, you may find yourself wearing down. You may be moody, distracted, depressed, easy to anger, and, in private, close to tears. The disease is beginning to take its toll on you. People may begin to notice. They may ask if anything is wrong. You may want to answer, "Everything is wrong, but I can't tell you anything about it."

RISING INTENSITY OF FEELINGS

The intensity of your emotions may shock you sometimes. You may find yourself suddenly lashing out at a clerk in a store who is keeping you waiting. You may have little or no patience at work. "Just get it done," you snarl. You may find yourself yelling at your friend with AIDS. "Why the hell don't you eat? You're making me crazy." You never felt so strongly about everything before.

Hugh spoke of a particularly difficult time he and John experienced: "Life turned into a nightmare. I had to get up in the morning and give him his special foods—there was something to put bacteria back in his stomach. I'd wake up in the morning, and we'd fight. Once I threw my beeper at him and busted my beeper, and it took me a year to get another one. Talk about making life difficult. Then I had to go to my apartment to get my messages. So I go to his apartment, go to my apartment, go all over the place to get food, and then try to make a living."

Jack describes what happened to him during a period when Bruce was very sick. "It was as if the pitch of my emotions became higher and higher, and I didn't notice it until something happened that made me see that I was getting close to crazy. I had stopped driving on the freeways, because I'd learned that I just couldn't deal with that. I didn't have an air-conditioned car—well, at least, the air conditioner wasn't working, and I didn't have the money to get it fixed. So sitting on the freeways, with the heat, the exhaust fumes, the bad tempers, was just something I didn't need to do. I had taken to getting up real early, leaving Bruce some breakfast, then driving on some local roads to the subdivision I was working in.

"One morning a delivery truck was blocking all but one lane of the street I traveled on to get to the bridge over Buffalo Bayou, when suddenly the car in front of me stopped and blocked the only open lane. I blew my horn. He got out and looked at his tire on the right front. So I got out and asked the driver what was going on. He said he was going to have to change his tire. I couldn't believe my ears. 'Look up the street,' I said. Cars were backing up for blocks, as far as you could see. 'You can't do that. Nobody can get by.' He said to me, 'You can all wait for the truck.' My blood was boiling, and I wanted to stomp his stupid ass into the pavement. After all, he could have pulled up in front of the truck. But I thought, 'I don't need more aggravation. There's got to be a way out of this.' So I got the car behind me to back up, and there was a wide, sort of flat, dry ditch on the side of the road. So I went down into the ditch, drove around the guy changing his tire and up again onto the road. Where I went back onto the road, the ditch was steep, and it banged and scraped the bottom of my car. That was too much. I flipped. I pulled over to one side because every car behind me was using the ditch as the street. I got out of my car—my door was just swinging open—and went over to the guy changing his tire. I grabbed him by his shirt and kept banging him against his car and screaming, 'You stupid asshole. Just say one word and I'll break your arm.' He was very passive, and I could see he was terrified. His shirt was all ripped. Then, I got over it and drove to work. That whole day I felt like I was walking on egg-shells. I was so mad. I hadn't seen so much craziness and violence in myself in years. It scared the hell out of me."

Denial and pain: The longer it has been since your spouse's or friend's diagnosis, the more likely it is that you will see him getting sicker. The reality may begin to gnaw at you. "This thing is real. This person I love is really sick. This could be a terminal illness that he has."

The more the reality intrudes on you, the more anxious you become. You won't want to think about it. But you have no choice. The reality comes over you suddenly, at times when you are not prepared to deal with it. You may feel yourself wanting to cry in the middle of a business meeting, on public transportation, in a restaurant. It is getting harder and harder for you to protect yourself

119

from the reality of the disease by denying its existence. Denial is no longer working for you.

All this is intensely painful. Expect it to be painful, and don't be afraid to hurt. Do not be afraid or ashamed to cry. Some carepartners have a friend they can cry with. Others cry with a family member. Some cry on their own.

Hugh describes the difficulty he and John had with denial. "I was confused at this point. He'd been really sick from October. He'd even been in the hospital. And some people were telling him he's got AIDS, and some people were telling him he hasn't got it. And now it was already Christmas, and we were still denying it—at some times, and not at others."

Marilyn talks about her husband Tim's denial of his illness and of her reaction to his denial. "Sometimes I thought Tim was losing his mind," she said. "He would sit there in his hospital bed telling me about all the great things we were going to do as soon as he got out, and I knew we weren't going to do any of them. He had already lost thirty pounds, and he was really weak. I'd ask the doctor what was wrong with him, why was he talking that way, and he'd tell me that Tim just couldn't face his illness. But Tim was just making it harder on me. I couldn't sit there making plans with him. I didn't even want to be sitting there after a while. I could see it happening. I knew it was real. I kept thinking, 'Why do I have to go through this?' "

Linda and her stepmother, Rose, cried often as Gary's illness progressed. "My mother and I seemed to be carrying the heaviest burden of Gary's illness. After a while we began to talk about the fact that he was just getting sicker and sicker. Every time something happened to him, he would get better after a while, but he was always weaker than before. One day we went to lunch so that we could talk, and after lunch, sitting in the car, we just cried and cried. That day we both admitted that we thought Gary's illness was terminal. It was almost too painful to bear. I kept thinking about how, when he was a little boy, he loved to show me things he'd discovered. He'd come running into the house yelling my name and then drag me outside to show me a big wasps' nest he'd found under the roof of the porch. I can't imagine what my mother was thinking."

Gary's stepmother, Rose, recalls that afternoon with Linda. "We got dressed up so we could treat ourselves to a really nice lunch, then we spent the whole time trying not to cry. I kept thinking that this couldn't be happening in my family. It all wasn't real. Here I was with my lovely daughter in this beautiful restaurant, and outside the weather was cold and clear. The day was beautiful. But back at my house was this terrible problem. This disaster was happening in my family. I had to admit it. I *had* to admit it, even though I wanted to scream and scream. My son is dying. My child is dying. I can see it happening. I see it every day, and there's nothing I can do about it. Sometimes I want to take him in my lap like I did when he was a little boy and he was hurting. I want to rock him back and forth and make him better."

Anger replaces denial: As your denial of the disease becomes less, it may well be replaced with anger. According to Dr. Kübler-Ross in her book *On Death and Dying*, this is often the case. Anger is part of the process that both you and your friend are going to pass through as you come to terms with what is happening in your life together. At this point you are facing the reality of the illness, even if you only sometimes face what the ultimate outcome of the illness might be. Your astonishment and disbelief upon hearing the diagnosis—"No, this can't be true. This can't be happening to us"—may now be replaced with a question: "Why is this happening to us?" The fact that there is no logical answer to this question provokes anger. Focusing your anger is the greatest problem now.

- You may be angry at the disease. "Why did it have to strike here? Where did this nightmare come from? How can we stand having the lives of these young people cut down like this?"

- You may be angry at governments on various levels. "Why did government officials let this problem reach this magnitude before trying to do anything about it? Are they telling us the truth now? Do we really know all the ways this disease is spread? Is there a deliberate policy on a national level to kill off all the IV-drug users and homosexual men in the country? Are concentration camps and quarantines right around the corner?"

- You may be angry at the news media and at newspapers and magazines that describe AIDS as "always fatal." "Don't they realize that half the people diagnosed with AIDS are still alive? Don't they realize that people with AIDS listen to the news and read newspapers and magazines? Don't they understand that these people need hope? Don't they realize the damage they are doing by creating the AIDS hysteria throughout the country?"

- You may be angry at your families. "Why do they have to be so narrow-minded? Why can't I be comfortable telling them about what I am going through? Would my brother have this fear of

121

telling our parents if his spouse had some life-threatening disease?"

- You may be angry at your friends. "I can't believe that the people I've told have run away. Why do I have to confront this and my friends don't? Why can't I tell all my friends about something that they might have to face too?"

- You may be angry at people in general. "Look at them, doing their silly, selfish things. They don't have the problems I do. They don't care about my problems."

- You may be angry at God, at your church or synagogue, and at the people who represent it, whether you attend this religious organization or not. "How could a good God let this happen? How can this religious organization continue to condemn relationships like ours where there is such love and concern? How dare these people even think, much less say in public, that this disease is the wrath of God directed against us? Can they possibly know anything about love and mercy and compassion—about God—and still say those things?"

- You may be angry at the medical profession. "Why don't they show more concern for us? Why haven't they found a cure for this thing? You can bet they'd be working twenty-four hours a day if the risk groups were Girl Scouts and U.S. senators."

- You may be angry at your sick friend. "How the hell did he get this? Has he put me in danger? Look at all the responsibilities I'm carrying, and all he does is make more and more demands."

Jack began to see his anger clearly, especially when Bruce was very sick. "I'm pissed about so many things I can hardly get them on one list. I'm pissed at Bruce, because he's such an asshole sometimes and so unfair with me, like I have an obligation to take care of him, or something. I'm pissed that this thing's been around for six years now, and nobody seems to know much more about how to cure it now than they did then. And I'm pissed at some of our friends who just didn't want to hear about it. And I'm just pissed in general. Why us? Why him and why me? Why did I spend all these years looking for a man to love, then fall in love with a man who had this damned rotten disease?"

Stella, David's wife, talked about a subject she came back to time and time again. "The news media is the world's worst. They started this stuff about how the saliva could be contaminated. Everybody got hysterical. So who wants to drink out of a water fountain now, after 'She drank out of it'? There's never been a case. But that's what makes it rough on people like me, people who have AIDS,

122

and people who have been close to someone who had AIDS. The news media is just unreal. I can't see plastering this stuff all over the front pages of the newspaper when you don't have any proof of casual transmission, not even one case."

Stella continued. "And the people in the hospital. We all went through that; when they'd show up covered from head to foot in plastic just to mop the floor or empty the wastebasket. But I done everything for David. I emptied the potty-chair. I cleaned the potty-chair. I changed sheets, I wiped behinds, I washed bodies, I fed through the feeding tube."

You and your friend have many reasons to be angry at this time. It's okay to be angry. Your main problem is to control this anger, not to lash out inappropriately and hurt people who may mean well, but whose actions don't measure up. Start to pay attention to each and every thing that makes you angry, and ask yourself a few questions. "What actually happened here? Would I ordinarily be angry about this? Can I control this anger either by expressing it rationally or by talking about it? If this situation is always going to provoke anger, can I avoid it?"

Don't think that you are going to eliminate anger from your life. If you look back, you will probably see that you always had a little anger in you, especially if you were a homosexual, IV-drug user, or a hemophiliac. You may always have felt you were oppressed, put down, on the outside. AIDS has intensified that. Your objective, when you examine your anger, is to bring it under control, to prevent it from interfering in your daily functioning.

Neil, Ron's lover, described his anger as a boiling caldron. "I would boil over at the drop of a pin. No one was safe, not a little old lady on the street, not a burly sanitation worker. I had such a need to strike out in any and every direction. The newspaper enraged me, seeing the president on TV enraged me, people who pulled away from a red light too slowly enraged me. One day I was griping about everything and anything to Ron, and he told me to come lie next to him on the bed. He put his arm around me like he was trying to protect me, and I put my head on his chest. I remember thinking how skinny his arm was and how strong it had been. 'Slow down, baby,' he said. 'Don't be so mad. I'm here, you know. I can help you be strong.' When he said that, I started to cry, and I cried for a long time. All the time Ron sort of rocked me. When I finished, though, I felt so much calmer. I actually felt stronger. Sick as he was, he knew how to do that for me.

"As time passed I started trying to take control of my anger. When I needed to be somewhere, I made up my mind ahead of time that I was either going to leave fifteen minutes early or be fifteen minutes late, so that traffic wouldn't make me crazy and angry. I avoided banks, stores, pharmacies, when I knew they would be crowded. I guess what I'm saying is that I started removing a lot of the occasions for outbursts of anger from my life—the underlying causes. Well, no one's been able to straighten out the world yet, not even God."

Fear: Many of the fears that you began to experience as your friend became sick may remain with you. They may grow more or less intense as the circumstances change, but they will be there, and they can disturb you night and day.

- You may be afraid of getting sick. "I've been exposed to this illness. There's no denying it now. I see how it's working. I could easily be next."

- You may be afraid of being abandoned. "What if I get sick? Will anyone be there to take care of me? My friend can't do it. He's too sick. I can't go to my family."

- You may be afraid of being left alone. "What if something happens to my friend? What will I do then? Will be able to cope? How will I be able to stand being by myself? What will I do with my time?"

- You may be afraid of the unknown. "What is going to happen next? Is my friend going to get better again? How will the illness change him?"

Mark's fears became more focused the longer he took care of Sam. "I kept thinking that I had always been the one to have little affairs, but never to let anybody get me into a relationship. I didn't want to be tied down. After a while, taking care of Sam, I was wishing I had gotten into a relationship. I ran through my mind the different men who had wanted me, or who said they had fallen in love with me. And I'd think, 'Wouldn't it be nice to know he was there for me, that he'd take care of me if something happened to me?' And of course, I realized that I didn't feel like I had anyone in the world I could count on except Sam, and he was sick. Sometimes I'd have this little film clip in my mind, about being alone and sick in my apartment and looking at the telephone sitting there next to the bed on a table, but having no one to call and ask for help. It was terrifying, so I'd put it out of my mind immediately."

Guilt: You may feel guilty that you are angry at your friend with AIDS. After all, here is someone that you love, and you find yourself angry at the demands he makes. You know he is sick, yet you resent the fact that you have to do everything in the relationship. Not only do you have to do all this work, but you may have to pay for it besides.

And you may feel guilty that your friend is sick and you're not. You may even think you gave him this disease. You also know that more than likely you are going to be alive at some time in the future when your friend may not be. Why should you survive and he not?

You think that you should not feel the way you do. That is the source of your guilt. "Everything I've ever heard since I was a child tells me that I should happily be doing these things for my sick friend, but instead I'm angry and resentful. Maybe I'm not a good person. Maybe I need to be punished for the way I feel."

Joan explained how she and Barry felt about guilt. "We know that there's this idea that parents should do anything for their children, and in a lot of ways we feel that way too. But this situation was different. David had put himself into a life-style that was against our religious beliefs and got sick because of it. We've provided him with everything he's asked for, and we've visited him twice in San Francisco, and I don't think we could have been asked to do more. Do I feel guilty? Yes, of course, I feel guilty. What mother wouldn't? He's my son. I feel that in some way what happened is my fault. I did something to be punished like this. I keep going over it in my mind, but I don't know what I did or what I could have done. Is he suffering for some sin I committed?"

WHAT ABOUT ME? WHAT DO I NEED?

At some point you have to stop and take stock. You have to pay attention to yourself. Too much is happening inside you now. This is a big thing you've undertaken. It is no doubt the most difficult, stressful, and painful thing you have ever done. So what are you going to need to cope with this? What are your needs, and how are you going to fulfill them? You absolutely must ask these questions now.

Every carepartner, spouse, or friend reaches this point. Now you have to shift the focus away from your friend with AIDS for a time. You have to focus on yourself. You have to make yourself more comfortable. If you don't, you're not going to be able to go on. It may be very difficult for you to sit down at this point and figure out what your needs are, but you must make an attempt. You have to sift through what you can do to lessen the tension and anxiety you feel. A great deal of your anxiety may come from or be reflected from the feelings of your friend with AIDS. So you have to start there.

Reacting to Your Friend's Feelings

One of the most difficult aspects of being a carepartner or caring friend is dealing with your partner's feelings and emotions. Many people with AIDS experience rapid, almost overwhelming emotional and mood swings. One moment they feel hopeful, the next hopeless. At different times they may be filled with anger at the injustice of the whole situation, guilty that they got the disease at all, depressed because they are helpless to change what is happening, or fearful of what the future may hold. Nor can they control these emotions which are totally new to them. You have to try to help your friend learn to deal with them. You have to learn to deal with them yourself.

Changed lives: When someone gets AIDS, the disease totally changes his life. This is true of your friend. Before the diagnosis, or before he became sick, your friend probably was an active, ambitious person. He was in control of his life, respected at work, respected in the community, loved by his friends and family. He had plans for the future. He saw himself as a valuable person with a definite and important place in society.

Now your friend may see himself as a social outcast. He may be unable to support himself because he is too weak to work, and all his dreams and plans for the future seem like dust at the foot of his bed. He feels that he is looked down upon, feared, and despised as a source of contagion by many of the people who should be supporting him, and that he has been abandoned by friends and family when he needs them the most. He feels helpless to control any aspect of his life; he is afraid doctors may not consult him about medical problems, you may not consult him about problems at home, and his friends and family may not talk to him about their lives or be afraid to talk to him about what is happening to him.

And to compound all these problems, he has too much time on his hands to think these things over and over and over. Added to his physical suffering is this terrible emotional suffering.

You get the brunt: And you, the carepartner or friend, are the person who is there the most. You are the one who must go through these mood swings with your sick friend. You might walk into your apartment one evening and bear the brunt of that whole day's frustrations. You may walk into the hospital room feeling great, and within five minutes feel that he has wrung you out emotionally, beaten you up, and pushed you to the verge of tears. He cannot help it, but he is making you deal with his feeling and emotions at a time when you might be finding it difficult to deal with your own. Of course, you may be doing the same thing to him, so use the rest of this chapter wherever it applies to you.

You can help: You can help your friend with AIDS to regain his sense of self-worth and a sense that his life still has meaning. To do this will require work, love, understanding, and patience with him and yourself.

But a caution first. You are not a therapist. You cannot and should not attempt to be one. The incredibly complex problems that may underly your friend's feelings—and your own for that matter—may well not be solvable by anyone, not therapist, priest, minister, or philosopher. There are no answers to questions like, "What did I do to deserve this? Why did this happen to me? How can a good God let this happen to me?" And it is no consolation to tell someone tortured by these questions that, "God works in mysterious ways," or, "This plague has been sent to purify us." Better no answers than these.

If your friend is suffering greatly, try to get him into an AIDS therapy group, so he can talk to other people with AIDS who share many of these same problems. If no group exists in your area, then try to find a therapist, a counselor, someone he can trust who knows how to deal with persons with AIDS.

Even with help the strain on you can be tremendous, but you are not helpless in this situation. If you cannot solve a problem, then to relieve the pressure, you must change your attitude toward it. A problem can cease to be a problem if you stop looking at it as one.

BOLD ACTION IS NEEDED NOW

You and your friend need to reduce your emotional suffering. You will not be able to do this if you approach the problem in a conventional way. You need to try new ways of thinking, new ways of looking at life. An extraordinary situation requires extraordinary approaches. Try the following four steps.

Divide big problems into small parts: The first step is to start learning about the philosophy of "one day at a time." This way of dealing with problems was developed by Alcoholics Anonymous where it has helped hundreds of thousands of people deal with problems that they thought were unsolvable. It is a way of dividing big problems into small manageable parts—daily parts. When a person first stops drinking, the craving for alcohol may be nearly overwhelming, and the thought that this is what life is going to be from here on out is very depressing. So Alcoholics Anonymous tells it new members, "You can put up with this for one day. You can

127

put up with anything for one day." Then, the organization sets up support systems for people to call when things get tough. This formula for dealing with big problems has been enormously successful, as thousands of recovering alcoholics can attest.

The Alcoholics Anonymous philosophy means this: Each day we deal with that day. Yesterday is over and is the past. We cannot act in the past. Tomorrow is the future and is not yet here. We cannot act in the future. What we can act upon is the here and now, today. So we concentrate on the day. Solve the problems you have that day. Don't worry about problems you may have in six months. As glib as it might sound, you know that today is the most important day in your life, and you should live it that way. Whenever something demands your attention or is on your mind, ask this important question, "What can I do about this today?" If the answer is "Nothing," try to put that problem out of your mind. This does not mean that you should not deal with problems that are coming up in the future. Of course, you must. But it is pointless to worry about a future problem if you can take *no action* today to begin solving it. You can begin today to plan a trip in six months, but it makes no sense to begin worrying today whether your friend will be well enough to take the trip when the time arrives.

Tom and Mart used this philosophy to deal with Mart's illness. Tom said, "Mart had been going to AA for about a year, so he had already internalized the ideal of 'one day at a time.' That really helped me get turned around, too. While he was in the hospital, I was being driven crazy by ideas of what we'd do if this or that happened. What about the business? What are we going to . . . ? How are we going to . . . ? I just stopped that. I started saying, 'Let's get through this. Let's get through that. Just take things as they come.' And the AA philosophy helped me to do that. We've been doing it ever since."

Mart said, "I also feel that, if it weren't for AA, this illness would have been much more difficult for me. AA gave me a certain discipline. If I had come down with AIDS and I had been drinking, I would have made a mess of myself. In the hospital, I started praying. Although I've never been very religious, I would pray to my Higher Power. I started thanking my Higher Power for having had another day. At the end of my prayer, I would always pray for a cure, and I would thank God for the day and for Tom. I still do that every day. Thank God for the day, and thank God for Tom."

You make the rules: The second step involves a radically new understanding of your situation. Talk to your friend with AIDS about this concept. When your friend was diagnosed with AIDS, the rules were changed. Since that time he cannot, and should not, judge himself by what other people in the world are doing who do not have AIDS. Nor should he judge himself in terms of what he used to do or what he planned to do. All that is over. The day your friend was diagnosed is also the dividing line between two lives: his life before AIDS and his life with AIDS.

People with AIDS are—and should think of themselves as—in a special category that sets them aside and sets them free. The rules that apply to everyone else do not apply to them. No one can tell a person with AIDS what he should do with his life, what he should try to accomplish. That is entirely up to him. So you and your friend are free to make the new rules yourself. Don't be weighed down with what could have been—what we could have done. All that is wasted energy. No amount of "what if's" and "if only's" is going to change one second of your lives, or is going to enrich you in any way.

You are free. You make the rules. What, realistically in the present circumstances, can you do to make your lives richer, happier, more fulfilled?

When you start to think this way, when you start to look around you, you will discover that the world is filled with opportunities for happiness, with chances to make life better. *Stop and smell the roses.* They've been there all along; you just never noticed them.

Your quality of life: The third thing you should do is to decide to make the best of the rest of your lives. No one—not one person in the world—has any guarantee that he will be alive tomorrow, a week from now, or a year from now. You have no such guarantee, and neither does your spouse or friend, so length of life is really not under anyone's control. *But what you do with today, and especially how you feel about it, is under your control.* You can passively allow yourself to be miserable and depressed, or you can decide to work actively against depression, choosing actively to do this or that which will make you both feel better, which will make your lives a little bit special, a little bit richer.

You may say to your friend, "Neither one of us knows how much time we've got together, so let's get everything out of that time that we can. Let's think from minute to minute, hour to hour, day to day, of those things that give us a sense of fulfillment, that make us happy, that make us feel good about ourselves. And let's do them." You can volunteer to help other people in need, pray, go on vacation or away for the weekend, clean the windows, paint a wall, or go to that restaurant where you always wanted to eat. Or you can do little things, like buy a beautiful flower or sit under a tree in the warm breeze. You can touch each other, speak only about what's on your mind to each other and to your friends, and watch the sunset over the harbor or bay. The choice is yours.

Jack and Bruce had to make a conscious decision about the quality of their lives together. Jack said, "Bruce and I were fighting all the time. I was sick of him and his acting like a baby, and he was sick of being sick, and sick of me bitching at him, so we were both walking around the house sulking. Finally, one day he was feeling pretty good, and we just took off in my car and went down to the coast. It wasn't too warm a day, but we were sitting on a blanket watching the waves in the gulf, and it was like we used to be before he got sick, only much closer. I felt really close to him. Bruce said, 'You know, I was just thinking about all the reasons I fell for you in the first place, pain in the ass that you are. I used to look at you sleeping. I'd think what a strong man you are, and yet you've got all these soft edges. You're still like that. Only a lot more now, when I need you so much. I really love it that you're like you are.'

"I was surprised, because he didn't say much about our relationship. But I needed him to say something like that to me," Jack said. "I answered, 'Talk about a pain in the ass—since you've been sick. Like a spoiled baby.' Bruce just laughed. 'I never said I wasn't a baby,' he said, 'just a tough one. And that's what you've wanted all along.' We laughed then, and it was like it was when we first fell in love. That seemed like forever ago. 'So let's take it easy on each other,' Bruce said. 'I love you and I'm willing. Let's make every day like today.' You can bet I agreed, and things got much better after that."

Set goals: The fourth and final step to help relieve emotional suffering is to set goals. Always have something in the near future to look forward to, even if it is just a little thing, like a nice dinner, a friend coming over to visit, or going to sleep that night. Try to have more than one thing to look forward to so that, when one goal is accomplished, there are others. The psychology of this is simple. When the present moment becomes painful or boring or depressing, your mind can move ahead to a situation where the present discomfort is gone. This makes the present moment bearable and often lifts the depression.

To sum all this up, we are saying here that you and your friend must take as much control over your emotions and feelings as you can. You do not have to be passive victims of depression, helplessness, or hopelessness. You can be active creators of happiness, control, hope, and love. And you must do it on a daily basis, from day to day. Just recognize the limits, and work within them. There will be plenty of room.

130

But if you or your friend can't do it sometimes, if you just need to be depressed, if you're having a hopeless day and you can't or don't want to do anything about it, then that's all right, too. Just recognize that nothing is perfect, no one does everything perfectly all the time, and forgive yourself. Learn what you can from the day and move on. If it's okay to be brave and courageous and making the best of it sometimes, then it's okay *not* to be brave and courageous and *not* making the best of it sometimes, too. You make the rules, so you decide what's okay.

DECIDING TO END THE RELATIONSHIP

Some caring friends and carepartners decide at a certain point during their friend's illness that they can't go on, that they are simply not capable of dealing with the relationship, and that they are doing themselves and the person with AIDS more harm than good. This is an extremely difficult decision to make, and it must be made together with the person with AIDS. You may find yourself in this position.

If, instead of feeling closer to the person with AIDS and he to you, you feel alienated from each other, then the disease has become a wedge between you. If you have stopped telling each other how you feel, or what you need, or if you never started this process of communication, then your relationship is in trouble. If you find that you are both angry and resentful and you are constantly questioning what you are doing, then it may well be that you should not be together.

Jerry and Arnold had seemed much like a solid couple, even during the first months of Jerry's illness. Then, during their trip to London, something seemed to happen to both of them. "It was like Arnold found out that there was a huge world out there," Jerry said, "and it didn't need to have me and AIDS in it at all, especially me with AIDS. He got a lot of attention in London, and since I got sick, we hadn't been going out much at home. So all of a sudden, when we got back, we were fighting. We weren't talking. He would go out and not come back till the next morning. I always understood Arnold, that he was very selfish, vain, and his feelings weren't very deep, but that had always been fine with me. I was probably the same. In his own way he loved me, and I loved him. We were happy together for a long time, and that had worked for us when that was what we both needed. Now it was just over. This illness demanded a different kind of relationship. It sounds so easy, doesn't it? But it was horrible.

"So finally, I said to him. 'Are you staying with me because you'd feel like a rat leaving me, after all these years, while I'm sick, and you think everyone we know will think you're a rat too?' He just looked at me for a minute, almost as if he didn't understand what I was talking about. 'I don't love you anymore,' he said. 'It's that more than anything else. I haven't let your sickness get in our way before, but I don't want to be with you anymore.'

"That was kind of how it ended. I was terrified for a while about being sick and alone, and I cried out of loneliness for weeks. But I've found lots of support, and my friends have been wonderful, and best of all my health seems to have withstood the breakup. I still sit and look at the wall and ask myself, 'How could anything that lasted that long have ended that easily?' I guess what I'm really saying is, 'Was it that shallow?' "

Try everything: Sometimes, when the relationship cannot be salvaged, because there was not much to it in the first place and the strain of AIDS tears it apart, the situation becomes impossible. But before you make that decision, take precautions that you will not regret it later. Do everything you can and involve your person with AIDS in every step.

- Try to have a therapist or counselor mediate the problems between you.

- Tell your partner your problems.

- State how you feel clearly and without fear of hurting your partner. He must know how you feel, and he will not fall apart upon hearing it.

- Demand that your partner tell you how he feels and what his problems are. Be prepared to be hurt. He may see what you're doing in an entirely different light than you do. What you think is generous, loving behavior, he may see as selfish, inconsiderate, and demeaning.

If after doing everything you can to salvage the relationship, you decide that you cannot go on, and especially if your friend with AIDS agrees, then you must leave. Understand clearly that your friends and family, your therapy group, even your therapist, may feel a need for you to stay in the relationship and may exert great pressure on you to remain. But you alone, together with your friend with AIDS, know what you should do.

9
GETTING THE HELP YOU NEED

Taking care of someone with AIDS is not something you will be able to do alone. You need to examine those things you can control and those you cannot, those things you can do alone and those you cannot. You are going to need help. This chapter will help you find it.

Despite your optimism and the hope that you keep in your heart, you know you cannot control the disease or its progression. You can get the best medical care and supervision for your friend, and you can lavish on him all your love and attention, but the disease and its opportunistic infections strike as they please, no matter what your efforts. So it is pointless to agonize about the disease or when it will strike. You will have sufficient anxiety when it does strike. You have no control here.

Although you may spend great amounts of time with your friend, you may feel lonely and abandoned. Large parts of what used to constitute your relationship are now gone. Even though a new and different relationship is forming between the two of you, you still feel alone, as if you are carrying the whole burden. You may feel that the friend you had before the illness has now left you, and you are just now learning who this new person is. You may crave assurance that you are doing the right things, that someone, some-where, recognizes what you are doing. You may need to feel that someone is looking out for you, that someone will be there for you when *you* need a friend. You need support, and this is something that you can control—by reaching out.

You may need a place to go to vent your feelings. You need to express your sadness, your anger, your happiness, your awe at the enormous changes that are going on in your relationship—and yet friends and family may be willing to listen to only so much. What is pressing on your mind may simply make them uncomfortable if you try to have extensive conversations with them about it. Again, in many circumstances, this is something that you can control, by reaching out.

Jerry, whose KS appeared to be in remission, described the reactions he got from his family when he tried to tell them how he felt. "For a while I was so confused I didn't know who to talk to, and I'd call my mother or sister and try to talk to them. But after a few times, I realized from their reactions that I was just causing them pain, and I wasn't feeling any better myself. I knew I had to find someone else to talk to. But, you understand, not many of your friends, especially the gay ones who are afraid, want to be talking about this illness. Arnold, my lover, often acted like I didn't have it at all. Eventually, I got a volunteer I liked from one of the agencies, and we used to talk for hours."

Reaching out is very important to a carepartner or friend of a person with AIDS. Many times what you cannot do or bear alone, you can do or bear with help. And there are many people out there who are willing to help you. You just have to find them or allow them to find you. As you know, whole organizations have been set up to help people with AIDS and their friends and families.

REACHING OUT TO YOUR FRIEND

You may well feel that you spend all your waking hours outside work caring for your friend and his needs, and that you seldom pay much attention to yourself or your needs. Neglecting your needs will simply cause you to be resentful, angry, and depressed. Eventually you will not be able to go on.

The first person you must reach out to is your friend with AIDS. You may have to say, "Look, I need your help. I feel like I'm doing this whole thing all by myself, and it's wearing me down. Please help me out." And there are many ways that your partner can help you.

Unreasonable demands: Your friend with AIDS can think twice about asking you for things, especially things he may not need or has no use for. Discuss it first, but then when you feel his demands are unreasonable, ask, "Are you sure you want me to do this? Are you sure you need this?"

James had to confront this problem with his brother Earl. "When Earl came home from the hospital after the toxo, he was pretty weak. He didn't do much, and he just slept and watched a lot of TV. He wasn't out there like he used to be, even sick, making things happen. He started calling me at work and asking me to bring him sports magazines or food like fried chicken and 'a pound of my favorite potato salad' from the deli on the corner. After a while I noticed that the magazines were never moved from where I put them down and all the food was in the refrigerator. So I said to him, 'You know how much money I make. I can't be spending money on magazines you don't read and food you don't eat.' 'I want them,' he said to me, but I think he understood. After that he'd call me, and I'd bargain with him until I got him down to one magazine, and I'd bring him as much food as I myself was willing to eat the next night. So when he didn't eat the food, I'd eat it the next night as my dinner. He didn't seem to mind and that worked for both of us. My only problem was I was eating only the food he liked."

He can complain less: Your friend with AIDS does not have to tell you every feeling and every pain in his body all the time. You know his condition. He does not have to complain to you about all the problems in the hospital, or at home, or with medical professionals, especially those problems you can do nothing about.

Jeffrey and Paul went through a very difficult time when Paul seemed to focus entirely on himself and his illness. "For a while after he moved in, he was doing well. He did telephone work at one of the AIDS agencies in town, and he and I went out fairly often. Then something happened. Maybe he got really depressed. But he started telling me about every little ache and pain in his body. He would call me at work to tell me that the joint in his knee hurt, or he'd just had a pain flash across his forehead, or his guts were growling. And he almost never stopped. He would even wake me up in the middle of the night to tell me that he couldn't sleep, or that this or that hurt. Finally, we went to all his doctors, but no one could find anything, and then we went to a therapist to see what he could tell us. He said Paul was depressed, but we already knew that. It was driving me crazy. I said to him, 'Paul, you have to start thinking about something else besides your aches and pains. You have to talk to me about other things.' It took a while, but he became conscious of when he was complaining, and the more conscious of it he became, the less he did it."

He can give you free time: Your sick friend can demand less of your time. He can be understanding if you need an occasional evening out, or can only spend a short time in the hospital now and then. If your whole life is made up of going to work and taking care of him, you are going to have less and less to give him as time goes on.

Hugh and John had a particularly difficult problem with time, because Hugh's work as a contractor doing renovations made many demands on him, and John was very jealous of his time. "When I got to the hospital, John sent me out for a sandwich. It was the beginning of the old go-out-and-get-it routine. When I got back, the doctor was there interviewing him, so I told John that I'd be back in the morning and I left.

"When I got there the next morning, John started crying. 'How come you left last night?' he asked. I said, 'You know, the doctor was here.' He said, 'I thought you left because you wanted to go out. You didn't want to stay here.' So I stayed most of that day.

"So every night I'd go by the hospital at visiting hours and stay an hour or so. John would get mad and ask why I couldn't stay longer, and I'd tell him that I had things to do. I think after a while he got used to that, because I just couldn't spend more time there. At least he didn't complain about it as much."

He can demand less attention: Sometimes it's not enough for you to be physically present; your friend with AIDS also wants all your attention focused on him. If you're cleaning the apartment or doing some work, he will interrupt you to tell you about an item in the newspaper or in a magazine, call you to look at something on TV, and otherwise let you know that he wants you focused on him. Meanwhile you're getting frustrated because you're not getting done what you wanted to do.

You and he can solve this problem in several ways. You can simply focus on him if you wish. He can invite someone over for an evening to keep him company while you do work in the house or work on something you brought home from your job. He can participate in whatever it is that you are doing to whatever degree he is able. Or he can have projects of his own to do.

Jack and Bruce had to solve this problem because Bruce was driving both of them crazy. He didn't know what to do with himself when he was alone, and he wanted all Jack's attention when Jack was around. Bruce was too healthy to have nothing to do, but not healthy enough to have a job. "You know," Jack said, "we lived in this big old house I had bought for the price of an old car when I first came to Houston, and there were millions of things that needed doing around the place. Finally, I told Bruce, 'Look, I'm going to teach you how to do things around this place, and you're going to make this a decent house to live in.' At first he grumbled a lot, but after a while he got into the swing of it. He could work with wood. He could take off and put on wallpaper. He could paint, scrape, repair windows, fix the porches. I just taught him how to do it as we went along. What a change it made. I'd come home, and he'd have been working, and he'd be so proud of what he'd done. I can tell you, during the times he was well, Bruce really made that house a place to be proud of."

136

He can show you his appreciation: Your friend with AIDS can let you know that he is aware of what you are doing and that he appreciates you. He can let you know that he loves you, and that he knows you love him. Sometimes these are hard things for people to express, but in these extraordinary circumstances they need to be said. You need to hear that he is concerned about you, just as much as he needs to hear that you are concerned about him.

Marilyn tells about her confrontation with Tim, her husband, when she told him she was prepared to leave. "All he was doing was moping around the house, sulking and feeling sorry for himself, and ordering me to get him this and get him that. Meanwhile, who was I? I work all day, I pay the bills, and at night I get to be the maid, without so much as a thank-you once in a while. So finally one day I said to him, 'Remember me, Tim? I'm Marilyn. I was Marilyn before you got sick, and I'm still Marilyn right now. Around here you act like I'm the maid.' He gave a look and said, 'But everything's changed. Don't you realize what's happened? This terrible thing has happened. We're outcasts.' I said to him, 'I realize better than you what's happened, but I'm still Marilyn, and you're still Tim.' I started to get angry. 'I'm still here, Tim. You want me to leave? I'll run out the door. Start paying attention to me. I need you to pay attention to me.'

"But he just sat there staring at me, so I got dressed and went out for the evening. When I got back, he was waiting up for me, and he snuggled up to me when I got into the bed. 'I've been thinking about what you said. You know, you're pretty special to still be here. When I think of all the shit I've laid on you, and you're still here. You didn't walk out the minute you heard I was sick.' "

Marilyn smiled and concluded, "He actually made me feel good that evening, for the first time in months. That was the beginning of something. A few new things started to get better for us after that."

Stella knew without any doubt that David loved her and was concerned about her. "One of the things that David worried about the most was that he thought I was going to die too. That worried him more than anything. He used to ask me, 'Are you going to die when I die?' And I'd say, 'No, David, I'm not going to die when you die.' And he worried about our being in the house by ourselves, and that I couldn't pay for the house. Every day I hugged David and told him that I loved him and that I'd always love him, and he did the same thing for me, every day."

Neil did nothing but concentrate on helping Ron after he became sick, but Neil couldn't see what Ron was giving him in return.

"I guess I really wasn't looking. I was feeling sorry for myself. Then, when we had to go into the hospital for the second time, I realized what he really was doing. When I got home that first night from the hospital, the apartment seemed so cold and empty. I shivered when I went into the kitchen, and it was the middle of summer. It struck me how warm the apartment always felt when he was there. I looked forward to seeing his face when I came through the door after work. And I missed terribly not having him to hold me at night before I went to sleep. He had been giving me so much love and strength for such a long time, but I hadn't been able to see it."

You both may need help: You and your friend must communicate on a more and more open basis. You have to be able to tell each other your needs, and to feel that the other is listening and is willing to make room for your needs.

If you find that you cannot talk, and that the tension is rising in the relationship, involve a third person—a therapist, a buddy, or someone you both trust—to meditate between you. Before you go to such a session, though, know what you want to get out of it. More than likely you are going because you are in pain, the relationship is not working, and you need assurance that your friend loves you and appreciates you. The whole purpose of going to a session like this is to express your feelings to your friend. Be sure that you can do so. It's easy not to. It's easy just to be a suffering martyr.

You may also find at this time that both you and your friend need to see a therapist individually or go to a group. Often, attending a group for caring friends, carepartners, or persons with AIDS is all the help that a person needs. Sometimes, however, it is not. Groups have limitations. Some people cannot express their intimate feelings in front of several other people, or their problem can be so complex that the group cannot deal with it. Groups are generally best at helping a person deal with immediate problems. They are usually not so good at solving deep-seated psychological problems.

Setting up support systems: Discuss with your ill friend whether you want to tell members of your family or any of your friends about the illness. Make this decision together. It can be another step in gathering together the help you need.

Sometimes, soon after they are diagnosed, persons with AIDS do not want anyone to know. They have any number of reasons. Often, they are in deep denial, and telling others is admitting it to themselves. Sometimes they do not want to be treated as a sick person; they want people to relate to them as they always have. And they may be afraid that everyone will abandon them. Each of these is a valid reason to keep the illness a secret at least for a time.

For some people with AIDS and their friends and carepartners, whom to tell about the illness is not an issue. If a person was sick for a long time before diagnosis, or has been very open about what has been going on with family and friends, everyone who needs to know may already know. But this is not always the case.

Eventually you both must agree to tell at least some people that he has AIDS. You will be taking chances—big risks—because the help you are going to need can only come from people. If some people abandon you, so be it; don't worry about them anymore. There will be others—people you may never have expected—who will be there for you. Only under the most extraordinary circumstances will you have to go through this alone. Help will come from unexpected quarters.

REACHING OUT TO YOUR OWN FAMILY

As a friend, lover, spouse, carepartner, relative, or even a caring parent, there may well come a point when you must talk to your own family and the ill person's family. Some families, if not every member of these families, will try to support you and your friend in this difficult situation. They will do more than express sympathy and phone once or twice in six months. A few will not even do that much, but they are the exceptions.

How to tell: It is usually best to give people news of this nature in person. Your friend should tell his own family. If he is well enough to travel, he could visit them so that he can tell them. If for some reason you must telephone them, tell them that he is sick, and ask them to come to visit. Only if they insist, or if you have known them a long time, should you tell them that he has AIDS.

Len tells how Molly, Evan's mother, telephoned and insisted that he tell her what was happening. Len said, "I had never had a conversation with her, but when I told her that I would get Evan, she said, 'No, I want to talk to you. Evan won't tell me what's going on and I need to know. Why is he sick all the time?' Evan was in the room at the time, and I put my hand over the receiver and said, 'It's your mother. She wants to know what's going on with you.' Evan shrugged his shoulders as if to say tell her what you want, and so I did. He had ARC at that time, but he had been really sick for months. I told her his symptoms, what they meant, what the doctor had told us, and what we were doing. 'You let me know if you want

139

me to do anything,' she said. I told her that I would, and then I gave the phone to Evan.

"She came up to stay with us four or five times over the next year and a half. During Evan's bad bouts of sickness, I don't know what I would have done without her. She even slept in the hospital with him."

Your family's position is ambiguous: The role of your family—the family of the carepartner, spouse, or friend—is an ambiguous one. The relationship between the sick person and your family is not by blood and is probably not even by marriage. Your family may feel in no way connected to the sick person. In fact, they may not even know of his existence if you have not shared your relationship with them. You may, for example, have told only your brothers or sisters that you are homosexual, and not your parents.

When you tell members of your family that your friend or lover has AIDS, they may feel at a loss. What should they do? Is there anything they can do? In fact, there may be nothing you can ask of them, except to love you and understand what you are going through. If they are nearby, they can provide you with a place to go, a refuge for dinner or a Sunday afternoon. If they know your partner, they can come to visit. If you are lucky, they will treat him like a sick member of the family. But this is unusual. Many times your family will wonder out loud why you are doing what you are doing. "Why don't you send this person back to his family?" they ask. "This is not your responsibility." And you may wonder out loud, "Would you ask my brother to send his wife to her family if she got a possibly terminal illness?"

Tom tells about his trip to the Midwest when he told his parents about Mart. "We were gathered around the breakfast table, my mother, my father, and I. My mother started asking me about Mart and the business. They had been very concerned about his health. I told them that he was getting ready to sell the business, because he really couldn't face the stress of another tax season. So I finally said, 'Listen, there's something that I really have to tell you . . .' My mother said, 'I think I know.' I said, '. . . that Mart has AIDS.' And she said, 'I was afraid of that.' I asked my father if he had suspected, but he said he hadn't, although he knew about AIDS.

"So it was absolutely a breeze. They made it easy for me to tell them. We began talking about what his illness meant for us, for Mart and me, and how we were coping. They were wonderfully supportive. They kept saying, 'If there's anything you need from us, just let us know—if there's anything we can do.' I said, 'I can't tell you how much this means, just to know that. I don't know what you

140

can do. But just to know that you're available, that you're thinking about us, is the support we need.' "

Families may have problems: Your families may already be burdened with a recent death or a serious illness. You may feel that you cannot add to the burdens the family is already bearing by telling them about your friend with AIDS.

Bruce, Jack's lover, felt that he couldn't tell his family about his illness, because his father had died only a year before and his mother and two older brothers were still running the wheat farm. Jack explains, "Bruce said, 'My mom doesn't need this. They were all pissed enough when I left. I can't figure what they're going to think when they find out about this.' So he was sick more than a year before he told his family.

"I never knew what to expect from my family," Jack went on. "I never knew if I wanted anything from them. They all live out in East Texas and they have their own lives to live, you know, families, businesses, all that. My brothers know about me, and they know about Bruce and his illness. They always say, 'If there's anything we can do?' But what can they do? I don't even know what to ask from them."

Howard, in his late forties, points out how difficult it is as you get older to expect much from your family. "I haven't really spelled it out completely, although I have told my mother and my brothers. I told my brother Max about it, but he's got his little business, his family, he's got other things in his life. And my mother is an old woman. While Alex was sick in the hospital, she was in the hospital with gall bladder surgery, so it wasn't possible to tell her anything."

Stella describes her family situation in these words. "My dad died when I was three, and my mother died when I was ten. I was raised by a lot of different sisters and brothers, and every year I'd go live with this one or that one. And the next year it would be, 'You're going to have to stay somewhere else.' And on up, until David and I got married. My family doesn't live here, but they weren't around when David was sick either. Some live in eastern Kentucky, and some live in Ohio, and some in Indiana. I have a couple of sisters who call pretty often, but other than that, they have their own lives. They probably would have acted differently if David had had some other disease. But if they had been in the same situation I'm in, if their husbands had had AIDS, I would have been the first one there. But I never asked them to take care of David."

Michael tells about a visit he made to his family when he needed their assurance. "Their reaction was wonderful. I said to them, 'I've got something to tell you. My roommate, Joe, died of AIDS this summer. He was living with me, and I was taking care of him, because his family told him that he couldn't come home. It was a very intense experience, and I learned a lot about myself.'

"And as I was explaining all this to my father and stepmother, my father turned off the TV, which is always a sign that this is something serious. He interrupted and said, 'I want to tell you something right now. We love you. We don't see anything wrong with you. We'd never turn you away or reject you for any reason whatsoever, whatever it was, whatever you had, whatever you told us, whatever you'd done. If you want to be here, you can be here. We don't reject you. We love you. So what can we do for you?' And I said to him, 'Nothing. You've just given me exactly what I want. Thank you very much.' "

REACHING OUT TO YOUR FRIEND'S FAMILY

The position of the family of your friend with AIDS is much clearer. The sick person is a blood member of this family. You can and should make demands on them. You can ask them to come to visit even for extended periods of time. You can ask them to help out with your friend's care in the hospital and in the home. You can ask them to help you share all the burdens of his care—emotional as well as physical and financial.

An IV-drug user: If your friend was an IV-drug user, you may have great difficulty explaining this to his family, especially if you played a part in his behavior. However, in many cases the family has already had to deal with your friend's drug problem, in one way or another, long before you came along. They may have denied that he used drugs intravenously, and they may deny it to you. Don't let them blame you, if you didn't cause the problem. If it is apparent that he became infected by using needles, admit it if they ask you. This is not the time to try to make up stories.

Marilyn was very angered by Tim's father's reaction. "He just sort of barged into the hospital room like he was the gestapo or something. To the doctor he said, 'What's going on here? Are you sure this is AIDS? What are you doing to cure him? Should I call in a doctor who knows what he's doing?' To me he said, 'How did he get it? Did you give it to him? I hear that soldiers in Germany are getting it from prostitutes.' To Tim he said, 'Maybe there's a mistake here. I know buyers in your business expect a snort of coke now and then. That creep I never liked from Chicago caused this, didn't he?'

"I wanted to say, 'Take your choice, Mr. Win-Friends-and Influence-People. Your son has shot up occasionally. He has had sex with male buyers and sometimes with models. Prostitutes, present company excluded, he liked to pick up late at night when he was drunk, another one of his charming habits he learned on his daddy's knee. You tell us how he got it.' But I didn't say anything. He's such a selfish son of a bitch; all he could hear was what he was saying anyway. Before he left, he had Tim crying, and his father was telling him that he was going to get it all fixed up. You know they can fix up anything in New York's garment district."

A homosexual relationship: If you and your friend are in a homosexual relationship, that fact will become clear to the family when they are told of the disease. They may accept this knowledge with little overt fuss, but few will want to discuss with you or with their son the relationship that exists between you—especially now that illness has struck. If they are around at all, they will recognize that you are a couple, but they may be too embarrassed or even angry to acknowledge it.

It is usually better not to try to force the family who are under the stress of recently learning about the illness, into accepting a homosexual relationship that they are not comfortable with. Under these circumstances, you have a right to expect them to express care and concern for their sick son, but changes in attitude or conviction are much harder, if not impossible, to elicit. Yes, his parents should treat you as the most important person in your friend's life and should consult you as they would any significant other in matters pertaining to your friend, but they may not be ready or able to accept you as they might a son- or daughter-in-law.

However, they may recognize at the very beginning what you are doing and who you are, and be grateful.

Jack said, "I told Bruce that he had to do something about telling his family. He said, 'I been on my own since I was sixteen. My family's got a tough enough time scratching a living out of that stingy soil up in the Panhandle without my laying this thing on them.'

"But I insisted anyway, because he really couldn't see how sick he was, and finally he did call his mother and brothers. I think their reaction stunned him. His mother flew down to Houston and stayed at the house with us for almost two weeks. She needed to know everything that was going on. I can tell you, too, the house sparkled for those two weeks. When she left, we were both sad. The whole thing, from the phone call till she left, was something really special."

143

Howard found it difficult to share his apartment and his life with Alex's mother, but during one period he did it for six weeks. "She was supposed to stay for only three weeks. When she was here, his mother went to both doctors to see how they treated him and examined him. She went right into the examining room to see what the lesions looked like. Around here she took care of him and fixed foods that she knew he liked when he was a child."

Some families will not accept you: Families may have various reasons for not embracing or even tolerating you and your homosexual relationship with their son, but the main reason is usually a moral one. They think the relationship is wrong, or sinful, or perverse. They are ashamed and guilty that their son is involved in such a relationship. Irritating and offensive as these beliefs may be to you, keep your mouth shut. You cannot deal with this, and you should not even try. There is so much else of more importance to deal with. If they say anything to you indicating their disapproval, simply say, "The problem here is that your son has AIDS. The problem is not our relationship. I am here now because I am helping your son deal with a life-threatening disease. At least we have in common our concern for your son's health."

James and Earl had a particularly difficult problem because they had the same parents, who lived almost two thousand miles away. Both men were homosexuals, and they had lived together off and on for years since they left home after high school. But they had never been lovers. James explains, "We couldn't afford to go there to talk to them, and they couldn't afford to come to see us, so we talked about it by telephone. I know they got the message that Earl has AIDS. I don't think they want to know how he got it, because they kept talking about how God takes care of these things, and the idea that we might be lovers would just be too heavy for them to even look at."

Social stigma: Families may also be terrified of the social stigmas they perceive will be attached to them if their neighbors learn that their son not only has AIDS, but is a homosexual or an IV-drug user. This, too, is their problem. Do not try to deal with it, and do not let them shift the problem to you. Given time, they may find the courage or resources to deal with any ostracism they encounter and still care for their ill relative.

Joan and Barry had avoided their greatest fear—that they would become outcasts in their own town because of the stigma of AIDS—when they told David, their son, that they could not take him home after he became ill. But the problem did not go away. "One day after he'd been living in San Francisco for about six weeks," Joan

144

says, "David called me. He told me that he really couldn't live in his friend's house anymore. 'It's just not working out. It's a mess.' He started crying on the phone and yelling at me, 'I can't stand it. Do you hear me? I can't stand it. I'm sick. I've got to get out of here. I've got nowhere to go and nobody to help me.'

"When he said that, I couldn't stand it either. I had felt so rotten and so guilty so long, but I felt Barry was right that we couldn't bring David home. Why hurt him and us at the same time? So I said to him, 'Just calm down. I'm still your mother. You can count on me. I'll come out there on the very next plane. I'll get everything straightened out for you.' Then I added before I really thought about it, 'I can stay there with you and get you well.' David didn't say anything like he didn't believe me.

"Barry and I had a good cry together as I packed to leave. I hadn't seen him cry since his father's funeral almost ten years ago. 'When will you be back?' he asked. 'What am I going to tell everybody?' I told him he knew as much as I did, but if I didn't do this, the rest of our lives wasn't going to be worth anything. I said, 'The Reverend can say anything he wants to about God's punishment for their wickedness, but when it's my son lying there so frail and weak, then I just know it's not true. God wouldn't do that to David. I read the other day that babies get AIDS and female homosexuals don't. How does the Reverend explain that?'

"When I got to San Francisco, I went to the house where David was staying. He was in a room with two other people, and they were all very sick. David was sleeping, so I didn't wake him. But he looked so sick and weak I could hardly believe my eyes.

"You could see that whoever was running the place was trying hard. It wasn't that the place wasn't clean, but it was just too crowded. The people in it needed much more care than anyone was providing. It was like someone was running a hospice or nursing home in a private house without any training. The man who had visited David in the hospital was there; he looked very tired and haggard. 'You know,' he said, 'these are all people who had no place else to go. I started trying to help out one or two men, but it got out of hand. So many people have such great need. I have seven men living in my house now, and I just can't handle it. Thank God the city provides nursing care and various other people come to help out, but it's not working.' I thanked him for helping David out as long as he had.

"I went out immediately to find an apartment for David. It took me the rest of the day to find something and then to go get at least a bed to put into it. I could have rented a mansion back home for the price of that tiny apartment. I moved David the next day by taxi."

You may be abandoned: Be prepared for abandonment and rejection. A few parents reject their child with AIDS outright. Those who do are the exception, not the rule. However, if your friend's family says they will not come to visit, and they do not want to see him at their home, their sick son will feel that rejection deeply and painfully.

Marilyn tells how Tim's father's rejection was covered in only the thinnest layer of subtlety. "After he came to visit that first time, he just didn't come back. You know, he lives right here in New York, and he works about twenty blocks from the hospital and only a little farther from where we live. So Tim would call him, and his father was always in a hurry to get somewhere. Then he started with his secretary saying he was never in the office. Tim said to me one day, 'I was always his go-getter son. He was always slapping me on the back and parading me up and down in front of all his friends. Now what am I?' I didn't say it, but I thought it, 'To him you're a sick, drug addict, faggot-loving jerk married to a whore, and you'll be lucky if you ever see him again at all.' But I sat on the bed and held him and told him I'd be there. But he never could get over his father's reaction to him. His father just confirmed to me every rotten thing I had ever thought of him."

James and Earl's parents began sending them religious literature about the sins of homosexuality and the hellfire awaiting them. "When that stuff first started coming, Earl read it over and then sat around trying to write Mom a letter telling her why he thought it was bad stuff. But when we talked to them on the phone, we could hear that they couldn't hear anything. So when the letters kept coming, we just started throwing them away without opening them."

Michael explains Joe's reaction to his parents' rejection of him and how he grew from the experience. "Joe was furious. But Joe had always been furious. For the first time in his life he expressed his fury toward his parents. He did that through therapy. This thing with AIDS brought all that to a head.

"In this crisis he had to acknowledge his love and his anger toward his parents. And that made him such a better person. He stopped being mad at everyone else and stopped blaming everyone for all his problems. In the last few months of his life, Joe was a different person. Without being real complicated about it, he started expressing his feelings. He would say, 'I feel this,' or, 'I feel that.' Before he got sick, he would say, 'I think I feel this,' or 'I think I feel that,' and it would always be bullshit. He was calmer, nicer, more thoughtful. He was much better to me. Everybody noticed it."

Draw closer: If your friend with AIDS has been rejected by his family to one degree or another, assure him that you are there.

146

Draw closer to him if you can, and be as strong as you can. The more alone you two are, the more you will cling to each other. Physical closeness may be very important right now. If you watch TV together, try to sit where you can touch each other. Call friends and invite them over. Realize, though, that some pain will remain in your friend, and there is nothing you can do about it.

Not every member of a family will act the same way, and you and your friend will probably maintain contact with those who did not abandon him. Often, when parents cannot deal with the situation, brothers and sisters, and sometimes close cousins, can. If only one parent calls, it will almost always be the mother.

Michael said, "Joe talked to someone in his family about once a week. One of his sisters would call, or his mother. He's got four sisters. But his father never called."

If you feel great anger toward those members of his family who abandoned your friend, that is entirely natural. If your friend wants to express anger, he should. So should you, although neither of you needs a big quarrel with families right now.

What to expect: Once families have been told, experience has shown they will react in several ways.

- They may reject you and your partner completely. They do not want to see either of you and will not visit. This is unusual.

- They may maintain limited telephone contact.

- They may grudgingly visit a few times, staying perhaps a few hours or a day. They make it clear that this is all that they will do, except to bury your friend in his hometown.

- They may offer some financial help, but not usually.

- One member, usually the mother or a sister, may begin to take an active part in the care of the person with AIDS. She may come to spend long periods of time with you to help in the care of the sick person, and she may make herself available whenever she is needed. She can be a great help. She can relieve you of much tension and many burdens. Do not be afraid to ask for whatever you need.

- They may ask the person with AIDS to come home to live, where they can take care of him. This is unusual.

- One of the parents may move in with their child with AIDS and care for him. These parents are also carepartners. This usually happens when the person with AIDS does not have a significant other and lives alone, and the parent lives alone in another city.

147

Most parents love their children, regardless of whether they are homosexual or heterosexual, and all parents, whatever their religious or moral conviction, will suffer great distress upon learning that their child has a possibly terminal illness. But regardless of their distress, most families will be reluctant to deal with AIDS, homosexuality, or IV-drug use.

REACHING OUT TO YOUR FRIENDS

Many pages in this book have been devoted to helping people like you overcome the fears associated with being the friend of a person with AIDS. Now we need to look at the situation from the other direction. What reactions can you expect when you are a person with AIDS, or the caring friend of a person with AIDS, and you reach out to friends for help and support?

Some friends come through: Some friends will stick by you, and you should not feel ashamed to ask them for help and to try to make time for them. Stay close to those people. They are valuable friends indeed. Sometimes your partner has friends who are more his friends that yours. Cultivate these people also. Ask them to come by on a regular basis, perhaps once or twice a week, and if you want, go elsewhere when they visit. If your partner was independent before he became ill and went out and did things with his friends without you, he should continue to do this as much as he wishes and can. You should be thankful to friends who go out with him. They provide you with time to spend on yourself.

Hugh tells about some of John's friends who amazed him. "John had this friend, a straight guy, who came to the hospital every day. He used to sit and talk to John and take care of him. He was somebody that John worked with. And he'd have these conversations with John. There was another guy, a religious friend of John's, who used to come and pray with him. An Episcopal priest came too, and he did touching. He came and ministered to John.

"About this time people from John's labor union and some of his friends got together to help us, and they started a fund. They raised a lot of money. I loved it, coming home and finding checks in the mail. It really helped."

Jack and Bruce had two friends they came to depend upon. "Larry and Fred met each other through Bruce and me," Jack said. "They just took to each other and to us. They never let us down. When Bruce was in the hospital, one or both of them were there every day, and when he was out, we saw them almost every weekend. Sometimes they'd come over and cook for us, or take us

148

to their place for dinner. They were what I would have thought brothers would be when you're in trouble."

Michael and Joe had a mutual friend, Mark, who had offered to take Joe in, when his family had told him he could not come home. Michael says, "I knew that Joe didn't want to stay with Mark, because he didn't like his roommate, and because he would be more comfortable in my house, since he'd lived there before. Then, when Joe was very sick, I called Mark up and he came right over. He and I sat on the sides of Joe's bed, and Mark rubbed his back. Joe was getting real stiff and cramping up, and Mark massaged him while I talked to him, telling him to relax. And then Joe started to relax, and Mark and I sat in front of the window and hugged and cried and cried and hugged."

Stella tells of a little boy who came every day to bring David the mail. "There were times when he had a cold, and he'd come to the door, but he wouldn't come in. He'd say, 'I got a little sniffle today, and I don't want to give you anything.' Thank God for people like that."

Unexpected help: You may have the following experience; many friends and carepartners of persons with AIDS have shared it. You call a friend, one that you may not feel particularly close to but want to tell about what is happening. Much to your surprise, that person comes to visit. She calls, returns to visit again, brings flowers, arrives on an evening to give you the evening off, brings a dinner prepared at home. You are surprised, even stunned, and very pleased.

Cultivate this person. You may not know her motivation, but unless it is unhealthy in some way—and that will become clear very quickly—accept it. People who want to help like this are often people with big hearts, who are shy and whose kindness is ordinarily hidden but needs to be expressed.

Some will abandon you: Not all your friends will stick by you. As a matter of fact, if the majority of your friends are there when you need them, count yourself lucky. People in a crisis situation, as you are, expect friends and family to rally around, to be willing to help when they are needed. But many people do not rally around. Instead, they run away. They cross off your name in their address book. Many friends, carepartners, and people with AIDS complain bitterly that they have been abandoned by their friends.

One of the most depressing reactions might go like this. Upon learning of the illness, your friend is most concerned. He comes immediately to ask what he can do. You think this person has come through, but the initial burst is all there is. This friend does not want to hear about it anymore. He does not come to the hospital, does not come to the house, does not call or return calls. You feel, rightly so, that the friend has cut you out of his life. His obligation to you was fulfilled by his initial show of concern.

Stella tells of the isolation she and her family felt after David was diagnosed with AIDS. "David was a fine person. He took care of a lot of widows and helped everybody out. He always joked with me. He'd say, 'I haven't seen you in three days.' He'd be going this way, and I'd be going that way on the highway, visiting people. It's really ironic for the person who helped so many people out, that just when you need a friend, nobody's there. I'm not saying that David didn't have any friends after he got sick, but it's people's nature to be fearful. It's the way we were born, and it's the way we'll die too, I guess. Some of it's just plain stupid, and it hurt David before he died. We were in our family room talking one night, about two o'clock in the morning, and he said, 'You know, I can count on my fingers the number of friends who have come up here to see me since I contracted AIDS.' That really hurts, especially when you're someone like David.

"I can go somewhere, and I want to just put my head down like that, because I know everybody is saying, 'Her husband is the one who died of AIDS.' But I'm the kind who'll just stick my head up and go on. I take one day at a time. I'll probably feel like that for the rest of my life. If we had had a lot of support from our friends when David got AIDS, I'd probably feel different. But when David got AIDS, it was as if David and I and the girls were in our own little world, and we stayed in our own world for over a year until David died. David's been dead for over a year now, and the girls and I are still in our own little world."

Marilyn spoke over and over again about her disappointment with friends who abandoned her and Tim. "I don't know if it would have been different if Tim hadn't gotten AIDS, or if we had kept up with our really old friends. I guess part of it was our fault, because we had so many friends, we really didn't have any friends. People you party with and see at openings and fashion shows, you don't expect to see in a hospital room. And after a while, those were the only friends we had."

Rose, Gary's and Linda's stepmother, explains her disappointment in some of her neighbors. "We had lived in the same house since the children were little—right after I married their father—so all our neighbors knew all our business, and it wasn't long before everyone knew that Gary had AIDS. I was really surprised at some of them. A few of Gary's friends from high school and college came by, but only two of them came more than one time. And my husband's and my friends seemed a little embarrassed around us. We had always had a bridge game at the house once a month, but that stopped because, I think, people were afraid. Of course, our very closest friends were there whenever we needed them. I have one friend who came every time I had to leave the house and didn't want to leave Gary alone. She took care of him like he was her own son. She spent almost as much time in the hospital as I did."

Howard also pointed out his hurt. "The support we got from our friends has been a disappointment. A lot of our friends have just blotted us out. They don't want to deal with the illness or with us. Some people wouldn't even return a phone call. I've called them and practically begged them to help Alex during the day when I'm working; he needed someone to help him with food and medicines and all. But these people have nothing but excuses. You know they're just excuses. These are people with plenty of time and money, who could adjust their schedules a little bit, but they won't. I believe they think they're safe from this illness if they just don't pay any attention to it and never think about it."

ORGANIZATIONS THAT CAN HELP

Even if you are not getting the support you need from family and friends, you can still get help. The gay and lesbian community has organized itself to help those whose lives have been affected by AIDS. They have been joined by many heterosexual people as well. The organizations these people have set up have made the homosexual community aware of AIDS through vast education programs, and have done more than any other institutions, including all levels of government, to help stop the spread of HIV, human immunodeficiency virus.

At the back of this book in Appendix D is a list of organizations that are active in helping persons with AIDS in one way or another. If you need help, call the number of the organization closest to you. The people at that number will know where to refer you if they can't help you. If that fails, call the organizations in one of the large cities, such as New York, San Francisco, Los Angeles, Houston, or Miami.

Organizations Set Up to Help You

In every major metropolitan area of the country, there are organizations set up by caring people to help those with AIDS, their friends, carepartners, spouses, and family members. Do not hesitate to call on these agencies. The whole purpose of their existence is to help you and your friend with AIDS. Even though agencies may have originally been set up primarily for homosexual men, many now provide services for everyone involved with AIDS and for all persons with AIDS, including IV-drug users, heterosexual women, hemophiliacs, and anyone infected through infected blood products. No matter what your situation, if you are involved with a person with AIDS, you can find help.

Services from AIDS agencies: Here is a list of the services AIDS agencies provide. This list includes everything you are likely to find in all agencies combined, so you may not find some of the services at the agency nearest you, or you may find it in a different form.

- Support groups and therapy groups for people with AIDS. Anyone is welcome in walk-in groups; in closed groups, only group members may attend. These groups may meet once a week for an hour or two. Here, people with AIDS have the opportunity to talk about their feelings and their experiences.

- Support groups and therapy groups for carepartners of persons with AIDS. There may be special groups for friends, spouses, parents, siblings, female friends, and those whose friend with AIDS is an IV-drug user or is a child. These groups usually meet once a week for an hour or two. Here, too, people express their feelings and exchange experiences.

- Medical referrals to doctors or hospitals that are experienced in dealing with AIDS patients.

- Spiritual counseling referrals for those in need. The agency will put the person in contact with a religious person who will try to help.

- Buddies, both male and female, who are volunteers and who try to help the person with AIDS and his carepartner in any way they can, from visiting to cleaning the apartment, shopping, running errands, and providing a shoulder to cry on. These people are usually trained by the agency.

- Crisis counselors, who are called in when the person with AIDS is in an emotional or mental crisis and needs immediate help to get himself under control.

- Referrals to individual therapy. When someone needs this service, the agency puts the person in touch with the therapist.

- Financial help on a limited basis, when the need is great.

- Help with finding housing when persons with AIDS have no

place to go, or referral to another agency that provides this service.

- Lawyers or referrals to lawyers who will draw up wills and deal with employers, insurance companies, and landlords who might try to fire or harass a person as soon as they learn he has AIDS.

- Social workers, or referrals to social workers, who will help persons with AIDS, their carepartners, and friends get all the social services, Social Security, and other payments from governments that they are entitled to under the law.

- Recreation committees who help set up activities for persons with AIDS, who get tickets to plays, movies, and concerts, and who provide a myriad of group activities and services.

- Education departments to collect and disseminate information about the illness and progress made in combating it. Sometimes educational departments may have information about experimental drug programs to which they can refer persons with AIDS.

- Visiting nurse services or referrals to visiting nurse services or home-care workers. These are often provided by state agencies or the Red Cross, which also provides transportation under some circumstances.

- Hot lines for people with a need to talk or with a need for information. There are state and city hot lines set up all over the country. Just ask the operator.

Services from hospitals and other agencies: Some hospitals have a hospice or outreach program that can also provide many services to you and your person with AIDS.

- Visiting nurses and home-care workers can be arranged for when your friend with AIDS leaves the hospital but continues to need nursing care.

- Patient representatives will arrange for social workers who can help you get aid from city, state, and federal agencies.

- Hospital workers may be assigned to serve in the same capacity as buddies.

- Living accommodations can sometimes be provided for homeless persons with AIDS.

Some churches or synagogues in the larger cities have programs for persons with AIDS and their carepartners. Dignity, an organiza-

153

tion of homosexual Roman Catholics, has chapters in many cities across the country, as does Integrity, the Episcopal lesbian and gay ministry. The Metropolitan Community Church, a Christian church for homosexuals, has congregations in many cities, large and small. Find out if your church or synagogue has an organization for homosexual members or for persons with AIDS.

By attending some religious services, you will discover if you need and want the comfort that religion can provide. Many people with AIDS, and their carepartners and friends, do return to church, sometimes after many years, and often for new and different reasons. Instead of going to church to tremble with fear and guilt before the wrath of an avenging and self-righteous God, who threatens people, makes them sick, and punishes innocent babies with AIDS, they find there a merciful, compassionate God, who tells them that he loves them, accepts them, forgives them whatever they think are their sins, and has prepared a home for them in his kingdom. All he asks is that they love one another.

TAKING ACTION

The whole point of this chapter is to let you know that you cannot do this thing alone, that you are going to need help, and that help will be there when you reach out for it. But you must reach out. Here is a summary.

- Your friend with AIDS can and must help you through this crisis.

- Families may well come through for you when you ask them, at least some member of your families.

- Some of your friends will help you bear the burdens and share the joys of your deepening relationship.

- Organizations, such as the Gay Men's Health Crisis and the AIDS Resource Center in New York, the Shanti Project and the Gay Men's Health Clinic in San Francisco, can be invaluable in helping you. So might hospice programs attached to hospitals, such as St. Vincent's in New York, as well as an increasing number throughout the country.

Carepartners' groups: Reach out to a friends' or carepartners' group if one is available in your area. There you will find people in your exact situation. You will find a place to vent your feelings to people who will not get tired of listening to you. You may find in these groups the people you will need to help you through this crisis. You may find there the friends to replace the ones who abandoned you.

You share a very large and widespread experience with other friends or carepartners, so seek them out wherever you are, even if there are no carepartner groups. Often you can meet them in the hospital visiting their friend with AIDS. Keep in mind that they may need you as much as you need them.

Groups for the worried well: Many cities have groups for those worried about AIDS infection. These people are called the "worried well." Groups for these people seek to lessen their anxiety with education about AIDS and its transmission, and by teaching them how to stay safe. If you feel you could use this help, call an AIDS organization for more information.

What now? If you are following the path that most caring friends and carepartners take, as it is outlined in this chapter, then you have been assessing your needs and setting up support systems to help you care for your friend with AIDS and yourself. Although you have suffered much pain and anxiety in this process, you have also learned a great deal about people, friends, family, the value of the moment, the value of relationships, and, most importantly, about yourself. Your experience up to this point has already enriched your life more than any other experience could have and has prepared you to care for your partner when he needs you most.

10

WHEN YOUR FRIEND IS VERY SICK:
Taking Care of the Relationship

The longer you and your friend with AIDS are together and the longer he is sick, the closer you'll be drawn together. Your love deepens and grows more profound. You'll find yourself sharing more intimate moments than you ever have before. This is a great learning time for both of you, the carepartner or friend and your friend with AIDS. During this period of your partner's illness, you'll learn more about love, relationships, compassion, feelings, courage, and caring than you have ever learned before. Cherish every moment of this time.

"Evan's sick now," Len says, "and I've fallen back in love with him. How could it have been otherwise? How can you be this close to someone every day, how can you go through this much with someone, and not love him? No, you either love, or you go away. And the more difficult things become, the more you love, because love alone makes it possible to bear. So you hold him. You cuddle him. You tell him of your love. And all the while you fear the loss, you fear the emptiness you might someday feel."

"The relationship got deeper—closer," Michael said of his friendship with Joe. "I think Joe and I really began to love each other in a way that was really ... I think Joe began to love me for who I really am, and I started to love Joe for Joe, not for what we wanted each other to be or projected the other to be. We were vulnerable to each other, and acknowledged our vulnerability to each other as we never had with anybody else or to each other before."

Suzanne, Michelle's mother, tells about feelings she had that puzzled her. "Cleaning Michelle and taking care of her at the last part of her life was the most intimate experience. I remember once, as my parents were leaving after a visit, they dropped me off on New York's West Side Highway, and I walked over to the hospital. It was the beginning of spring. I felt like I was going to meet a lover. I remember thinking, what a strange way to be feeling. I wanted to be alone with her. I could see the time that we

156

had together. I wanted the intimacy. I wanted it to be mine. I would go to get the things to change her. I would close the door. I bought different powders and nice smelling soaps."

Jack said this of Bruce. "It was hard to watch someone so full of spunk and life—and so strong—getting his ass whipped by this disease. He seemed to shrivel up. To sort of dry up like a dying cactus. First he had pneumonia. Then he had something the doctor thought would make him blind. But they had a new drug for that, so he went only partially blind. Then he got that cancer of the lymph glands. I was there, sitting right next to him, when the doctor explained what was happening to him. 'Bruce,' Dr. Bill said, 'we've got to take a hard look at this thing. If I send you to a doctor to get drugs for this lymphoma, the drugs are going to make you really sick and knock out what immune system you've got left. I'm telling you that the drugs will probably kill you indirectly.' 'And if I don't get them, the cancer will kill me directly,' Bruce said.

"That's the picture,' Dr. Bill said. Bruce and I looked at each other. He reached over and put his arm around my shoulder and pulled me against him. 'Some choice, we got, lovin' Bubba,' he said to me, using a name he never used in public. 'Maybe we should try the drugs a time or two and see how bad it is. I hate to go out not fighting.'

"He was part of me from that minute on. We had shared something so intimate that for a long time I felt like what was happening to him was happening to me. We just got closer and closer. It got so I took him everywhere, and when I couldn't be there, we had a nurse come to the house every day. At night he curled up against me when he slept, and I could feel the tremors in his body. I used to think the tremors were what I could feel of the war going on inside him. Once or twice I just had to cry when he was around, and he said, 'Be sad, lovin' Bubba. God knows I got a load of it inside me, too.' "

FORMS OF INTIMACY

The growing intimacy you may feel toward your friend with AIDS may be expressed in many ways, either in the hospital or at home. You may find yourself doing things that you never dreamed that you would do for any person. You may change your friend's clothes when he is incontinent and clean him, not feeling repulsed by this. You may learn how to use a bedpan. You may have to learn how to make a bed with someone in it. You will be doing these things out of love and not in any way feeling resentful. And in among the chores and the meals on trays, you may be talking about things you never dreamed you would talk about with anyone.

Personal Physical Services

One of the most concrete ways of expressing intimacy is by touching your friend. As one who has long since felt like a pariah, he will find touching even more important than before. You may touch him simply to touch him, or you may be touching him through performing services for him that he cannot do by himself anymore.

Massage: When your friend with AIDS is confined to a bed for a long time and is very sick, he may be feeling that he is ugly, repulsive, and isolated. The touch of your hands brings him reassurance and comfort. It does much good just to sit and hold his hand.

You might discover that giving your friend with AIDS a massage while he is confined to bed not only lets you touch him, but makes him more comfortable and is medically positive by helping to prevent bedsores. You do not have to know how to give massage. All you have to know is how to knead your friend's muscles and skin lightly—he will tell you the correct pressure—and how to show your love by performing this service. You do not have to massage his whole body, maybe only his neck and back or his hands and feet.

"John loved massages," Hugh said. "It made him feel better, and I don't like to give them—I don't even know how. But this friend of mine, George, gave John a really great massage and it felt so good. When George couldn't come regularly, I started hiring this woman to come to give him massages. It was so important to him."

Michael tells how Joe also loved massages and asked for one when he was very sick in the hospital. Massages had become an expression of love between Michael and Joe. "At one point he asked me to give him a back rub. He'd always loved to have his back rubbed. And that last summer when he was bummed out about something, or just needed a lift, or I wanted to give him a treat, then I'd rub his back. And I would always think, 'If I were Joe, how would I like my back rubbed?' And I would always rub his back that way. It always seemed to work.

"One evening when he asked me to rub his back, I thought to myself, 'If I were Joe, I'd want my back rubbed real gently tonight.' But to my surprise, when I started, he said, 'Not so hard.' And then I realized that I was just a witness to his death—that we weren't experiencing any of the same things." At that moment Michael realized how weak Joe really was.

Elimination: Another way that you may show your intimacy with your friend with AIDS is by caring for his needs for cleanliness, especially when he can no longer take care of these needs himself.

Probably your friend with AIDS feels most helpless, embarrassed, and even ashamed when he can no longer control the elimination of wastes from his body. You can help his feelings by not making a fuss when your friend is incontinent and by simply accepting it as a part of the illness. It takes all your love and compassion to perform these services for someone.

If a person has control, but cannot get out of bed, use a urinal bottle for urine and a bedpan for bowel movements. To use a bedpan, have the person roll gently over onto his side, then put the bedpan under him and roll him onto it. If he is stronger, you can have him lie on his back and slide the bedpan under him by helping him to raise his hips. Use gloves during all these procedures, not because of fear of infection, but simply for cleanliness. Empty the bedpan and the urinal bottle in the toilet. Use wet paper towels or disposable washcloths to clean him up after a bowel movement. After washing him, use a powder or cream to prevent the skin from becoming irritated.

If a person has lost control of his bodily functions, try to get disposable underpants and have him wear them when necessary. Also place a disposable cotton pad under him in bed. Be sure that his pajamas are out of the way and always try to be prompt and thorough in changing the pads when they are soiled. Of course, if a person loses control of his bladder, the hospital can always have a catheter inserted, but this is sometimes a painful procedure, and your friend may be even more uncomfortable with it than without it. Discuss this with your friend.

Stella tells how she cared for David in the hospital. "I felt like he was mine, and I was going to care for him. And that's what I was at the hospital for. Some of these situations involved wiping behinds. David felt more comfortable with me doing it, than with some other woman that he saw only sometime during the day."

Bathing and cleanliness: Your friend with AIDS can become most uncomfortable when he does not bathe regularly and when the bed itself does not seem fresh. When someone is sick, one of the most uplifting feelings he can have is to be freshly bathed, with his teeth brushed, wearing clean garments, and lying on clean sheets. You can raise your friend's spirits by helping him with all these tasks.

If he can get out of bed, help him to the shower. Sometimes he might want to sit on a chair in the shower—do not expect seriously ill persons to stand in the shower. You might help wash him as he sits. Turn on the water to wet him. Shut it off to soap him and shampoo his hair. Then turn it back on to rinse.

Len describes how he and Evan handled this problem when Evan was in the hospital, still very sick and weak from PCP. "Evan didn't want to be bathed in bed, but he couldn't stand up in the shower. So we got a metal and plastic chair and put it in the shower. He'd sit up on the edge of his bed, and I'd help him undress. Then he'd lean on me till he got to the chair in the shower. I always had the water going ahead of time to warm up the shower. I also didn't want to be adjusting the temperature of the water while he was sitting there. First I'd wet him. Then I'd push the nozzle against the wall so he could soap himself. He always wanted to do everything that he could by himself, and I wasn't trying to make him more dependent on me. When he wanted to be rinsed, I'd aim the water back on him, turn it off when he asked. Then he'd dry himself sitting there. Later, when he got stronger, he'd dry himself outside the shower. I can't tell you how proud we both were when, two weeks later, he took a shower by himself."

If your friend cannot get out of bed, bathe him in bed. It is best to do this in the morning, and before you plan to change the sheets. Use a cotton washcloth that is damp, but not dripping wet. That way, the mattress itself will not get damp. Wear gloves for cleanliness, not fear of infection. Make sure, of course, that the room temperature is not too cold, and that the water in your bucket or pan is not too hot or cold. Use pure soap without deodorants or perfumes, as these are less likely to dry the skin.

Have your friend first lie on his stomach. Wash an area of his body, then dry it, and cover it with a towel. When you are finished with the back of his body, rub on skin cream to prevent drying. Then, help your friend with AIDS to roll over, and wash the front of his body. Be sure to wash the genital area thoroughly as this part of the body can become most uncomfortable very quickly. Use powders here to prevent itching and rashes. When the bath is finished, help dress your friend in fresh garments; put on socks if his circulation is not good and his feet get cold.

It is not difficult to change the sheets while someone is in the bed. If it is a large bed, help your friend roll over to one side. Take the soiled sheets and, beginning on the empty side of the bed, roll them toward the person's back. Then replace them with clean sheets and roll these toward the person's back. Then roll your friend onto the clean sheets, pull the dirty sheets off, and make the other side of the bed. If it is a small bed, be very careful your friend does not fall. If it is a hospital bed, raise the side rails.

Help your friend brush his teeth, or better, to clean his mouth. You can do this with a toothbrush and paste, but if that becomes too messy, use a cotton swab and a mild solution of hydrogen peroxide. You can ask in the hospital or the pharmacy if they have anything specifically made to perform this task. If your friend has thrush, be sure to consult with the doctor about how to clean his mouth for him, as toothpaste or hydrogen peroxide may not be good for him.

Finally, comb your friend's hair if he cannot perform this task himself. This will make him feel better, even if his hair becomes mussed again after only a short while. If you need to wash his hair, do it before you begin to bathe him, and simply use a slightly soapy washcloth and rub it through his hair until it is damp. Then rinse the hair with a wet, but soapless, washcloth. Finally, when the soap is removed, dry his hair with a fresh towel.

Sometimes you may need to give your friend with AIDS an alcohol bath to bring down fevers. Put alcohol, a little water, and some ice in a bowl. Rub the damp, but not wet, washcloth gently over his body. You can feel the heat being absorbed by the washcloth. Sometimes you must do this for a long time to reduce the fever. Bringing a person's fever down this way replaces taking drugs and will probably spare him the discomfort of having night sweats.

Grooming: Sometimes, when a person is sick for a long time, his hair grows long, his mustache or beard becomes unruly, and his fingernails and toenails become long and uncomfortable. Contact your local AIDS agency to see if they have barbers who will come to cut your friend's hair. You can trim his toenails and fingernails, and if necessary, trim his hair and facial hair. Remember, your friend with AIDS may be quietly suffering and embarrassed because he cannot do these things for himself, and because he still wants to look presentable, so be sure you do them as best you can with compassion and love.

Howard described Alex's feeling when Alex became too weak to take care of himself. "You know, a lot of things that you and I take for granted, like putting on your socks or signing your name, have become an ordeal for him, and it's totally discouraging sometimes. How do we keep our spirits up? It's very difficult sometimes. He feels terrible, but he doesn't want to tell me. He's become so

161

dependent. He was the most independent of people, very strong-willed, very headstrong, and now he's become very dependent on me and on his mother when she was here. It's very difficult for him. I don't know how he's managed it. You have to be very strong to change your whole life-style so much. He has trouble buttoning his shirt. One day he complained that the tuna fish was too hard to mash. Watering the plants, cleaning the apartment—forget about it. He'd be happy if he could dress himself."

Keeping Company

Intimacy takes myriad forms. You might sit with your friend in silence, or read to him as he listens or dozes, and feel yourself bursting with feelings—love, compassion, and pain.

You might sit or lie on the bed and let your friend lean against you and hold you, or you hold him so he feels secure and is not afraid, or so that you are not so afraid.

You might have moments of great revelation toward each other, in which he will tell you something about his feelings or his present state, feelings that he has never revealed before, or you may do the same with him.

James and Earl, who have lived together for most of their lives, found their relationship vastly changed as Earl became sicker. "You know, man, he and I sort of got wrapped up in the cocoon together, and everybody else who came into our lives just didn't seem to make a lot of difference. After he had toxo, he came home and he was such a mess. The nurse would come every day to give him his medicine, and this buddy from the agency would come to get him lunch. I put the phone right next to the bed, so that he could get it and I could call him from work during the day. But sometimes he couldn't pick up the phone or he'd drop it, and then I'd be going crazy wondering if he was all right, but I couldn't just leave my job. We didn't need me on unemployment. Finally, I talked to a neighbor, Barbara, who was home most of the time, and I'd call her to go over to see him when I couldn't get him on the phone.

"We pulled our beds together so that we were really sleeping together, and lots of times during the night I'd wake up, and he'd be holding onto me. Once I woke up, and he was crying, and I said, 'Hey, what's this all about?' He said, 'You been here all my life, and now I see that you're my man.' It was the middle of the night, but he began to tell me how he felt when we were kids and in high school, how sometimes he loved me so much it scared him, and other times he hated me because I always got everything and he got nothing. 'When you'd get those good grades, and everyone would be saying how great you were, I'd just want to choke you right there where you were standing.' I said to him. 'And when you did your thing playing basketball, and the girls would all be gathered around and everyone would be telling me my brother was so wonderful, I wanted to be somebody else.' Earl said to me, 'And now we got each other, and that's what we got.' He was crying. I loved him so hard at that minute that I wanted to squeeze the breath out of him."

Your friend may tell you how strong his hold is on life, if he feels it slipping away. He may tell you how he wants you to react after he is gone. He may tell you that what you have done for him is more than he could have expected from anyone in life and that part of him will live in you and part of you will live in him.

"One weekend," Rose, Gary's stepmother, said, "Bob was visiting and he was upstairs with Gary. Usually I could hear them laughing and talking, but this day they seemed quiet and to be talking in soft tones. After a while, Gary called me to come upstairs. When I went into the room, I saw that both of them had tears in their eyes. 'What's going on here?' I asked.

" 'I've been trying to get him to talk about what's going to happen after I'm gone,' Gary said, 'and it just makes us both so sad. But we've got to talk about it. I need to talk about it. I need to be sure that he'll be all right when I'm gone.'

"In some ways I felt like I didn't belong in this discussion," Rose said, "but I knew what Gary needed from me, even if he wasn't sure. I said to Bob, 'You're part of our family now. We love you like our own child. You'll always be welcome in this house, and I hope you'll spend holidays with us and things like that.' "

Religion: You may find yourself going back to church or synagogue. You may not go for the reasons you remember as a child, but extraordinary times often cause us to look back for sources of comfort.

"How are we doing?" Howard asked rhetorically. "We have hope. We went to church this morning. Although it's not my religion, we prayed. The first time Alex was in the hospital, I even went into a Roman Catholic church to say a prayer for him. I figured it was his church, and I would be saying his prayer for him. If he could go, that's where he would go, so I was just acting as his messenger."

"I have a lot more faith in God now," Suzanne says. "I was quite angry before. As I became more and more tired, I really had to let go, and I just had to hand myself over. I began to see that it was

163

going to be taken care of. Over and over again, I saw things fall into place, and they were taken care of. I was always afraid that Michelle would die without me there. Then Michelle said, 'It's going to be this week, Mom, and I would like you to be here more, because I know it's going to be this week.' I would have to have faith that God would see to it that I was there."

Tom talked about his renewed interest in prayer. "I pray a lot too. I never used to pray at all, just once in a while. Because St. Paul's is right near the hospital, part of my visits to Mart were stops at St. Paul's before and after. I'd light candles. A lot of things I needed to sort out got sorted out that way. Two blocks away from where I work there is a church. Two or three times a week I stop in there. It's amazing how your spiritual feelings start to flow when you have a crisis. You look for help at that point, and that's one of the ways you get it. I get some kind of strength from visiting a church. I can feel an inner strength that comes from that."

"Evan often goes with me to the mass that Dignity holds every Saturday night, even though it's not his religion," Len said. "Dignity is the Roman Catholic organization for homosexual people, and we found a lot of comfort there. People there know him from the hospital, and he always gets a warm and loving welcome. We started going maybe two months after he was diagnosed. I remember we went to the mass on Christmas Eve, and I got such good feeling from that, seeing all these gay people praying together and being told that God loves them as much as He loves any of his children. I thought, 'Why have we allowed ourselves to be deprived of this experience, when we have such love to share?' "

Precious moments: You and your friend with AIDS might share little stories, cherished flashes of memory from childhood that you have never revealed before.

"Sometimes Gary tells me the most incredible things," Linda said of her brother. "Once I was sitting in his hospital room, and he told me how, when he was little, he would look for excuses to run up and hug me or to jump on me when I was sitting down because he loved the way I smelled and how I felt soft. And I remember being embarrassed at the time because he seemed to like to put his head on my breasts. I always thought he was just being a pain in the neck. Now he tells me he was being intimate. Of course, I think he stopped doing that stuff when he got to be around eight, maybe older. But now he seems to want to share things from the past with me, and I do the same with him."

All of these moments are precious. The closeness you feel with this person is something so painfully valuable that you may never have felt it with anyone before. People who see you two together may see the intimacy. They may wonder how it is possible when one person is so sick. Be aware that most relationships never reach this degree of intimacy in a lifetime. This is a shared experience of carepartners and caring friends of persons with AIDS.

Intimacy with friends: Sometime your friend with AIDS has other friends, or relatives, who have stayed by his side through this long process. The same things will be happening in their relationships with your friend as are happening in yours with him. He may want to share his feelings and knowledge with them too. Try to leave them alone together as much as you can. Let your friends and family draw close to him if they wish. Often, the person with AIDS has much to share and wants to share it with all those who are close to him. Be sure to allow it.

"Bob started coming to see Gary not only on weekends, but during the week sometimes," Linda explained. "He'd drive out on Wednesday evening, then get up very early on Thursday, and drive back. He and Gary would just sit for hours talking and reading, and Bob would take care of him while he was there, giving everyone else, especially my mother, time off. She loved Bob because he loved Gary so much. He never missed a weekend, and we all left them alone as much as they wanted, because you could see how important to them the time was that they had together."

AS THE ILLNESS GROWS MORE SEVERE

Often long periods of hospitalization occur as AIDS grows more severe and complex. Your friend with AIDS may have two or more opportunistic infections at the same time; he may be taking an array of drugs that staggers the imagination, most of them toxic and experimental, their side effects half-known and their interaction with each other completely unknown. If KS is one of your partner's problems, he may be undergoing terribly debilitating chemotherapy or radiation therapy that leaves him barely able to move or talk. All this, and more, becomes part of the disease. When AIDS grows more severe, the medical aspects seem to become more desperate, less under control, as the doctors try this and that in their attempts to do something—anything—to help.

You may be witnessing the slow—or even rapid—decline of this person you love. You may see him or her becoming thinner and thinner. He may lose his hair, have terrible rashes, and be afflicted with chronic herpes sores and thrush. His body, which may once have been beautiful, may become little more than a skeleton with skin

165

stretched over it. You will find looking at your friend is not repulsive, only enormously sad and painful.

Besides the physical decline of your partner you may begin to notice the mental decline as well. He may seem less alert, less able to find words, less interested in anything. In some cases, the destruction of nerve and brain cells first causes the loss of voluntary functions—your friend may become very clumsy and perhaps eventually lose the ability to speak—and then later it causes the loss of involuntary functions, like blinking, and even breathing.

"John was just wasting away," Hugh said, "and he was in terrible pain all the time. And it was actually to the point that you could see the outline of his spine by looking at his stomach. This black stuff used to come out of his ass, like it was his guts just dissolving and oozing out. And nothing that anyone was doing was doing him any good, and there wasn't anything anyone could for him. So the doctors got together with me and everyone and just decided not to continue to prolong John's life. We were going to stop all the medications.

"I was with John that night, and his nurse came in. You know, John had tubes for glucose and water, tubes for this and that, all connected to his neck, and the nurse just came in and disconnected everything and threw it into the garbage, except for one bottle. And she stuck herself while she was doing it. John said, 'What are they doing?' I just started crying at this point. I said, 'There nothing else they can do, John.' And John said, 'You're back to the same thing, when you said I had AIDS. I'm going to die.' John used to drift off and come back. Sometimes he didn't seem to believe that he had AIDS and that he was dying."

Stella said, "David was so sick toward the end. He had cytomegalovirus in the lungs. His adrenal glands had shriveled up and died. He had toxoplasmosis also, and that caused all kinds of brain problems. The part of his brain that controlled his temperature had just withered away. He had microbacterium tuberculosis, and just a lot of lung stuff.

"I wouldn't let them put David on oxygen or on a respirator, or anything that would prolong his life artificially. At that hospital, when someone goes on a respirator, the family can't stay with them or anything. And I wasn't going to let them do that to David to prolong his life for two days or so. He'd have been alone and frightened. David and I talked about it. We had already made up our minds before he got really, really bad, that if it came down to the point where he was going to have to live on a respirator, and hooked up to all this tubing and all that, he didn't want it. Everything he wanted is what I tried to do. The only thing I couldn't do was let him die at home."

Suzanne describes Michelle when she finally agreed to go into the hospital. "She could barely walk around at this point. She had kept herself going to work. God knows how she did it. God bless her. When I look back on this, she must have known it in her heart. She did the things she wanted to do. She loved her job; she kept on going to work; she went to the office Christmas party. God, she was so thin and so frail. Her coloring was horrible. She had lost most of her hair. She was plagued by these huge herpes sores on her face. She tried to cover them with gauze bandage."

Michael describes how Joe was never really sick after his first bout with PCP. "What happened was that life was going on here much as usual, and we had gotten through the summer, and we were beginning to talk about what we were going to do, now that winter was coming. Because this is a small place, and we're going to be inside a lot, and it was going to be a lot more crowded, what improvements did we need to make in here for life to be more bearable? Then Joe started to get little symptoms that something was wrong, like bleeding around his teeth and little blood specks where his capillaries were bursting. So they put him in the hospital, and we found that his platelets were down. I knew what platelets were. I didn't understand that you couldn't live without them. I don't think Joe did either. He was scared shitless. When we brought him back to the hospital, he knew something was very wrong. We both thought, 'Okay, this is the first of those hospitalizations that are going to happen.' We talked about it, and we expected it. Now it's happened. They were going to put him in the hospital, torture him a little, then send him home a little weaker. And everything will be okay until it happens again.

"So we went on that assumption. He was only in the hospital seven days. But on the fifth day, things weren't happening the way they were supposed to. The situation wasn't getting any better, any clearer. The doctors didn't know why the platelets were down. They not only didn't know why it was happening, but didn't know what to do about it either."

Less Denial and Anger, Greater Pain

As a caring friend, you will react at this stage of your friend's illness in very complex ways. On the one hand, you are drawing closer to your partner, but at the same time being closer is causing you increasing pain. Moreover, it is becoming harder and harder for you to deny that you are witnessing your partner's physical and possibly mental deterioration. It is no longer possible to say that this is not happening. It is happening, and you cannot avoid it. Your pain is great because you are realizing that you may soon lose a person who has become intensely valuable to you.

You will survive: You may feel guilt now, too. You are beginning to realize that you will survive this relationship. You probably know people, perhaps from a carepartners' group, who have already survived the death of friends who had AIDS. Now that you have had to look at serious illness, and at death and dying, as realities, you realize—consciously or unconsciously—that every person who dies probably has someone who loves him intensely, much as you love your friend. These people survived the loss. They suffer, but they go on.

The separation begins: You must look after yourself, even as you see your friend slipping from you. Of course, you are taking the best possible care of your friend. You are loving him to the best of your ability and will continue to be there, holding him, touching him, telling him you love him, no matter what.

But you may begin not just to feel, but to *fear and dread* that you are going to lose this person. You may fear not just the loss, but the resulting emptiness in your life. After all, you know that you are—and have been for a long time—spending enormous amounts of time and energy dealing with your friend's illness. What will you do with that time and energy if you do not have your friend to care for? You may have heard from other carepartners and friends about the great void they felt when their ill friend died.

So you begin now to build bridges across that canyon. These bridges may take a thousand forms: new and old friends, work, places to go to feel and be yourself, volunteer work, family, whatever you need. You are consciously aware that you are building outside the relationship. Your friend is not included here. But you are doing this for your own health, although sometimes you don't feel good about it.

Pain and sadness: However intense your pain and sadness, these feelings are natural. You may have to go off, away from your ill friend, to express them, either in group, with a friend or family member, a therapist, or alone. But do not be afraid to express your sadness or pain. You need to express these profound emotions. They are not a sign of weakness. Actually, when you express these emotions in whatever way, you will feel stronger afterward.

Jeffrey said, "For some reason I got on the phone with my friend Ben, and I broke down and cried with him more than anyone else. He said, 'I'm coming down this weekend, no if's, and's, or but's.' I needed a friend to cry with."

Less anger: You may be so filled with emotion for your friend, with gratitude toward those friends and family who have supported you, that you have little room for anger toward those who have abandoned you, or for anger at the disease itself. That anger, those people, are not relevant now. At some point in the future you may return to this anger and deal with it. But for now it is not important.

Sharing with your friend: If previously, you had resentment toward your friend with AIDS because you were carrying more and more of the relationship, that too may be fading into the background. Now you accept him at exactly the point where he is, and you ask him for whatever support you need that he is capable of giving. You may need only for him to touch you, to tell you that he loves you. When decisions have to be made, consult with him, because at this time he may be feeling—he may well know—that he has less and less control over his illness, and consequently over his life. Help him to feel as much in control as possible, especially regarding life-extending therapies.

"When Bruce went into the hospital that August," Jack said, "he had so many problems that it was hard to believe he was still alive. He had tried the chemotherapy for the lymphomas for a while, and everything just came apart. In no time, he could hardly breathe, and they started treating him for the pneumocystis again. He'd been in the hospital two days when Dr. Bill came in and asked, 'If it comes down to it, do you want us to use a respirator?' Bruce responded, 'What's that mean?'

" 'It means,' Dr. Bill said, 'that if you can't breathe on your own, then we'll hook you up to a machine that will breathe for you.'

"I interrupted at that moment. I asked, 'You put him on the machine to help him out while the drug works, so he can breathe on his own again?'

"Dr. Bill said matter-of-factly. 'That hasn't happened yet, at least not in this hospital. When we put somebody with pneumocystis on the respirator, they don't come off it.' Just like that, I thought, he'd told Bruce and me that Bruce was going to die soon. I looked at Bruce, and he looked at me, but I couldn't read his face.

" 'Tell me later what you want to do,' Dr. Bill said, and he left the room. 'You take a walk, too,' Bruce said to me. 'I need some time to myself.'

"So I went down the hall to the phone, and I called Bruce's brother up in the Panhandle, and I told him what was happening and asked him to come down. 'Of course,' he said. 'I'll leave on the first plane I can get.' He hesitated for a moment. 'If something should happen to him before I get there, I wouldn't put him on

169

that machine,' he said. 'It's a terrible thing. They did that to our father when he had cancer. He was conscious, and he was hurting real bad, and he couldn't talk, and he kept looking at us with his eyes beggin' for something. And his wife—not my mother—and I finally figured out that he wanted off that horrible machine. But Bruce should do what he wants.'

"His brother was on his way, and I went back to Bruce's room. He didn't move when I came in, and he was lying there with his eyes closed. I pulled a chair up next to the bed and sat on the arm of it and put my head lightly on his stomach and my arms sort of around him. He didn't say anything to me but began stroking my hair and my neck."

In many ways those who love the ill person are most fortunate when that person can participate in the decision concerning artificial life-support systems. There is no rational place then for regrets later.

"I went to the hospital the next day," says Michael, "and Joe told me what the doctor had told him. They didn't know what was causing his platelet count to be so low, and there was nothing they could do about it. I burst into tears and hugged Joe, and we cried. That was the only time we cried together. And I told Joe that I didn't want him to die and why. And we just held each other and cried. Then, events began to take control of the situation, and a lot of momentum built up. At that point the doctor came back into the room, and we had a replay of her conversation with Joe from the night before, where she outlined to Joe all the procedural alternatives. Joe took her through all those alternatives, and each one of those alternatives came to the same conclusion: None of them would make any difference; he was going to bleed to death, regardless of what they did. So he said, 'I just want to let nature take its course.' Joe was not going to fight the inevitable at that point. He knew he was going to bleed internally till he died."

Suzanne said, "I asked to see what a respirator was. And I said to the doctor, 'This is not likely to be.' I did not like what I saw. It seemed so ridiculous, it's maybe for two or three days. It may be that early in an illness—there are miraculous cases—people have been saved by a respirator and lived another two years. But Michelle had just deteriorated. She was incontinent. She really couldn't eat anymore. You could almost see the fungus growing in her mouth. When she breathed, we were constantly cleaning her mouth. So I talked to her about it, and she asked me, 'What would you do, Mommy?'

"I said, 'You know me, I guess I like natural things. I don't think I would do anything like that.' She said. 'That's the way I am too. That's what I'm going to do.'

"Because there was no machine, I was able to hold her and touch her constantly those last few days. I was able to lay my head next to her and to whisper to her about how I loved her."

Unresolved issues: In every relationship there may be many unresolved issues. These could be as important as an affair that hurt one or the other of you, but that you have never really talked about or worked out, or it could be the disposition of a favorite book or trinket that you shared. Sometimes your friend may want to talk about these things. If so, allow him. Let him resolve as many of these issues as you can. Talk about anything and everything your friend wants to, whether or not it is painful to you, so that you and your friend feel at ease and at peace with each other. The more of these issues that are resolved, the more accepting both of you will be. Sometimes it is extremely difficult for an ill person to let go, no matter how desperately sick he is, if he feels he is leaving behind a lot of unfinished business.

DEALING WITH YOUR FRIEND'S FEELINGS

As your partner becomes sicker, he, too, may begin to let in the reality of what is happening to him. His denial may become less and less. Often he will come to this point before you do. Sometimes, as persons with AIDS begin to face the reality of their possible death, they try to prepare and even protect their carepartner or friend. They will make quick little jokes about their death. They may refer to your life and what it will be like after they are gone. In the beginning, you need to respond with great diplomacy when your friend pulls this on you, because he may be testing you, wanting you to tell him that he is not going to die. You want to hold out hope, yet you want to help yourself and your friend come to terms with the reality of what is happening.

Your partner, spouse, child, or friend may also need reassurance that you will be all right after he leaves. He probably loves you as much as you love him, and he may be afraid for you after he is gone. He could easily be as worried about you, as you are about him.

"Earl started saying things to me," James said, "and I made like I didn't understand at first. But he wanted me to listen. 'This is getting too hard to do,' he told me once, out of nowhere. And I didn't hear him. 'You got to get yourself ready,' he said to me another time, and I just did what I was doing. But one day we had to talk. When we got down to it, he told me that he had to go, but he was scared for me. 'I don't have any memory that you're not

171

there,' he said. 'I can't put your picture together in my head and I'm not there. But that's got to be.' I couldn't talk to him about that. 'I hear you,' I said. 'I been hearing you all along.' "

Emotional Stages

You may witness your partner going through the emotional stages of a dying person, as these stages were described by Dr. Elisabeth Kübler-Ross, who worked with hundreds of dying people. Dr. Kübler-Ross described a process that most people go through as they approach death. Of course, stages of the dying process do overlap, and a person will move from one stage to another then back again, but what Dr. Kübler-Ross has described is the way many people make peace with approaching death, an event they may fear more than any other.

Remember, many people may not go through these stages at all. No one has to. Remember, too, these stages are very similar to what we may be going through as we face the approaching loss of our partner.

You should realize that you and your friend have probably been going through these stages in varying degrees since he became sick. If you go back through this book, you can see that we have passed through some of the stages outlined below—and you can see them in the reality in your life. First, you and your friend had to accept the fact of his illness and what that meant, now you are trying to accept the probability of his death and what that reality means.

These stages are: denial and isolation, anger, bargaining, depression, and acceptance. Here is a brief description of each of these stages, what they mean, how you can help your friend, and how knowledge of these stages can help you.

Denial: When you and your friend with AIDS were first given the diagnosis, denial was a big part of your reaction. Denial protected you from a reality that was too painful to accept. Now, you have probably long since accepted the fact that your partner has AIDS, as has he, but denial of death can still be very strong. "No, this can't be getting so serious," he'll say. "Let's try another treatment. Let's call in another doctor." As the reality of the illness grow stronger, you may discover that your partner becomes quiet, sullen, and withdrawn. He doesn't want to talk about anything much. He may just be numb. You may be numb yourself in denial. If so, let it be. This phase may pass for both of you, but it doesn't have to. Many people have died denying that death could happen to them. They may have stared at the door of the room right up to the end, full of hope—perhaps even knowing—that at any minute someone was coming through that door with the miracle cure they had been praying for. Denial is some people's way of coping with death.

Just let your partner know that you are there. It will be more painful for you if your friend remains in denial, but do not try to bring him out of it unless he is in great emotional or physical pain. If so, get professional help. But stay calm. Go off and cry now and again if you feel the need. Try to have friends and family be there to support both of you at this time.

Anger: Denial is often replaced with anger. The person may be asking, "Why is this happening to me?" and, in the process, striking out at whoever is nearby and convenient. Your friend with AIDS may accuse you of not caring for him; he may accuse the medical professionals of killing him. He may hurt you and everyone who has stood by him.

Allow him this anger. Try not to be hurt or strike back. Most of all, if this is possible, try not to take it personally. The person feels angry because he is afraid of dying, and he focuses his anger on you because you are there. Try to empathize. Say, "You have a right to be angry. Being angry may help you. Go ahead and yell at me." But look out for yourself. If you can't take the anger any longer, then leave. Come back later. Simply say, "Your anger is too much for me right now. I'll come back later when I feel stronger." You, too, may be feeling great anger, wondering why you must lose this person you love. But you know there is no answer to this question. If possible, go to where you can express your anger—to your therapist, group, special friend, or even at home alone.

Bargaining: This is only a brief stage, where the person seems to take a step in the direction of accepting what is happening, but is grasping for straws to prevent the change. "If this doesn't happen to me, then I'll spend all my life taking care of other sick people." Or, "I just want to live until the end of winter. I want to see one more spring."

Your friend with AIDS might seem peaceful at this point. Enjoy this time together, and let him bring up any issues or problems that he wants resolved.

Depression: When your sick friend stops bargaining and knows that he is dying, he may become extremely depressed. "So this is going to happen to me after all." He is sad, overcome with a great sense of loss. The depression may arise when your friend looks back at all the things he has left undone, and sees empty spots in

173

people's lives that he will not be there to fill. He may be very depressed that he is so thin, that he's not attractive anymore, that he has lost the physique he spent years building up in the gym. Try to help him overcome this depression by complimenting him in any way you can. If he has a nice smile, tell him; if his impish grin is still there, tell him.

The other part of this depression, according to Dr. Kübler-Ross, is due to the fact that the ill person now knows that he is about to lose everything and everyone he loves. He is going to have to let go of what he has and knows: life, you, his friends, his family, his whole familiar world. We can imagine how great this loss must appear to him by comparing our own reaction to the loss of only one person in our lives. The depression is a preparatory depression, a grief over the loss of life and relationships. You, too, may feel this great depression, as you prepare yourself for the loss of your friend.

Allow your partner to be sad. Do not try to cheer him up, but sit with him and allow him to express his sorrow if he wishes. Hold his hand, and if he wants to be quiet and doesn't want other visitors distracting him, then follow his wishes.

Allow yourself to be sad, too. Sit quietly. Try to be there as much as possible, and if you need company, ask your friend if you can have someone sit with you in the room. Tell him that you love him and you understand how he feels. Touch him a lot. Your partner's death may be weeks, months away, but he knows it is coming. So do you.

Acceptance: Oftentimes, when the person accepts the fact of his approaching death, it is like a giant sigh of relief. "Okay, so it's going to happen to me." Your partner is no longer depressed or angry, nor is he devoid of feeling. He is more at peace, calmer, quieter, more concerned with what's going on inside him than what's going on outside. Your response is to be there. To hold his hand, to reassure him that you will be there.

Where to Die

Sometimes a decision must be made about where a person should die, at home or in the hospital. This is a very big decision, and sometimes difficult to make, because the sick person might prefer to die at home. But because the care of a dying person is all-consuming, many carepartners decide that it is not possible for them to continue their own lives, and at the same time allow their partner to die at home. *Coming Home: A Guide to Home Care for the Terminally Ill,* by Deborah Duda, a book you might find at your public library, could be very useful, if you should decide to do this.

174

Everything that has been said in this section to carepartners and caring friends applies equally as well to all friends of persons with AIDS. It may become very difficult for you to stay around when you are told that your friend is dying. Your instinct may be to run away, to hide, and to emerge again when it is all over.

Please be careful as you read the following pages in this chapter. You may find some of the information and personal stories of dying too painful to read right now, and not immediately helpful. Read these sections only when you need to—only when facts and testaments about death can strengthen and sustain you.

If someone with AIDS asks you to sit with him, or his carepartner asks you to be with him, try to be there. Despite your fear, you know that you have been asked to enter the most intimate chambers of these people's existence, to share their most profound times and experiences.

James was terrified as he saw his brother Earl dying in the hospital. "He had been paralyzed almost completely for two weeks, and what was happening to him, I couldn't stand. He had stopped eating, and they had a feeding tube down his throat. He had huge bed sores on his butt and on his shoulders and heels and elbows. I spent all my time there when I wasn't working. I even slept there on the floor. Finally, I couldn't do it alone anymore. I said to Earl that I needed someone there, and he signaled with his eyes that it was okay. We didn't have many friends, but I called the woman who used to look in on him during the day for me. She didn't hesitate. 'I'll be right there,' she said. When she came, we went to the visitors' lounge awhile and I cried. You know that woman never left his room without asking Earl first, and she stayed there all day while I was working. In two weeks, I came to love her as much as I ever loved anyone."

People need to know that you are there, that you can be counted on. They need you to touch them, to hold them, to comfort them, to fuss over them. You can get them food or something to drink.

When Your Friend Approaches Death

At some point you will know that a crisis is here. You will be able to see it. The doctors will inform you. At that point, tell everyone who should be told. If he is able, talk to your partner or friend. Tell him that you would like some visitors to be with you. Whom does he want to be there? Most people are aware when they are dying, even if only in the back of their minds, so your friend will know what you are talking about when you ask who he wants you to call. If he doesn't seem to recognize how much in crisis he is, then, of course, don't alarm him.

If you have been largely abandoned by family and have few friends you can call upon, then get people from the hospital hospice program to sit with you. Call you local organization that helps persons with AIDS. Or you may want to be alone with your partner or friend.

Sometimes, although the person with AIDS is very, very sick and is suffering greatly, he clings to life. He may be young. Sometimes he may repeat over and over that he loves you, because he may know he is going to leave you and he feels guilty. He may need assurance that you will be all right, that you do not want him to stay and suffer on your account. Many times he needs to know that it is okay for him to go. Here are some experiences with death.

Suzanne: "Michelle died a terrible, terrible death. She began to decay, and she was still living. The last night, the night before she died, we had asked the night nurse not to turn her again, because we were so sure she was going to die that night, and it was so upsetting to watch them turn her at this point, that we asked them please do not do this, that we'd take care of her.

"So the next morning they had to turn her; she had not died. The nurses who had the day off were calling in to find out how Michelle was, and they were terribly distraught. Even one of the doctors cried. Michelle was such a little girl at this point. She weighed maybe seventy or eighty pounds. But still she would say something. She would say she loved us.

"The nurses told me to go," Suzanne said. "They said, 'You're keeping Michelle here. You're making it harder for her to go.' I said, 'I can't go home. I can't leave now . . .'

"But sometimes you have to go away and leave them alone. I thought about Michelle and how she had to go upstairs and listen to music and be alone, and that made sense in the overall picture of her life. So I told my daughter, Camille, that she had to lie down and I would lie down too. So we lay down on the cot that was in the room, out of Michelle's sight, and I put my arms around her and we went to sleep.

"The last night that Michelle was alive, before I went to sleep, her fever went up to 105. The nurse was very busy. She had three people on respirators. She was out of her mind. So she set me up with alcohol and all these things, and I washed Michelle and washed her and washed her, with ice and alcohol. She must die a peaceful death. None of us could cope with this otherwise. I finally got her fever down. The nurse kept coming in and trying to help me. And I kept saying, 'I know what I'm doing. Go take care of those other people.'

"I said to her then, I whispered in her ear, 'Michelle, you're too sick now. I don't want you to stay. I want you to go.' I knew she could hear me. Then I just lay down and went to sleep.

"When Bob, my husband, woke me up, Michelle was dying. Her hands just unfolded, and she stopped breathing, very peacefully."

Michael: "Then the night began. Our friend Cecile came to visit Joe for a while. He got to say good-bye to Cecile. Some people called. He made some phone calls. He spoke to his sister, who was racked with guilt, and tried to make her feel better. We got through the night. He got progressively weaker and weaker, and it became apparent that the estimate of two weeks was wrong. I didn't know how short a period of time it was going to be, but Joe seemed to know. After the third time he said, 'I can feel the energy leaving my body.' I realized that he was not speaking about something metaphorical, but he was indeed describing an actual physical sensation of energy leaving his body. I felt just the opposite of what Joe was feeling. I felt energy pouring into my body from every available corner of the universe, like I'd just taken some drugs—which I hadn't—but I felt acutely aware, totally energized.

"Our communication became very basic. We didn't talk about anything. He'd ask for a drink of water. He said he felt sorry for his sister, and he cried about her. But I just sort of helped him through the night. He began to have physical pain. His stomach was hemorrhaging and that was causing a lot of pressure in his bowels, and it hurt him, and he had to use a bedpan. He was very happy that I'd had experience using a bedpan.

"Then in the morning his father called. Joe spoke to his father and said good-bye to him. I was totally exhausted; my eyeballs were burning. I was drained, and I didn't know what was going on, because we had made it through the night and it was day again, even though Joe was as weak as a newborn kitten.

"I started having a lot of anxiety about our friend Mark. He and Joe go back a long, long way. Joe and he had had a falling out, but they had been patching it up over the summer. But Joe didn't trust Mark to be able to deal with the situation, and had sort of kept him away. I knew Mark was afraid, but that he could deal with it. So, finally, I said to Joe, 'I'm really uncomfortable about something. I think we need to attend to it now.' And Joe said, 'I'm okay,' in a weak voice. And I said, 'Not you, dummy, it has nothing to do with you. It's Mark. I think we should tell Mark what is going on right now.' 'If you have to,' Joe said. So I called Mark up and he said he was coming right over.

"At one point, Joe opened his eyes—they were sort of rolling around in his head—then he focused on us, and he saw Mark and asked, 'Mark, what are you doing here?' Then, he seemed to understand what was going on, and I said to him, 'You look really stoned.' He smiled at me and said, 'Yeah.' Then he closed his eyes and went back to sleep, and his breathing just got softer and softer. And we were crying and amazed, and Mark informed me later that I kept saying, 'This is so beautiful.' He understood what I meant.

"And then Joe stopped breathing. It was hard to say which was his last breath. It was as peaceful as it could be. And then it was over. He wasn't there anymore. Whatever it means to be dead, it had happened to Joe."

Jack: "Bruce's brother had been with us for a couple of days. He stayed in the hospital during the day when I was at work, then he'd leave when I got there after work with the car, and he'd come back about eleven and send me home. He slept on a cot in Bruce's room. He looked just like Bruce, this big man, who didn't have a pretension in the world. He was a heterosexual man with a wife and two children, but he didn't seem to have any opinion about the relationship between Bruce and me. About all he said to me was, 'My brother tells me you been real fine to him, caring for him and all that, and I want you to know that me and my family is real grateful.'

"But on Wednesday night, when his brother came back to the hospital, Bruce asked me not to leave. 'I want you here tonight,' he said. 'Both of you. Something's happening. I'm scared.' I think at that moment both his brother and I knew that he was going to die that night. I said to him, 'Course, I'll stay.' But I was suddenly terrified. I felt my skin crawl. Was he really telling us this was it? What about the cure we knew was coming? What about finishing the work on the house? What about us? So I went down to the lounge and got a comfortable chair and brought it to his room and put it right next to the bed so I could hold his hand. I took off my shoes and tried to get comfortable. When the nurse came by, she brought me a blanket.

"And that's how the night began. Sometime later, when there was only the light in the hall, and the hospital and the world outside were as quiet as the desert at midnight—I was sort of dozing—I heard Bruce sort of gasp, first softly then loudly, and then he squeezed my hand. I jumped up and saw that he was wide-awake. His brother jumped up too and turned on a light.

178

Bruce was trying to get his breath. He whispered in my ear. 'Get someone to help me.' His brother went to the door. 'You stay here,' he said to me. 'I'll get help.' So I heard him go down the hall, and I grabbed Bruce and held him because he had begun to go into convulsions. Then I started to cry and I kept saying over and over again, 'I love you, Bruce. I love you, man.' He went limp in my arms.

"Before I realized what had happened to him, all hell broke loose in the room. It was the respiratory team, or some group like that that went into action when someone died; I think they try to revive him. So they shoved me and Bruce's brother out of the room, and we both stood there in the hall while all this noise and activity went on in the room.

"After a few minutes, they came out of the room and told us he was gone. His brother rushed back into the room, but a young woman grabbed my arm and pulled me to the side. 'I just wanted to tell you that I was the first one in the room. He had died when we got there. I want you to know that he died in your arms. I hope, when my time comes, I have someone like you who loves me to hold me.' So I started to cry again, and I went into the room, and his brother and I sat and I talked to him. In a while he said, 'I've got to call his brother and my wife.' He got up and left the room."

Stella: "I was probably more prepared for David's death than most people who have AIDS in the family. I was prepared by the nurses for every step of David's dying before it happened. When it got down to the last days, they said, 'Do you want to be with him when he dies? Do you want to be out?'

"I said, 'David and I started this together by ourselves, and we'll end it together by ourselves.' It was my request that I be in the room by myself with David when he died. That was my time. It took David eighteen hours to die, and I stood by the bed and held him for eighteen hours. Some of his family was there and of course they poked their heads in and all that. They let me know they were there. But it was my time with him. Even though somebody's in a coma, he can hear. So I talked to him. I told him how much I loved him. I told him how much I cared. I told him I didn't have the disease. I told him over and over that I didn't have the disease and that I wasn't going to die, and I was going to take care of our kids. The one thing I told him, 'When these girls grow up, I'm going to tell them what a good daddy they had. And I'm going to tell them how proud you were of your girls. The one thing I'll always teach my kids is to never, ever, feel degraded because your dad had AIDS. To hold your head up and be proud of your dad.' I said, 'I'll tell them that. You'll never have to worry about that.'

179

"About an hour before David died, they came in and told me I could change my mind, and put David on a respirator. I said, 'No way.'

"David was in a coma for most of the eighteen hours it took him to die. But it was pretty rough because he started having seizures really, really bad. But he could be having a really bad seizure, and I could talk to him, and he'd calm down. I always let David know that I loved him.

"David had a close friend, Les, who was a state trooper. They was raised together, went all through school together; he was just like a brother . . . for that eighteen hours David was dying, and I knew he was dying, and I kept praying, 'Just let him live. Just let him live a little while longer.' We called Les. But right before he got there, I started praying for God just to take David on. He'd suffered enough. And when he heard Les's voice, David died. It was like he was waiting for Les to come to take care of me and the kids before he died."

11
RESOLUTION:
Conquering Your Grief and Loss

When you suffer the loss of someone very close to you, you will probably go into a state of shock and denial. It may last for hours or a few days. Your mind rejects reality. You want to believe there's been some mistake, that all this will turn out to be a dream. This is how you cope with the beginning of your grief.

Even in shock, however, people's reactions are as different as their personalities. You may burst into tears, you may grab the person closest to you and hug him or her fiercely, you may need to leave the room because you can't breathe, you may feel faint, dazed. Or you may feel very calm, relieved, peaceful, thankful that this person with AIDS will suffer nothing more. There is no way to predict what your reaction will be. But from the very first stages through to resolution, your grief is *your* grief, and you will suffer it as you alone would suffer it.

People have been suffering the loss of loved ones since they first learned to love, but still, after thousands of years, each person's grief is something new. Below, some of our friends in this book share their early grief with us.

Hugh: "John had been lingering between life and death for almost two weeks. Every day someone different in the hospital would tell me he was going to die that day. 'It's going to be today,' they would say. But one day I went to the hospital around noon and the nurse, Ellen, was crying. She said, 'You better come quick.' I knew she meant that John was dying. And I knew she was right.

"So I called our friend Armando and I said, 'You should go to the hospital because John's going to need some help. He's dying.' Armando came and put candles all around the room and lit them, and he had death chants playing. It was really beautiful. I was in such turmoil that I had to go out and walk and walk. I got back to the hospital just as John expired. He was like this"—Hugh folded his hands on his chest, his voice barely audible—"and his eyes were wide open, looking straight up. I was glad for John. He looked

181

unbelievable, so gorgeous. I couldn't believe it; it was so extraordinary. Edith, the nurse who had disconnected all the tubes from John's neck that night, was sobbing. She wanted to close his eyes, but I wouldn't let her. I just stayed in the room, and it was the time when the hospital shift changed, so everyone was there. And a lot of John's friends started coming by. The nurses said, 'Hugh, why don't you let us change him?' I told them, 'Go ahead and change him.' They said, 'No, we don't want you here. It's bad enough. Go down the hall, and let us get him cleaned up, and then you can come back and be with him.'

"So I went down the hall and I wasn't crying. I felt this incredible relief. I wanted to let people know John died. I called his mother, but she wasn't home. I called his brother, and we made pleasantries. Then I went back to the room, and they had John tied up, his head tied to keep his mouth closed, his hands tied, his feet tied, and his eyes were still wide open.

"Everybody left, one by one, and said good-bye to John, and then I talked to John. I felt very good, you know. I didn't feel terribly sad. I felt extraordinary. I went downstairs to the chaplain's office and talked to the chaplain about having the funeral there."

Jack: "I was never a big man with words, but, you know, a carpenter has a lot of time to think about things while he works. I'd thought a lot about Bruce and what we had together and about his sickness. And there were just a lot things I wanted to tell him, I needed to tell him, because I hurt so much.

"After a while, Bruce's mother went to call her sons again so they could make arrangements to take his body back home, and I was in the room with Bruce alone. I felt as if he were still there in some way, but I could see that his body was dead, because the blood vessels in his arm began to change. 'I'll never forget you,' I said almost in whisper in his ear, 'not now, not in ten years. I love you, big Mister. You're the man who taught me how to love a man if I wanted to love him.' I kept thinking about his swagger, about how big and handsome he was, and how proud he was to be a tough man from the Panhandle. I said to him, 'I keep thinking how proud you were of me. You always made sure that everywhere we went everybody knew I belonged to you. I was proud just to be with you, to know that you were mine and you loved me and didn't want anyone else. We had something special, you and I. I want to thank you for that, and to tell you that I forgive you for all the times you were a pain in the ass and a big baby.'

"Then I started to cry a little, and I told him how sorry I was about all the camping trips we won't take together, all the little projects we won't finish, all the times we won't spend holding each other in bed, and all the pain he had suffered, and that he had had to go away when he was so young. 'You know what's in my heart for you, Bruce, and that my heart just aches and aches and aches. I love you, big Mister. I love you with my whole heart.'

"I stayed there, crying a little now and then, until the nurses came to wrap him in gauze, and I didn't want to stay for that. I went down the hall and talked to his mother for a while, then we drove to my house. In a little while a few of my friends arrived, and they sat by the bed that Bruce and I used to sleep in, and I lay there and cried and cried. I needed to do that, and I needed them to be there while I did it. Around noon, the four of us went to get some lunch. We hadn't even had breakfast."

PRACTICAL MATTERS

Immediately after your friend's death, while you are still in shock, you may have to deal with many practical matters, especially if you have been the primary care giver. Most of this you will do almost automatically, since there will be people around reminding you that this, or that, has to be done. They, too, contribute to the process of grief.

- Make arrangements with a funeral home or with a place to have a funeral or a brief service. Make sure you have chosen the clothes in which you want the body seen and buried or cremated.

- Arrange to get the death certificate, in multiple copies if possible. You will need many copies for numerous tasks later on, like collecting insurance and closing bank accounts. They must all be stamped and signed by the coroner's office. This matter is usually handled by the funeral director, so speak to him about obtaining extra copies.

- Telephone people. Call family, friends, coworkers, anyone who you think should know of the death. Be sure to call people who will help you. You need people around for yourself. And even if it is painful to discuss the death of your friend, it will grow easier with repetition—repetition will become part of the grief process and help you accept your friend's death. You'll be grateful for the loving contact of others around you.

- Contact the executor of the will, if it is someone other than yourself.

- Arrange for the burial or cremation, and the transportation to where the body will be buried if it is in another town or state and if this is a task you are called upon to do.

There are other tasks to perform in the next few days. You can do them yourself or people who are helping you can do them for you.

- Order flowers or omit them.
- Prepare the eulogy.
- Prepare an obituary.
- Have food at the house or apartment for those who will be coming by after the service.
- Arrange places for people to stay who are coming from a distance.

Later, when there is time, you or the executor will have to:

- Contact insurance companies.
- Contact all people to whom your partner owed debts.
- Tell the landlord, if your partner was renting and you are not staying at the apartment. Contact utilities.

There are, of course, a thousand other things to do, especially if you lived with the person with AIDS or were his primary care giver. You may have to see to the disposal of his clothing and furniture, his papers, medicines, and other personal belongings. This may be a very difficult and painful task, and you may put it off, as if disposing of the deceased's belongings is disposing of the person himself. But you can draw strength from all these small duties, and however difficult the ritual may be, sometimes it is an opportunity to remember your friend fondly and to ease you through your own grief.

GRIEF AS A PROCESS

Grief is a process of healing. It is a painful process that many times we try to avoid, but cannot. The more we try to avoid grief, the longer our mourning takes and our wounds may not heal. It's a hard thing for us to allow ourself to feel pain, because nature tells us pain means something is wrong, and we should do something immediately to relieve it. But this is a case where we must, for our own benefit, feel the pain.

Tears: You may remain in a state of shock through the funeral and immediately after when there are many people around. Occasionally, during this time, you may cry and otherwise be able to express your sorrow and pain. Many people, especially men, have been told since childhood that crying is a sign of weakness, but crying is a sign of your strength. You need to cry because you hurt, and tears are a means of relieving hurt and tension. If you can cry with friends, that is fine. If you cry alone, that also is fine. Do not feel ashamed.

Remember, too, that you can't and shouldn't cry and mourn all the time. Even in the first days, there will be times when you and your friends and family will laugh and have fun remembering the person who is gone—and when, to your own surprise, your life seems to resume of its own accord. You may think this is strange, but it is entirely natural.

Sharing grief: If you are a friend to someone who has lost a significant other, then share your grief. Don't try to make the person feel better; that's not necessary or desirable now. Just say, "I too feel a terrible loss. I have a big hurt inside me." If you need to cry, do so. In a way, your crying will help you, the carepartner, the caring friend, or the family.

If you, the carepartner, feel angry with the person who has left you, that is natural too. Most people suffering a loss feel this anger at one time or another. You may feel—like a child who has lost a parent—that your friend with AIDS has abandoned you. You might think, "If he truly loved me, he wouldn't have left me like this." Express this anger as a thoroughly justified and understandable reaction. Get it out and over with.

Sitting on a sofa, with his elbows on his knees and his head in his hands, James said, "Damn you, Earl. Damn you for your rotten habits. Damn you for getting this disease. Damn you for putting us through this. Damn your leaving me now. Damn you for making me feel so alone."

Emptiness: When their person with AIDS dies, carepartners and friends feel an intense void. Until the death, their lives had been filled with activity and urgency, constantly concerned with caring for their sick friend. Suddenly that stops. Now vast periods of time in the day are empty. They have nothing to do, nowhere to go. This sudden vacuum in their lives creates another source of pain and sorrow.

"It got to the point, just a few days after John was buried," Hugh said, "that I started having panic attacks, like I was going to die or something. I couldn't even leave the house to walk down the street. I couldn't sleep. I couldn't believe it. I honestly couldn't believe that all that had happened. I would lie in bed playing it over and over and over and over. The situation had been twenty-four hours a day, and suddenly I had nothing. It was my job for eight months, and it was over. I felt totally alone."

Image and presence: This sense of emptiness can lead to your own preoccupation with the image of the deceased. You might hear his voice, or feel his presence in the room, or see him looking through the curtains as you come up to your house. You might see him sitting in his favorite chair, petting the dog, or catch a glimpse of him passing the end of the aisle in the supermarket. You might smell him in his clothes and be very reluctant to throw anything of his away. You might find yourself looking into a room to see if he is there. In your mind, you know that he is gone, that he is not there and will not be. But however difficult and painful it seems, these images help you to get accustomed to your loss. You are not crazy. You are not losing your mind. The jolt you get makes your loss real to you, more manageable. If your preoccupation becomes inappropriate, someone will notice and say something to you. But you may notice yourself.

"There are so many memories here in this house," Stella explained, "that we just can't live here anymore. We see David sitting on the couch. It took me up till two months ago to realize that David wasn't coming back. People might think I'm crazy, but it did. I can pull up in the driveway, and it seems like somebody opens the drapes. And at night, I can hear him walking around the house. But it's getting better than it was."

This is an intensely emotional period for you, the carepartner or friend. You are searching for the absent person. Your feelings can range from relief to terror, to profound loneliness over the loss. You may feel that your friend is reaching out to you.

"I must have been in our apartment a week after Earl died," James said, "when I realized I couldn't live there anymore. I could see Earl everywhere. I reached for him in bed. I'd wake up and hear him calling me to help him in the bathroom. I called the phone during the day and let it ring. Every little thing was a picture of him. I'd get depressed just walking into the place, but I didn't have any money to move. My parents told me I should move, but I told them I couldn't and why. So without saying anything, they sent me a check with a letter, saying it was a loan that I could pay back when I could. I started looking that day for another apartment. It just needed to be. There was no other way to make a separation."

"I always loved my house," Jack said. "After Bruce died, it was like a refuge to me. I used to love to go look at and touch the things that he'd worked on while he was sick. It was like he had made the place richer for me. He had put little bits of himself here and there. You know he did everything his own way. I could say, 'No, Bruce, that's not how to miter a corner, here's how.' Then I come home and see he'd mitered all the corners his own way. It wasn't as if what he did was wrong, it just wasn't right. I love finding those Bruce things in the house now."

What if . . . ? You may wonder if you did everything possible to help your friend to live. You may have a million "What if" questions. "What if I had done this or that, would he still be alive today?" You can also question whether you fulfilled all the needs of your partner prior to his death. This experience of questioning is almost universal among carepartners and caring friends.

"I don't let a lot of things bother me, but there are a lot of issues I still wonder about," Jack says. "What if Bruce had stopped work earlier? What if we had tried one of the experimental drug programs? What if he'd just learned to take it easier, and not try to do so much all the time? But I know we wouldn't do things different now than we did then."

Suzanne tells about a woman in her group whose son had died a week after she arrived in group. "We asked her to come back to group; we wanted to talk to her. She finally told us that she didn't want to come back. She had seven other children, and she did a lot of volunteer work, and she was able to move on with her life, without questioning a lot of things. She was a very religious woman, and she felt that her son was taken care of and was peaceful. She was comfortable with that. I wish I could do that. I mean, there are a lot of things I feel uncomfortable about, especially as a parent. How I failed. What if this? What if that? The unending, 'what if's.' "

"That's why I went to group," Hugh said. "I don't think my friends, my family, and John's friends were able to deal with my grief. I don't think I share a lot with people. One of John's friends, the wife of the very religious guy, wrote me a note with a two-hundred-dollar check in it. In the note she said, 'Surely John is in heaven, because of you.' I needed someone to say that. Someone had told me I'd done the right things.

"That's why I just wanted to be in group. I really didn't want to talk about it. I still get very confused about it. I guess that's natural after people die. What if? What if? What if? You know that stuff doesn't get you anywhere anyway. What happened is what happened."

Guilt: Sometimes you will feel guilt. But guilt for what? More than likely you did everything you could, probably more than

187

anyone, including your partner or friend, could have expected. You have nothing to feel guilty about. If this remains a problem, talk to a counselor or therapist about it. Discuss it with a friend or in group. The real basis for your guilt may be in the fact that you are still here and your friend is not. Deep inside, you may feel unworthy of living and somehow responsible for your friend's death.

Late one night, James talked about his dead brother. "I feel like I'm half of somebody. He was there. He was always there. Everything I ever did wasn't finished until Earl knew about it. Now I'm mad at him. I'm mad at me, too. Why am I here? Why didn't I die, too? You know, he and I, we were brothers. Everything was always James and Earl, never just James, never just Earl." James began to cry softly. "I shouldn't be alive. There should be no James if there's no Earl. What did I do? What could I have done different? I just know, if I'm here, he should be too. And I keep thinking it's my fault. It's my doing that he's not."

Hugh talked about the fact that he suffered greatly, for a long time after John's death. Was there something he didn't do? Did he let John down in some way? "No, I didn't let him down. It was the intensity of it, you know. I did everything I could. I didn't know my way. I took care of everything pretty much alone. I didn't really take good care of myself, my own needs, but some things I couldn't do. They almost overpowered me. I remember when they were going to put that thing in John's neck, he wanted me to stay. I just said, 'No, I can't.'

"I don't have any regrets about anything I did. I did the best I could. I wonder sometimes—maybe for a second—if I would have done it, if I'd known what the aftermath was going to be; if I knew how bad that was going to be."

Depression: Suddenly, you cannot see any future for yourself. The days ahead seem endlessly dreary. "What's ahead for me?" you ask. "More sadness. More loneliness." You may find it hard to concentrate; you might feel exhausted and dread getting out of bed in the morning. You may not feel like doing anything. You may want to sleep eighteen or twenty hours a day.

Depression and the resulting lack of will to act—these, too, are part of the grieving process. It will pass with time. But you must be patient with yourself. Try to remember events in the past that you thought you would never get over: the breakup with a person you loved, losing the best job you ever had, the death of one of your parents. You survived these events. You know—more than likely you know with absolute certainty—that your friend wanted you to go on after he left you. Take your time. Slowly you will move again, as you realize that *shedding your grief is not the same as discarding the intense memories of someone you loved.*

You can also work actively against this depression. Let yourself feel it, as you must, then make yourself move. Do positive things that give you a feeling of accomplishment, even something as simple as doing the dishes accumulating in the sink. Force yourself to call a friend you may be neglecting and go out to dinner. Make a visit to a church or synagogue. Take a walk or a bicycle ride. Go to the gym.

It's important that you not dwell too long on the fact of your depression. Movement will take it away for a while, but ultimately it will play itself out.

More frequent illness: As you grieve, you may get more colds, more ill-defined feelings of sickness. This also can be part of the process of mourning, and it happens to many people. They have stomach problems, back problems, headaches. As your grief lessens, your normal health should return. But while you are mourning, take special care of yourself. Your resistance is low. Of course, if you had a sexual relationship with the person who has died, you may fear that you are coming down with AIDS. Have your health checked if it reassures you.

Panic attacks: Sometimes, too, you may suffer overwhelming anxiety or terror. Suddenly, for no apparent reason, everything seems out of control. You may feel that you are going to die at that very minute. You may break down crying in the most inappropriate places. You may be seized with the desire to run. You may be talking out loud to yourself as you walk down the street and never realize that you are doing it. Sometimes you act very crazy. You do things that you would never do otherwise. "Why shouldn't I vacuum my apartment at four in the morning if I want to?" you say, defending your strange behavior.

This, too, will pass. The pressure and strain of your loneliness and grief produce distortions in your mind and your perceptions. As the strain lessens, you will return to normal. Probably, you will not even know that you passed through this period.

REVIEWING THE EVENTS

You know in your heart that you and your friend with AIDS were strong and courageous for enduring what you have gone through. Yet you may have a great need to go over in your mind the whole course of the illness from the time your friend was diagnosed to the end—reviewing the events as they happened, with each hospitaliza-

189

tion, each crisis, as if it had happened yesterday. Many carepartners and caring friends do this.

This review may be necessary to help you to digest what has happened, to go over your feelings about the events at each stage of the illness and to make peace with them. It is important as you do this review that you bring into it people who were around when you were going through the events. You may need assurance from the people who make up your support system that you did everything you could and that your partner did everything he could. You need to accept some facts: that your emotions were what they were, that you couldn't stop the loss, and that you expressed your love for your partner in the hundreds of ways that you cared for him. You may need to be told that you should be feeling the pain you feel. This pain is not a sign of weakness. It is the other side of the love that you have lost.

"My eyeballs are still intact," Suzanne said, describing how she feels months after Michelle's death. "It's extremely painful. It's like being stabbed a hundred times. I go over every little thing. Night after night, I wake up back in that hospital again." Suzanne snapped her fingers. "Every little detail."

"I've been over it and over it and over it," James said. "And it hurt me as much the tenth time as the first. I keep saying it wasn't like Earl wasn't there anymore. It was like I wasn't there anymore either. Everything I ever did, it was like 'I can't wait to tell Earl about this.'

"Then one day something started to happen. I was going over things, and it seemed like for the first time those things were things *that had happened.* Those things were back there. But I was here. I hurt, but I was right here on this chair. And who was I? I was somebody. I have arms, and legs, and I can move around. I said out loud, 'Okay, Earl, maybe I'm getting ready.' "

Anger: You might also be feeling anger about the disease itself, about those people who abandoned you and your friend, and you might feel a need to settle with those people. Let this be. If the opportunity arises and you still want to settle, then do it, but don't go out of your way, unless your need is very great. Better to direct your anger to activities that are more positive, like lobbying the government for more money for AIDS care, or when you are ready, being the kind of friend to others that you wish others had been to you.

Gradually, over a period of months, your pain will grow less intense. You will not think about and feel your loss twenty-four hours of every day. You have allowed yourself to feel your hurt; you have been working through your pain. A whole complex of issues is being resolved inside you, and without any loss of that mental memorial you've made, your life begins again.

You start new relationships: You will become more active in life again. Whereas before you might have spent much time alone, or at least in mental solitude, now you begin to seek out new relationships, new people, new points of view, and new activities that give you fulfillment. This is part of growing beyond your loss.

This movement, away from death, may take you about a year. But you will learn again to enjoy life without your partner, and you will know that you have a right to have survived, you have a right to go on with your life. You have this right because you know you could not have prevented your friend's death; you were not responsible for the course of the disease; you could not have taken your friend's place, even if you had wanted to. You could not have done more for him or loved him more. You gave all to him; now you must do so for yourself. Your life can no longer linger in the past.

You keep your friend in your memory: You may begin to feel uneasy that you do not think about your friend all day, every day. In some way, you feel that you are betraying him, because your love has been so intense and now it seems a little distant. If you feel this way, understand that it means that you are growing emotionally, that you are no longer obsessed about the loss of your friend. Your partner will always be with you, but as a memory, not as an everyday presence. You must leave him behind, even though it hurts you to do so. It hurts you to let go.

"You feel guilty about moving away from the person who's gone," Suzanne explained. "Your whole time thing is all mixed up. Michelle would have been twenty-five in May. I'm going to get older, but Michelle is not going to get older. If I move away from her and try to pick up the pieces of my life, I feel guilty. I feel like I'm leaving her in the past. Somehow you want to carry her with you; it prevents your own healing."

Rose described a visit she had from her son Gary's lover, Bob. "One day I was home alone—Gary had been dead about seven months—and the doorbell rang. I wasn't expecting anyone. I opened the door, and it was Bob, looking robust and healthy. I almost burst into tears when I saw him, and I just grabbed him and hugged him.

I want to tell you that I love him like my own—anyone who could bring such happiness to my son when he was sick. 'I need to talk to you, Rose,' he said. 'I'm really confused. I don't think anyone but you can understand what's going on with me.'

"He came in, and I made coffee, and we sat in the kitchen. 'Sometimes during the day,' he said, 'I get wrapped up in what I'm doing, and I completely forget about Gary and what we had together, and how I still love him. The same thing happens to me in the evening. I go out with some friends, or a friend, and I don't talk about Gary like I did. I don't think about him as much.' He paused for a while like he was thinking or finding it hard to admit something. 'I feel like that's wrong. He's not part of my life like he was. I feel guilty, as if I'm killing him in another way now that he's dead. You know I love him, and how I loved him. I get rid of some of his things, and I feel like I'm betraying him.'

"While he was talking, I thought about my brother who was killed in the war, about my parents, and about my little girl from my first marriage who had died at three. Now Gary. I knew Bob had come to me for strength. He wanted Gary's mother to tell him what he was feeling was all right. I could feel his need. 'I have the same feelings,' I said. 'My son is gone. I can't send him a birthday card this year. He won't call me on Mother's Day. For a while after he died, I wanted to seal his room so nothing would ever change, and I kept the door shut so I could pretend that he was sleeping in there, and I'd even tiptoe by so I wouldn't wake him.

"But after a while, I knew I couldn't do that forever. I knew that it was all right for me to do that for a while, but not forever. The door is open now. I went in one day and rearranged the furniture and took his things off the walls. And I cried while I did it. I thought of his head on my breast when he was a little boy. I thought of all the time with him that I had been cheated out of, the Thanksgivings, the birthdays, those afternoons he'd drop by when he was on his way somewhere. But I had to tell myself that that was over now. It was going to fade into memory, and I had to let it. My husband needs me. My children and grandchildren need me. You need me and I need you.'

"He just sat awhile with tears streaming down his cheeks, and he thanked me. When he got ready to leave, I held him a long time and we cried together, but I knew he was going to be all right. That was the least I could have done for him."

Letting go: Letting go is perhaps the hardest thing you will have to do. You have to say in your heart to your deceased partner, "I will always love you. You will always be in my heart and in my mind. But I have to go on now, the way you wanted me to." If you are having trouble with this step, if you feel you cannot let go—you cannot dispose of your partner's things, or you cannot bring his affairs to a close—then get help. Go to a bereavement group in your area or to a counselor.

"I had so many good times with John," Hugh said, "times I've never, never had with anyone else. John was really proud of me. I was excited about these contracting jobs, and he'd encourage me. He'd talk to friends about what I was doing. He'd talk about working together on projects, and we'd plan things and talk about ideas a lot. I was excited, and I'd go see his jobs. I guess what I'm afraid of most—that's what hurts the most—I feel that I'll never, ever, have that again. I keep thinking that I need to see John again, to talk to him. I told that to my shrink once, and he said, 'What would you say to him?' I said I'd walk up to him and say, 'Hello, how are you doing?' That's the problem you know, letting go. I haven't let go. I still talk to him. I say, 'Hi,' to him. I miss him."

Many times letting go means admitting we are not in control of life. If were in control, we would not have suffered this loss; we would not have this pain; we would not have to remake our lives to fill the void left by our friend who is no longer there. If we need to ease ourselves into letting go, then we can do it a little each day. You can resolve to yourself, "Today, I will allow myself to go on. I will experiment to see what my new life could be like."

Who are you?   You will begin to redefine the person you are. For a very long time you defined yourself as a carepartner or caring friend to a person with AIDS. That was your purpose in life and what you did. Now, after a period of time when you simply took care of yourself and your pain, you will begin to look again at yourself and ask what it is you want from your life. You may find that the values you thought important before this experience are not so important now. You will probably find that you place much greater value on the relationships you have with people. You know more about these relationships now, you know how to nurture them, you know how to help other people feel good about themselves. This experience will have made you a much more mature and sensitive individual; it has taught you the preciousness of time.

Hugh: "The shrink in my bereavement group said that this was an opportunity to look into our own lives. Everything certainly changes, and it's an opportunity to change your life. I feel like a totally different person since this happened. I'm a totally different Hugh than I was two years ago or four years ago. I feel much stronger. I feel like I could do anything or nothing. Things that I used to get upset about are nothing now. I think that I'm kinder and more loving now.

"I never thought of people before. I never, ever, missed people before in my life. I've said good-bye to people and never gave them another thought, you know. I moved out of my house from my parents when I was seventeen and never gave it a thought. I've broken up with people and never thought of them again. That's a big difference. I think more about people now. I'm a lot less selfish."

Suzanne: "I went to a training session at New York Hospital. I was asked to speak about my daughter's illness and then answer questions from the audience. There was another woman there whose son had AIDS, and she had come all the way from California to live in her son's one-room apartment to take care of him. The other speaker was a young man who had AIDS. I remember we were out in the hall when he arrived, and I thought that he couldn't be the one with AIDS because he looked so well. He was winded when he arrived, and he asked for a glass of water, and that moved something inside me. My heart just opened up. Maybe I can't go back to my old life. A boy asked me for a glass of water, and I was moved.

"I like the feeling of being with people who understand better than most of my friends, who believe it's okay to have cancer but it's not okay to have AIDS. The people who've had to deal with AIDS are set apart.

"My husband keeps saying, 'Why don't you quit your job and just see what happens.' But I'm not ready for that. I can't do that yet. I'm just beginning to move a little bit in that new direction. AIDS takes over your life in such a way that it's hard to shake it off. I've grown intolerant of situations that I feel are shallow. I want to say to people, 'Hey folks, there's something going on out there.' There's lots of people giving, in ways that most people aren't even aware that people can give. I don't know where I'm going, perhaps into something where I can help."

Michael: "I'm not nearly as scared as I used to be about whether or not anybody else loves me. I know that people love me. They love me because I love myself in a way that I never did before. I take better care of myself. I pay more attention to myself. I think about what my interests are, and that I didn't used to do. It sounds obvious, but I didn't pay any attention.

"I'll tell you how I identify the change in me the most. I wake up in the morning now, and I know what I'm feeling and who I am. I used to go for days, for weeks, even for years, walking around not knowing what I was feeling. Now in the morning, all the time, I know what I feel. I used to wake up and wonder what's going on.

Should I get up? Is there any reason to get up? I'm not like that anymore. I've become very aware of what's going on inside me all the time.

"While Joe was here, I kept thinking, 'I've got a center. I've got a focus in life. I feel like I've got a purpose in life. But I've got to extend this into the future. Joe has to be sick in order for me to be well? That doesn't make sense. And I thought about that a lot, and I feel like that's what happened. I extended that focus into the future. I feel like we create our own reality and make happen what we want to happen. I was given a situation, and I accepted a situation that had enough emotional and psychological content that it was able to support whatever I hung on it. And I hung a lot on it. I make it work for myself in a lot of different ways. I got a lot out of it.

"I developed a kind of self-awareness that I never had before. It feels real solid. It doesn't feel like something that's going to evaporate in the next minute. And my going to nursing school now—that seems to be the result of all this. Finding something I want to do. Something that will satisfy me, where I can contribute."

Stella: "What I'd really like to do is to go to nurse's training, and maybe take care of terminally ill patients, or ICU [Intensive Care Unit], or hospice work. You know, if David's illness has taught me anything, it's taught me patience. When something happens, I don't panic. I take care of that situation. Then, if another one arises, I take care of that one. And I tell you, since David died, it's been one situation after another, especially with the kids.

"One of the biggest things I'm concerned about is people's fear. I do everything I can on the education of this disease. I speak whenever I can. I'm willing to do anything. And somehow, it has been getting better. It's so important that our young children learn about this disease, and how to be safe.

"I realized that I wasn't going to have the money to go to nurse's training, but after a while, I got a job helping the mentally retarded. It's a wonderful job, and it helps me a lot to feel good about what I'm doing."

Rose: "The changes that Gary's illness and death made on all our lives has been amazing. I see my daughter Linda in such a different light. She knew exactly what to do. She did all the right things to make us a family and help get through this. My husband had a whole side I never knew existed. He accepted Gary. He accepted Bob into our home like a son. And me, I found all this strength inside me that had been waiting to be called upon. My relationships with all the people in my life now are much warmer, more open, more loving, and more honest."

Suzanne tells this story. "The day of Michelle's memorial service was the day of that huge memorial vigil that they had on Christopher Street, for all those afflicted with AIDS. They marched down to the river, and they had all lit candles. Well, I was totally exhausted from planning Michelle's service. But, I wanted everyone to come back to my house after the memorial service, so there was food there, and lots of people to help out.

"Timothy, one of the priests at my church, he's gay, and he asked me if I would come to the vigil. So, after our guests had left, I went back to New York that night and went to the vigil. When I left the house, I told my mother, my father, and my daughter Camille where I was going. They all came with me.

"While I was walking with Timothy, he told me that today was the tenth anniversary of his ordination. I thought that was astonishing. "We bought these candles—the money went to GMHC—and strangely enough, when we got down to the river, of the people I was walking with, my candle was the only one that was still lit. Camille said, 'Look, Mom, your candle is the only one that is still lit.' So we said Michelle's name and threw it into the river.

"Of the people that had come, only Camille and I had made it down to the river because there was such a crowd. My mother and father got too tired, so they said they'd sit on a parked car and wait for us to come back. On the way back, we were looking for them—there were people everywhere milling around, and some of them were crying—and then, off in the distance, I saw my mother and father sitting on the curb with a young blond man. He was crying like a little boy.

"We talked to him awhile and found out that he was from out of town, and he had come to New York with his lover, but his lover had gotten sick, and in about two weeks had died of AIDS. He was about Camille's age, so she talked to him. He didn't really know anyone, and he was staying at some friend's house.

"I still have a picture in my mind of that. The weird people who come together around this disease, people who would never meet each other. People who would never have anything to say to each other. This disease brings them together."

APPENDIXES

APPENDIX A
WHAT REALLY CAUSES AIDS?

Throughout the AIDS crisis, there has been a controversy about the real cause of the syndrome. Many publications, such as this book, identify HIV only as "the virus associated with AIDS." We have deliberately not used the term "the AIDS virus." Here are our reasons:

- There is no proof that HIV by itself can cause AIDS. Since the very definition of AIDS requires the presence of other infections, namely opportunistic infections or cancers, it seems unlikely that HIV is the sole cause of the disease.

- Other viruses such as CMV, herpes simplex and zoster, and Epstein-Barr are present in the majority of persons with AIDS, and it is not clear what part these viruses play in the onset of the disease.

- Kaposi's sarcoma remains an AIDS mystery, and its connection with HIV is unclear and undefined.

- The role of cofactors, such as intestinal parasites, other sexually transmitted diseases, recreational drugs, the general health of the person, and environmental conditions have not been clearly defined in relation to the onset of AIDS.

- The possibility of a link between AIDS and African Swine Fever virus has not been fully explored, even though there seems to be a correlation between outbreaks of African Swine Fever among hogs in places such as Burundi and Rwanda in Africa, Haiti and Brazil in the Americas, and Belle Glade, Florida, in the United States and large numbers of cases of AIDS in the same locations. The *New York Native*, a weekly newspaper for the gay community, has vigorously pursued this connection, but has not been satisfied with investigations to date. In early 1987, it published some evidence that AIDS could be linked to tertiary syphilis.

- The report in the *New York Times* on Sunday, August 3, 1986, of the discovery of a new virus found in the lesions and spleens of twenty-three out of twenty-four persons with AIDS by Dr. Shyh-Ching Lo at the Armed Forces Institute of Pathology in Washington, D.C., has only deepened the mystery of the causes of AIDS.

- We know little about the spread of AIDS in places like central and eastern Africa and Haiti, where most persons with AIDS are heterosexuals, half are women, and where up to 10 percent of the population in some locations is testing positive for antibodies to the virus associated with AIDS. We do not know why the risk groups are entirely different in other parts of the world or what this means about the causes of the syndrome.

In sum, AIDS is an incredibly complex medical condition and a problem that is not easily traced to a single source. The authors feel that worldwide attention to the AIDS epidemic and the intensification of medical research efforts will produce much new and useful information that may help identify and control the real cause of AIDS.

APPENDIX B
THE HIV ANTIBODY TEST: PROS AND CONS

In April 1985, the blood donated to blood banks throughout the United States began to be tested for antibodies to the virus associated with AIDS. The antibodies to the virus, HIV (HTLV-III or LAV), have been found in the blood of most persons with AIDS, although there have been a few cases of AIDS where these antibodies have not been found. The absence of the virus in these few has not yet been explained satisfactorily, and at least leads to doubt that HIV can be called "the AIDS virus."

Blood is tested by an ELISA (Enzyme-Linked Immunosorbent Assay) screening test. If it is reactive, it is retested again by the same method. If it reactive again, it is tested by a Western Blot test. If the blood is reactive to this more complicated test, it is removed from the blood bank because it contains antibodies to the virus associated with AIDS and therefore could contain the virus and possibly could transmit the disease. These tests are extremely useful to screen blood for blood banks.

What the tests show: These tests do not screen blood for the virus, only for the antibodies to the virus associated with AIDS. Since testing started in 1985, it has also been discovered that these antibodies are not detectable for up to six months after exposure to the virus, so there can be some blood in the blood banks donated by people who have been infected by the virus but whose blood is not yet showing antibodies.

To detect the virus itself is a long procedure involving cultures that are hard to grow because of contamination by other organisms. The presence of the antibodies does not guarantee the presence of the virus itself, but the assumption is that the virus is still present in the body.

What will the test show you? The tests will tell you if you have been exposed to the virus associated with AIDS. It will not tell you if you have the virus in your system, although, as stated above, the likelihood is extremely great that if you test positive, you have the virus.

The tests will not tell you if you might get sick. The tests will not tell you if you will develop ARC or AIDS.

Why take the test? If you take the test, you will know if you have been exposed to the virus associated with AIDS. If you have not been exposed, and you have been practicing safer sex, then you are probably in the clear. Continue to take good care of yourself, as discussed in Chapter 1 of this book, do not expose yourself to the body fluids of any other human being, or expose anyone to your body fluids, especially someone in one of the risk groups for AIDS, and you can be confident that you will not get AIDS.

If you test positive, you will know you have been exposed to the virus associated with AIDS. Out of respect for yourself and other people, you should take good care of yourself, not expose anyone to your body fluids, and not expose yourself to anyone else's body fluids. Your chances of getting sick are uncertain, but the risk has increased.

However, whether you test positive or negative, your behavior should be exactly the same: You will not exchange body fluids with anyone and you will take good care of yourself, so testing really should not make any difference in behavior.

What are the dangers of taking the test? AIDS is a reportable disease. That means that the names and addresses of persons with AIDS must reported to public health authorities. That is how the Centers for Disease Control issues it weekly numbers of AIDS cases.

At present, it is theoretically possible to get the ELISA and Western Blot tests under conditions of strict secrecy and confidentiality. Only clinics that do not take your name can make this guarantee.

But if you use blood banks or facilities that do take your name, there is no guarantee that what is strictly secret and confidential today cannot become reportable to public health authorities tomorrow. Even today, five states require that doctors report the names and addresses of persons whose blood tests positive to the antibodies of the virus associated with AIDS. They are Colorado, Idaho, Minnesota, South Carolina, and Wisconsin. There is also the possibility that other states will pass such laws.

AIDS hysteria and discrimination: If positive test results become reportable—and in most cases, even if they don't—they will somehow become a matter of public or semipublic record, so that at least some interested people will be able to use the results for their own purposes. Besides identifying the person as a homosexual or IV-drug user, in the present climate of hysteria and discrimination, a positive result could:

- if reported to an employer, cause a person to be fired,
- if reported to an insurance company, cause someone to lose insurance coverage, especially health and life insurance,
- if reported to a landlord, cause someone the loss of housing accommodations or at least become subject to harassment.

Recommendation: What the results of the test will tell you will make little difference, if you are living as you should be in the midst of this devastating crisis. But if you must know, arrange it between yourself and your doctor, or go to a clinic that identifies you with a number only. *Make sure that however the blood is identified, it can never be traced to you. Make sure that only you and your doctor will ever know the results.* And, before you even go that far, make sure the doctor is not required by law to expose you in some way.

APPENDIX C
SAFER-SEX GUIDELINES

Courtesy of Gay Men's Health Crisis, New York, New York.

Guidelines for safer sex should be followed by everyone. Anyone who is sexually active is at risk of exposure to the [AIDS] virus. The only exception is the couple who has been in an exclusively monogamous sexual relationship since 1978. To date, gay and bisexual men, IV-drug users, and their sexual partners have been most often affected by the disease.

Because many people already carry the [AIDS] virus (especially in New York City and other major urban areas), reducing the number of different sexual partners does not guarantee safety from exposure. All it takes is one infectious partner for exposure. But even if one has been exposed, it is thought to be important to avoid repeated exposure to the virus.

Risk reduction practices must always be followed in every sexual encounter. *Have all the sex you want—just be sure to always make it safer.*

AIDS is transmitted through the exchange of certain body fluids—you cannot get it from casual contact (hugging, kissing, sharing bathroom and kitchens).

The exchange of *cum* (semen) and *pre-cum* should be avoided:

■ **In oral sex**

- avoid putting the head of the penis into your mouth
- never allow anyone to ejaculate into the mouth
- use a condom for the greatest freedom in oral sex

■ **In anal sex**

- *always* use a condom, with water-soluble lubricants such as

204

KY. Some experts encourage the use of spermicidal jelly containing Nonoxynol-9

- withdrawing before ejaculation, even with a condom, is safest, since a condom can break

- under no circumstances should you ejaculate semen into the anus. *This may be the highest-risk activity for AIDS.* Use a condom

■ In vaginal sex

- *always* use a condom. If you use a lubricant, it should be water soluble, such as KY

- withdrawing before ejaculation, even with a condom, is safest, since a condom can break

The exchange of *blood* should be avoided.

☐ Fisting is dangerous! And it carries the risk of AIDS transmission through the exchange of blood. If you do it, always use a rubber glove

☐ If you inject drugs, never share needles, cookers, or other drug paraphernalia

☐ If you are bisexual, avoid contact with menstrual flow. Use a condom

What about *saliva?*

☐ The virus has been isolated in saliva, though rarely and in very low concentrations. The exchange of saliva is generally thought not to be a risk for AIDS.

What about *urine* and *feces?*

☐ Although the virus could theoretically be present in any body secretion, urine, feces, sweat, and tears are not known to be modes of transmission. Oral contact with fecal material (rimming) should be avoided to reduce the risk of other sexually transmitted diseases. One should use a condom, finger cot, or rubber glove in giving a rectal massage. Avoid oral contact with fingers after this.

Alcohol and *drugs* may impair your judgment and may compromise your system.

Poppers (amyl nitrite) have been linked to Kaposi's sarcoma, a cancer associated with AIDS. *Don't use poppers!*

Mutual masturbation, hugging, frontage (body rubbing), cuddling, showering together, and massaging do not involve the exchange of body fluids and therefore are considered safe.

These guidelines will help to give you enough information to make responsible choices.

Additional Precaution: Avoid oral contact with vaginal secretions, as these may contain varying concentrations of the virus associated with AIDS.

APPENDIX D
NATIONAL DIRECTORY OF AIDS-RELATED ORGANIZATIONS

Throughout the United States, homosexual and bisexual men and lesbian woman, together with their heterosexual friends and supporters, have banded together to organize resource centers to supply information, support, and all kinds of advice and counseling for persons with AIDS or ARC, persons caring for those with the disease or its symptoms, and for the worried well. Below is a list of organizations that can supply one or more of a variety of services to persons who have some need related to AIDS. The list begins with organizations or institutions that operate on a national level or that are part of our federal government. Remember, if the first organization you call doesn't supply the information you need, go to the next closest.

National

AIDS Action Council
Federation of AIDS-Related
   Organizations
1115½ Independence Avenue, SE
Washington, DC 20003
(202) 547-3101/547-3102

AIDS Medical Foundation
230 Park Avenue, Room 1266
New York, NY 10169
(212) 949-7411

American Association of
   Physicians for Human Rights
P.O. Box 14366
San Francisco, CA 94114
(415) 558-9353/673-3189

Centers for Disease Control,
   AIDS Activity
Building 3, Room 5B-1,
   1600 Clifton Road
Atlanta, GA 30333
Hot line: 1-(800) 342-AIDS
In Atlanta (404) 329-3534

Gay and Lesbian Press
   Association
P.O. Box A, Old Chelsea Station
New York, NY 10011
(212) 989-6622

Gay Rights National Lobby,
AIDS Project
P.O. Box 1892
Washington, DC 20013

Haitian Community Health
Project
391 Eastern Parkway
Brooklyn, NY 11213
(718) 773-1171

Haitian Coalition on AIDS
255 Eastern Parkway
Brooklyn, NY 11238
(718) 783-2676

KS Research and Education
Foundation
54 Tenth Street
San Francisco, CA 94103
(415) 864-4376

Lambda Legal Defense and
Education Fund
132 West 43rd Street, 5th Floor
New York, NY 10036
(212) 944-9488

Lesbian and Gay Concern
Committee, National
Association of Social Workers
110 West 86th Street
New York, NY 10024
(212) 799-3298

National Coalition of Gay
Sexually Transmitted Disease
Services
P.O. Box 239
Milwaukee, WI 53201
(414) 277-7671

National Gay Task Force
1517 U Street NW
Washington, DC 20009
(202) 332-6483

Crisis line: 1-(800) 221-7044
For crisis line in New York,
Alaska, Hawaii:
(212) 807-6016

National Hemophilia Foundation
Soho Building, 110 Greene
Street, Room 406
New York, NY 10012
(212) 219-8180

National Institute of Allergy
and Infectious Diseases
Office of Research Reporting
and Public Response
9000 Rockville Pike
Building 31, Room 7A32
National Institutes of Health
Bethesda, MD 20892
(301) 496-5717

National Lesbian and Gay
Health Foundation
P.O. Box 65472
Washington, DC 20035
(202) 797-3708

Public Health Service,
Department of Health and
Human Services
Washington, DC 20021
(202) 245-6867
Hot line (general information):
1-(800) 342-2437
Hot line (AIDS information):
1-(800) 447-AIDS

United States Conference of
Mayors
1620 I Street, NW, 4th Floor
Washington, DC 20006
(202) 293-7330
(Publishes *Directory o
AIDS Related Services*)

Organizations by State

Alabama

AIDS Outreach
Birmingham, AL
(205) 930-0440
Call Public Health Service:
1-(800) 447-AIDS, with
specific AIDS questions

Alaska

Anchorage AIDS Project
(907) 276-3918
Call Public Health Service:
1-(800) 447-AIDS, with
specific AIDS questions

Arizona

Arizona Step AIDS Project
736 East Slynn Main
Phoenix, AZ 85014
(602) 277-1929

Tucson AIDS Project
80 West Cushing Street
Tucson, AZ 85701
(602) 792-3772

Arkansas

Arkansas AIDS Foundation
P.O. Box 5007
Little Rock, AK 72225
(501) 224-4020

Arkansas State Department of
Health
4815 West Markham
Little Rock, AK 72205
AIDS hot line: 1-(800) 445-7720

California

AIDS & KS Foundation/
Sacramento
2115 J Street, Suite 3
Sacramento, CA 95816
(916) 448-AIDS

AIDS Team
P.O. Box 9773
Fresno, CA 93974
(209) 264-2436

California Department of
Health Services,
AIDS Activities
P.O. Box 160146
Sacramento, CA 95816
(916) 445-0553

Northern California
Bay Area Physicians for
Human Rights
P.O. Box 14546
San Francisco, CA 94114
Administration: (415) 558-9353
Medical inquiries: (415) 372-7321

Kaposi's Sarcoma Clinic,
University of California,
San Francisco Medical Center,
A-312
San Francisco, CA 94143
(415) 666-1407

KS Research and Education
Foundation
54 Tenth Street
San Francisco, CA 94103
(415) 864-4376

The Pacific Center AIDS Project
(East Bay)
400 40th Street, Suite 200
Oakland, CA 94609
(415) 420-8181

San Francisco AIDS Foundation
333 Valencia Street, 4th Floor
San Francisco, CA 94103
(415) 864-4376
Hot line: (415) 863-AIDS
Toll-free Northern California:
1-(800) FOR-AIDS

San Francisco People with AIDS
1040 Ashbury, #5
San Francisco, CA 94117
(415) 665-3787

Shanti Project
890 Hayes Street
San Francisco, CA 94117
(415) 558-9644

Southern California
AIDS Project/Los Angeles
837 N. Cole Street, Suite 3
Los Angeles, CA 90038
Office: (213) 871-1284
Hot line: (213) 871-2437

Beach Area Community Clinic
3705 Mission Boulevard
San Diego, CA 92109
(619) 488-0644

KS Foundation/Los Angeles,
Gay/Lesbian Community
Center
1213 North Highland Avenue
Los Angeles, CA 90038
(213) 461-1333

L.A. Sex Information Hotline
8405 Beverly Boulevard
Los Angeles, CA 90048
(213) 653-1123

Owen Clinic, University of
California
San Diego Medical Center
225 Dickinson Street
San Diego, CA 92103
(619) 294-3995

San Diego AIDS Project
4304 3rd Avenue, P.O. Box 81082
San Diego, CA 92138
(619) 294-2437

Southern California Physicians
for Human Rights
7985 Santa Monica Boulevard,
Suite 109, #165
Los Angeles, CA 90701
(213) 860-6611

Colorado

Boulder County AIDS Project
(303) 442-4318

Colorado AIDS Project
P.O. Box 18529
Denver, CO 80218
(303) 837-0166

Southern Colorado AIDS Project
2021 West Pike Peak's Avenue
Colorado Springs, CO 80904
(303) 633-8711

Connecticut

AIDS Project New Haven
P.O. Box 7
New Haven, CT 06473
(203) 239-7881

Hartford Gay Health Collective
320 Farmington Avenue
Hartford, CT 06105
(203) 527-9813

Yale Self-Care Network
17 Hillhouse Avenue
New Haven, CT 06520
(203) 432-0123

Delaware

Gay and Lesbian Alliance of
Delaware
P.O. Box 9218
Wilmington, DE 19809
(302) 764-2208 or
1-(800) 342-4012

District of Columbia

AIDS Action Project, Whitman-
Walker Clinic
2335 18th Street, NW
Washington, DC 20009
(202) 332-5295 or
(202) 332-AIDS

Commission for Public Health
Suite 1217
1875 Connecticut Avenue, NW
Washington, DC 20009
(202) 673-6888

St. Francis Center
3800 Macomb Street, NW
Washington, DC 20016
(202) 234-5613

Florida

AIDS Action Committee,
Florida Keys Memorial
Hospital
P.O. Box 4073
Key West, FL 33041
(305) 294-5531, ext. 4797

AIDS Support Group
c/o MCC Church
23rd Street & NE Biscayne
Boulevard
Miami, FL 33181
(305) 573-4156

Health Crisis Network
P.O. Box 52-1546
Miami, FL 33152
(305) 634-4636

Monroe County Health Dept.
Public Service Building
Junior College Road
Key West, FL 33040
(305) 294-1021

University of Miami Medical
School AIDS Project
Department of Medicine R-60
Miami, FL 33136
(305) 549-7538

University of South Florida
Main Lab, Medical Clinic S
12901 North 30th Street
Tampa, FL 33612
(813) 974-4214

Georgia

AID Atlanta (AIDA)
811 Cypress Street
Atlanta, GA 30308
(404) 872-0600

Centers for Disease Control,
AIDS Activity
Building 3, Room 5b-1
1600 Clifton Road
Atlanta, GA 30333
(404) 329-3473

211

Hawaii

Life Foundation
320 Ward Avenue, Suite 104
Honolulu, HI 96814
(808) 924-2437

Idaho

Idaho AIDS Foundation
P.O. Box 44123
Boise, ID 83711
(208) 345-2277
Call Public Health Service,
   1-(800) 447-AIDS,
   with specific AIDS questions

Illinois

AIDS/ARC Support Services,
   Howard Brown Memorial
   Clinic
2676 North Halsted Street
Chicago, IL 60614
Clinic: (312) 871-5776
Offices: (312) 871-5776
Hot line: 1-(800) 243-AIDS

AIDS Assistance Program
P.O. Box 578418
Chicago, IL 60657
(312) 539-2437

AIDS Foundation of Chicago
845 North Michigan Avenue
Suite 903E
Chicago, IL 60611
(312) 988-9005

Chicago House
500 North Michigan Avenue
Room 2000
Chicago, IL 60611
(312) 334-2346

Sable/Sherer Clinic
Cook County Hospital
621 South Winchester
Chicago, IL 60612
(312) 633-7810

Indiana

AIDS Activity Office
Indiana State Board of Health
Room 234
1330 West Michigan
Indianapolis, IN 46206
(317) 633-8406

Gay Switchboard AIDS Hot line
(317) 543-6200

Iowa

AIDS Hot line: 1-(800) 445-AIDS

Iowa Department of Public
   Health
Lucas State Office Building
Des Moines, IA 50319
AIDS information:
   (515) 532-3301

Kansas

Department of Health and
   Environment
Epidemiology Center
Forbes Field
Topeka, KS 66620
(913) 862-9360

Kentucky

Gay and Lesbian Hot line,
   Louisville: 1-(800) 654-AIDS

Kentucky Cabinet for Human
   Resources
STD Control Program
275 Main Street
Frankfurt, KY 40621

Louisiana

Crescent City Coalition
c/o St. Louis Community Center
1022 Barracks Street
New Orleans, LA 70116
(504) 568-9619/524-7023

Foundation for Health Education
P.O. Box 51537
New Orleans, LA 70151
(504) 244-6900

Maine

AIDS Project
48 Deering Street
Portland, ME 04101
(207) 775-1267

AIDS Line: 1-(800) 857-AIDS

Maryland

AIDS Hot line, Health Education
Resource Center
101 West Read Street, Suite 819
Baltimore, MD 21201
Metro Baltimore Hot line:
(301) 947-AIDS

Health Education Resource
Organization (HERO)
(301) 658-1180
Baltimore and Montgomery
County Referrals
Prince George's County Office:
(301) 386-4370
Montgomery County Office:
(301) 762-3385
Hot line: (301) 251-1164
(Metro Washington, DC)
Statewide: 1-(800) 638-6252

Gay Community Center Clinic
241 West Chase Street
Baltimore, MD 21201
(301) 837-2050

Massachusetts

AIDS Action Committee,
Fenway Community Health
Center
16 Haviland Street
Boston MA 02215
(617) 267-7573

AIDS Hotline, Boston
Department of Health and
Hospitals
House Office Building #3
818 Harrison Avenue
Boston, MA 02118
(617) 424-5916

Haitian Committee on AIDS
117 Harvard Street
Dorchester, MA 02124
(617) 436-2808

Mayor's Ad Hoc Committee on
AIDS
City Hall, Room 608
Boston, MA 02201
(617) 725-4849

Michigan

State Department of Public
Health
3500 North Logan
P.O. Box 30035
Lansing, MI 48909
(517) 335-8371

United Community Services
51 West Warren Avenue
Detroit, MI 48201
(313) 833-0622

Wellness Networks, Inc.
P.O. Box 1046
Royal Oaks, MI 48068
(313) 876-3582
Call statewide Hot line:
1-(800) 482-2404 ext. 3582

Minnesota

AIDS Support Group
c/o 2309 Girard Avenue South
Minneapolis, MN 55405

Minnesota AIDS Project,
Lesbian and Gay Community
Services
124 West Lake Street, Suite E
Minneapolis, MN 55408
(612) 827-2821

Mississippi

State Department of Health
Jackson, MS 39215
(601) 354-6612
AIDS Hot line: 1-(800) 826-2961
Call Public Health Service:
1-(800) 447-AIDS, with
specific AIDS questions

Missouri

St. Louis Task Force on AIDS
P.O. Box 2905
St. Louis, MO 63130
(312) 862-9800

Montana

Montana AIDS Project
Department of Health &
Environmental Science
Cogswell Building
Helena, MT 59620

Nebraska

AIDS Hot line
P.O. Box 3512
Omaha, NE 68103
1-(800) 782-AIDS

Gay and Lesbian Information
and Support Line
P.O. Box 94882
Lincoln, NE 68509
(402) 475-4697

Nebraska Department of Health
301 Centennial Mall South
P.O. Box 95007
Lincoln, NE 68509
(402) 471-2937

Nevada

AIDS information, Reno:
(702) 329-AIDS

Northern Nevada Task Force
on AIDS
Attn.: Trudy Larson, M.D.
1000 Ryland Street
Reno, NV 89502
(702) 322-2175

Sparks Screening and
Counseling Center
2345 East Prater
Sparks, NV 89431
(702) 358-6819

New Hampshire

Feminist Health Center of
Portsmouth
232 Court Street
Portsmouth, NH 03801
(603) 436-7588

Gay Information/AIDS Line:
(603) 753-9533

New Hampshire Division of
Health
Communicable Diseases Center
Hazen Drive
Concord, NH 03301
1-(800) 852-3345

New Jersey

AIDS Hot line: 1-(800) 624-2377

214

AIDS Education Project of
New Jersey Gay Coalition
P.O. Box 1431
New Brunswick, NJ 08903
(201) 596-0767

New Mexico

AIDS Hot line
P.O. Box 968
Santa Fe, NM 87504
(505) 827-3301

New Mexico Physicians for
Human Rights
P.O. Box 1361
Espanola, NM 87532
(505) 753-2779/984-1217

New York

AIDS RESOURCE CENTER,
INC.
24 West 30th Street, 10th Floor
New York, New York 10001
(212) 481-1270

Albert Einstein College of
Medicine, Pediatric AIDS
Information
1300 Morris Park Avenue
F401
Bronx, NY 10461
(212) 430-3333

Beth Israel Hospital, AIDS
Information for IV-Substance
Abusers
(212) 420-4141

Gay Men's Health Crisis
P.O. Box 274
132 West 24 Street
New York, NY 10011
(212) 807-6655

Gay Men's Health Project
74 Grove Street #2J
New York, NY 10014
(212) 691-6969

New York City Department of
Health
Office of Gay and Lesbian
Health Concerns
125 Worth Street, #806
New York, NY 10013
Offices: (212) 566-6110
Hot line: (718) 485-8111

People With AIDS Coalition
263A West 19 Street,
Room 125
New York, NY 10011
(212) 627-1810

State of New York Department
of Health, Office of Public
Health
Hot line: 1-(800) 462-0820,
or call your nearest AIDS
organization

AIDS Council of Northeastern
New York
Albany, NY
(518) 445-AIDS

Buffalo AIDS Task Force, Inc.
Buffalo, NY
(716) 881-AIDS

Central New York AIDS Task
Force
Syracuse, NY
(315) 475-AIDS

Children and Youth AIDS
Project
New York, NY
(212) 807-6655

Long Island AIDS Project
(516) 444-AIDS

Mid-Hudson Valley AIDS Task
  Force
White Plains, NY
(914) 997-1614

Southern Tier AIDS Task Force
Binghamton, NY
(607) 723-6520

North Carolina

AIDS Resource Project of
  GROW
P.O. Box 4535
Wilmington, NC 28406

AIDS Task Force of Winston-
  Salem
P.O. Box 2982
Winston-Salem, NC 27102
(919) 723-5031

GLH/AIDS Project
P.O. Box 3203
Durham, NC 27705-1203
(919) 683-2182
Call Public Health Service:
  1-(800) 447-AIDS,
  with specific AIDS questions

Metrolina AIDS Project
P.O. Box 32-62
Charlotte, NC 28232
(704) 333-2487

Triad Health Project
P.O. Box 5716
Greensboro, NC 27435
(919) 275-1654

North Dakota

Call Public Health Service:
  1-(800) 447-AIDS
  with specific AIDS questions.

Ohio

AIDS Volunteers of Cincinnati
P.O. Box 2615
Cincinnati, OH 45201
(513) 542-0943

Cleveland Health Issues
11800 Edgewater Street, #206
Lakewood, OH 44107
Daytime: (216) 822-2785
Evening: (216) 266-6507

Free Medical Clinic of Greater
  Cleveland
12201 Euclid Avenue
Cleveland, OH 44106
(216) 721-4010

Health Issues Task Force
P.O. Box 14925, Public Square
  Station
Cleveland, OH 44114
(216) 651-1448

STD Clinic, Ambrose Clement
  Health Clinic
3101 Brunet Avenue
Cincinnati, OH 45229
(513) 352-3143

Oklahoma

Oklahoma Blood Institute
1001 Lincoln Boulevard
Oklahoma City, OK 73101
(405) 239-2437

Oklahoma Department of Health
STD Division
P.O. Box 53551
Oklahoma City, OK 73152
(405) 271-4061
Hot line, Oklahoma City:
  (405) 525-AIDS

Oregon

Cascade AIDS Project
408 S.W. 2nd Avenue, Suite 420
Portland, OR 97204
(503) 223-5907

Pennsylvania

Division of Acute Infectious
   Disease Epidemiology
P.O. Box 90
Harrisburg, PA 17108
Hot line: 1-(800) 692-7254

Philadelphia AIDS Task Force
P.O. Box 7259
Philadelphia, PA 19101
Hot line: (215) 232-8055

Pittsburgh AIDS Task Force
P.O. Box 2763
Pittsburgh, PA 15230

Pitt Men's Study
University of Pittsburgh
P.O. Box 7319
Pittsburgh, PA 15213
(412) 624-2008

Rhode Island

Rhode Island Department of
   Health
AIDS Control Program
Room 105
75 Davis Street
Providence, RI 02908
(401) 277-2362

Rhode Island Project AIDS
22 Hayes Street
Room 124
Providence, RI 02903
(401) 277-6502

South Carolina

AIDS Hot line: 1-(800) 322-2437

AIDS Community Health
   Education Risk Reduction
   Project
Department of Health and
   Environmental Control
2600 Bull Street
Columbia, SC 29201
(803) 734-5482

South Dakota

AIDS Hot line: 1-(800) 592-1861

Communicable Disease Control
South Dakota Department of
   Health
523 East Capitol
Pierre, SD 57501
(605) 773-3357

Tennessee

Aid to End AIDS Committee,
   Memphis: (901) 726-4299
aids Response, Knoxville:
   (615) 521-6546
Nashville Cares: (615) 321-0118

Tennessee Department of
   Health and Environment
AIDS Education
100 Ninth Avenue North
Nashville, TN 37219
(615) 741-7387

Texas

AIDS Action Project
c/o Oaklawn Counseling Center
Suite 202, 3409 Oaklawn Street
Dallas, TX 75219
(214) 528-2181

AIDS Task Force
P.O. Box 190712
Dallas, TX 75219
(214) 528-4233

KS/AIDS Foundation of Houston
3317 Montrose Boulevard
Houston, TX 77006
(713) 524-AIDS

The Montrose Clinic
104 Westeimer
Houston, TX 77006
(713) 528-5531/528-5535

Safeweek/AIDS Committee
1713 West Mulberry
San Antonio, TX 78201
(512) 736-5216

Utah

AIDS Project/Utah information
  line: (801) 486-AIDS

Salt Lake AIDS Foundation
3450 Highland Drive #102
c/o Laurie Gregory
Salt Lake City, UT 84106
(801) 466-9976

Vermont

V.E.R.M.O.N.T. C.A.R.E.S.
P.O. Box 5248
Burlington, VT 05402

Vermont Department of Health
60 Main Street
Box 70
Burlington, VT 05402
AIDS Hot line: 1-(800) 882-AIDS

Virginia

Richmond AIDS Information
  Network
Fan Free Clinic
1721 Hanover Avenue
Richmond, VA 23220
AIDS Hot line: (804) 358-6343
Offices: (804) 355-4428

Tidewater AIDS Crisis Task
  Force
804 West 41 Street
Norfolk, VA 23508
(804) 423-5859

Virginia State Department of
  Health
STD Program
Room 722
109 Governor Street
Richmond, VA 23219
AIDS Hot line: 1-(800) 533-4148

Washington

Gay Men's Health Group
2353 Minor Avenue East
Seattle, WA 98102
(206) 322-3919

Harbor View Medical Center,
  STD Clinic
324 9th—ZA-85
Seattle, WA 98104
(206) 223-3000

Northwest AIDS Foundation
P.O. Box 3449
Seattle, WA 98114
(206) 527-8770/622-9650

Seattle AIDS Action Committee
113 Summit Avenue E1, #204
Seattle, WA 98104
(206) 323-1229

West Virginia

Call Public Health Service:
1-(800) 447-AIDS,
with specific AIDS questions

Wisconsin

Blue Bus Clinic
1552 University Avenue
Madison, WI 53706
(608) 262-7440

Milwaukee AIDS Project,
Brady East STD Clinic
1240 East Brady Street
Milwaukee, WI 53202
(414) 273-2437

Wyoming

Call Public Health Service:
1-(800) 447-AIDS,
with specific AIDS questions

Canada

AIDS Committee of Toronto
66 Wellesley East
Toronto, ONT M4Y 1G2
(416) 926-1626

National AIDS Center
Health Protection Building
B-7
Tunney's Pasture
Ottawa, ONT K1A 1B4
Attn: Greg Smith
(613) 957-1774

Ontario Public Education Panel
on AIDS
15 Overlea Boulevard, 5th floor
Toronto, ONT M4H 1A9
(416) 965-2168

South and Central America

Pan American Health
Organization
525 23rd Street, NW
Washington, DC 20037
(202) 861-4353

Worldwide

World Health Organization
AIDS Program
Geneva, Switzerland
Hot line: 91-21-11

World Health Organization
AIDS Program, Europe
Copenhagen, Denmark
Hot line: 290-111

Since AIDS resource locations
are constantly changing, readers
may wish to call or write the
National AIDS Network for a
local service listing.

The National AIDS Network
1012 14th Street NW
Suite 601
Washington, D.C. 20005
(202) 347-0390

GLOSSARY

AIDS (Acquired Immune Deficiency Syndrome): A complex disease characterized by severe damage to the body's natural immune system. A person with AIDS becomes susceptible to unusual opportunistic diseases and cancers that are not ordinarily a threat to people with normal immune systems.

AIDS-Related Complex: A health condition in which some of the symptoms of AIDS have appeared, but none of the opportunistic infections used to define the syndrome has appeared.

Amyl, or **Butyl Nitrite:** Known as "poppers," these nitrites are a fluorocarbon that is inhaled and a produces a temporary "rush" or "high" by dilating the blood vessels. Used mainly during sex.

Antibiotics: These are drugs that help the body to kill invading microorganisms, be they bacteria, fungi, or protozoa.

Antibody: A protein produced by the B-lymphocytes that combines with foreign substances or microorganisms that invade the body and helps destroy them. Once our body has an antibody to a particular substance, the cells remember what happened, and the person usually is immune to that specific substance or microorganism in the future.

Antigen: A substance or microorganism that the body (the immune system) recognizes as foreign and attempts to destroy.

ARC: AIDS-Related Complex, *see above.*

Arthritis: A health condition in which the joints of the bones or muscles become inflamed.

B-lymphocytes (B-cells): White blood cells that produce antibodies to attack certain diseases.

Bacterium: A small microorganism made up of a single cell. There are hundreds of different bacteria. Many can cause disease.

Biopsy: A procedure in which a small sample of some tissue or organ is removed for laboratory examination. Many biopsies are

220

performed with long needles with special tips that are pushed into the area or organ.

Bisexual: A person who has sex with both men and women.

Bone marrow: The spongy substance found in the hollow parts of the long bones in the arms and legs. It produces blood cells.

Brain tumor: A growth in the brain. It is benign if it is self-contained. It is cancerous if it is invading the tissue surrounding it, not just pushing it out of its way.

Brain lesion: Any abnormality in the brain tissue.

Cancer: The uncontrolled growth of the cells of the tissues of any organ in the body. Cancers can destroy the tissues surroundings them and can spread to different parts of the body.

Candidiasis: A fungal infection that is usually present in the mouth or throat. It is called thrush and is caused by a candida fungus.

Cell: The smallest independent unit of life that is capable of performing all living functions, and the smallest unit making up larger living organisms. Cells are made up of at least a nucleus, surrounded by cytoplasm and enclosed in a semipermeable membrane.

Chemotherapy: Treatment of cancer with drugs, or chemicals, mostly toxic.

Clotting factors: Substances in the blood that cause the blood to change from a liquid to a coagulate, or a solid. This stops bleeding.

CMV: *See Cytomegalovirus.*

Cofactor: Substances, agents, or other factors that increase the probability of a person getting a particular disease if the underlying cause of that disease is present, or which are necessary for the development of the disease.

Constitutional symptoms: A group of symptoms that can usually indicate a very early stage of AIDS. These include loss of weight, fatigue, fever, diarrhea, night sweats, and malaise over a period of months.

Cryptococcus: A usually harmless fungus that causes meningitis in persons with AIDS and is very difficult to cure because it keeps recurring and the drug to treat it is very toxic.

Cryptosporidiosis: A protozoan infection that is usually self-limiting in persons with normal immune systems, but which can cause severe diarrhea, dehydration, and malnutrition in persons with AIDS.

Cytomegalovirus (CMV): A virus in the herpes family that is found in persons with AIDS and in other homosexual men, but ordinarily does not cause disease if the immune system is normal. In persons with AIDS, it can cause disease in various organs, including the lungs, eyes, brain, and colon.

DNA: The substance in the cells that has all the genetic information of that living organism.

Encephalitis: Disease or inflammation of the brain, with a variety of causes.

Endemic: A condition or disease that is widespread or very common in a particular population or place.

Enteritis: Disease or inflammation of the intestines, usually the small intestine, as for example, CMV enteritis.

Epidemic: A disease or condition that affects many persons within a population at the same time when ordinarily they are not subject to this condition.

Factor VIII: One of the clotting factors in the blood.

Fungus: Tiny members of a group of organisms that includes yeast, molds, mildew, and mushrooms.

Gastroenteritis: Disease of the lining of the stomach or the intestines, usually characterized by inflammation.

Gene: The basic unit in which is encoded the heredity of a cell or an organism. Chains of genes in ordered sequences makes up the DNA of a cell.

Giardia: An intestinal parasite once common among homosexual men, which can cause severe diarrhea.

Gland: A group of cells—or organ—in the body that removes materials from the blood, alters them to produce a specialized substance, such as a hormone, and then releases it back into the bloodstream to act in the body in some way.

Hemophilia: A hereditary disorder of the blood that prevents it from clotting properly, and occurs almost exclusively in males.

Hepatitis: An inflammation of the liver that can cause the skin and eyes to turn yellow, and can cause malaise, vomiting, and pain. It can have any of several causes, but is usually caused by viral infections.

Herpes simplex: A herpes virus that causes cold sores around the mouth or genital area. These usually heal by themselves after a while. In persons with AIDS, however, these virus sores require the intervention of a drug to heal.

Herpes virus: A family of large viruses that contain a large amount of DNA. They include herpes simplex, herpes zoster, cytomegalovirus, and Epstein-Barr virus.

Herpes zoster: The virus that causes chicken pox and shingles. In AIDS patients, it can also infect sections of the body along nerve roots, presented as patches of red bumps on the skin.

HIV (Human Immunosuppressive Virus): The new nomenclature for describing the virus HTLV-III/LAV, adopted in Paris in 1986.

HPA-23: A drug that has shown some promise of preventing the replication of HIV in the body, but has numerous toxic side effects.

HTLV-III/LAV (Human T-cell Lymphotropic Virus, type III): A newly discovered retrovirus that is associated with AIDS and is largely accepted by much of the medical profession as the cause of AIDS. Also called *HIV*.

Immune: The state of being highly resistant to a particular disease because of the formation of antibodies to the disease.

Immune system: The whole system made up of cells and proteins in the body which fights infectious diseases that invade the body and probably cancers, too.

Immunization: The introduction into the body of a weakened form of a disease that cannot cause sickness, which induces the body to form antibodies against the disease. This is also called vaccination.

Incubation time: The time between the introduction of a germ into the body and the first sign of symptoms.

Interferons: Natural proteins made by the white blood cells in response to the invasion by some foreign organism into the body. Interferons are being tested in a variety of ways and apparently act in viral infections.

Isolation: A medical procedure which keeps patients with contagious infections separated from other patients who are sick but do not have the same disease. Often AIDS patients are isolated to a degree that is questionable, since the virus associated with AIDS is not airborne or spread by casual contact.

Kaposi's sarcoma (KS): A cancer of the small blood vessels, ordinarily first appearing on the skin of the legs or arms. In AIDS patients, KS is a more aggressive disease than it is in older men of

Mediterranean descent, in whom it usually appears late in life and progresses slowly. The link between KS and AIDS is not clear.

Latency: *See Incubation time.* The period between the introduction of a germ and the first symptoms.

LAV (Lymphadenophathy-Associated Virus): *See HIV or HTLV-III.* A retrovirus found in people with enlarged lymph nodes, who are also at high risk of contracting AIDS. It is the same virus as HIV.

Lymph nodes: Glands located in the groin, neck, underarms, and various locations on the body, which fight infections by filtering out microorganisms and producing hormones, and which contain large numbers of lymphocytes.

Lymphadenopathy: A condition characterized by persistent swelling of the lymph nodes, sometimes thought to be an early sign of infection with the virus associated with AIDS.

Lymphocytes: Specialized, small, white blood cells that are very important in immunity. Lymphocytes are manufactured in the bone marrow and are altered in other organs to become T-lymphocytes or B-lymphocytes.

Lymphoma: A cancer of the lymphatic system.

Meningitis: Infection and inflammation of the membranes that cover the brain and the spinal cord.

Microbes: Organisms that can be seen only under a microscope.

Opportunistic infection: Any of a number of infections that are caused by microorganisms ordinarily found in the environment, but which do not cause disease except in persons with damaged immune systems. *See Chapter 5.*

Parasite: An organism that depends on a host for food and hence for its survival.

Pentamidine: A drug used against PCP. *See Chapter 5.*

Plasma: The liquid part of the blood that contains minerals and proteins.

Platelet: A component of the blood that plays an important part in helping blood to clot. Without platelets any wound could result in death by bleeding.

Pneumocystis Carinii Pneumonia (PCP): A pneumonia caused by the protozoan parasite Pneumocystis carinii, which does not ordinarily cause disease in people with normal immune systems. It is a leading cause of death in persons with AIDS. *See Chapter 5.*

Radiation therapy: Treatment of cancer with intense beams of radiation. The radiation actually kills the cancer cells and any cells it must pass through to get to the cancer cells.

Retrovirus: A virus that contains RNA, and not DNA, as its genetic material. Retroviruses produce an analogue (a kind of mirror image) of their RNA by using an enzyme known as "reverse transcriptase." What results is DNA that incorporates itself into the genetic material of the cell that the virus has invaded. Scientists hope that by interfering with this "reverse transcriptase" they can prevent the retrovirus from replicating itself in the host cell.

Ribavirin: A drug being tested in persons with AIDS that has apparently shown, in a test tube, some success in protecting T-cells from infections with the virus associated with AIDS.

Risk factor: Some condition in the environment or in a person's behavior or makeup that increases the probability of contracting a particular disease.

Risk group: A group of people at higher risk of getting some disease than the general population.

RNA: Genetic material that is the analogue of DNA.

T-helper lymphocytes (T-4 cells): White blood cells in the body that are a key component in the body's defense against invading organisms. They help the B-lymphocytes to produce an antibody that enhances immunity.

T-lymphocyte: A type of lymphocyte that matures in the thymus gland and helps protect the body against a number of microorganisms, such as viruses, fungi, and parasites. T-lymphocytes also release substances that cause B-lymphocytes to proliferate.

T-suppressor lymphocytes (T-8 cells): A group of T-lymphocytes that regulates the antibody production of B-lymphocytes.

Thrush: An infection in the mouth, tongue, and throat caused by a candida fungus. *See Candidiasis.*

Thymosin: A hormone produced by the thymus gland that is important to the immune system. It is used as a drug in treating immune-deficiency diseases.

Thymus gland: A gland in the neck that helps in the development of T-lymphocytes and produces hormones that help in maintaining the immune system.

Toxoplasmosis: A disease caused by the protozoan parasite toxoplasma gondii. It is almost never a threat to persons with normal immune systems, but is a serious problem for persons with AIDS, often causing infections of the brain.

Transfusion: The introduction of whole blood or blood products into a person who needs them because of loss of blood or because the blood lacks a particular substance.

Tumor: Any abnormal growth, whether it is cancerous or not, a threat to health or not.

Vaccine: A weakened or dead virus or bacteria that is introduced into the body to cause it to make antibodies and increase immunity against that particular disease.

Virus: A submicroscopic organism that is not a complete cell and is composed of DNA or RNA and protein. It depends totally on living cells for survival and causes numerous diseases such as colds, flus, chicken pox, and measles.

White blood cells: Blood cells whose primary function is to fight infections.

BIBLIOGRAPHY

Altman, Dennis. *AIDS in the Mind of America.* New York: Acorn Press, Doubleday, 1986. The author offers excellent insights into the problems American society has had, because of its homophobia, dealing with the AIDS epidemic. Written from a gay perspective, the book fails only in that the author attempts to remain above the politics; he does not take a stand on many important issues, although his writing clearly demands that he take sides.

Black, David. *The Plague Years: A Chronicle of AIDS, The Epidemic of Our Times.* New York: Simon & Schuster, 1985. A book by an excellent writer who traveled the country extensively, learning from all the principal people involved in the AIDS epidemic. It contains a great deal of useful information about what is happening in various centers of AIDS activity and insights into what important people are thinking. However, the book rambles and becomes tedious when the author is unable to resist editorializing about his interviews and reminding his readers that he is heterosexual.

Brown, Raymond, K., M.D. *AIDS, Cancer and the Medical Establishment.* New York: Robert Speller Publishers, 1986. This book questions many of the commonly accepted "truths" about AIDS. The first and third sections are particularly interesting and useful. The first section discusses the probability that HTLV-III may be only one factor among many in the development of AIDS, and the third discusses the reluctance of many doctors to sanction their patients' use of alternative health and medical approaches to the disease.

CDC AIDS Weekly. Write to *CDC AIDS Weekly,* Department 1-B, 1409 Fairview Road, Atlanta, GA 30306-4611. This government publication is available from a private, nongovernment publisher on a subscription basis and contains the very latest information on companies and organizations involved in AIDS research. It records outbreaks of the syndrome and reports on research for vaccines, drugs, and other treatments. It publishes abstracts from studies, symposia, and articles, and has a calendar of upcoming meetings and conferences.

Department of Health and Human Services, Public Health Service. *Reports on AIDS Published in the Morbidity and Mortality Weekly Report June 1981 through February 1986.* Centers for Disease Control, Atlanta, Georgia 30333. This book includes all the articles related to AIDS that have appeared in the *Morbidity and Mortality Weekly Report,* published by the Centers for Disease Control. These articles, arranged in chronological order, track the reporting of information from 1981, when the CDC first published information on Kaposi's sarcoma and Pneumocystis carinii pneumonia occurring in young homosexual men. Much of this material is highly technical, but useful.

Duda, Deborah. *Coming Home: A Guide to Home Care for the Terminally Ill.* Santa Fe, New Mexico: John Muir, 1984. A useful guide to a difficult problem.

Fettner, Ann Giudici, and Check, William A., Ph.D. *The Truth About AIDS: The Evolution of an Epidemic.* Rev. ed. New York: Holt, Rinehart & Winston, 1986. This is a straightforward introduction to AIDS that makes the chronology of the epidemic understandable to most people. It covers the start of the AIDS epidemic, how it has evolved, the progress that has been made combating the disease, and the politics involved in all aspects of the still-unfolding AIDS crisis.

Greenly, Mike. *Chronicles: The Human Side of AIDS.* New York: Irvington Publishers, 1986. Mike Greenly has interviewed a great variety of people with many points of view and involvement in the AIDS epidemic, and he has indeed shown the human side of AIDS.

Gong, Victor, M.D. *Understanding AIDS, A Comprehensive Guide.* New Brunswick: Rutgers University Press, 1985. An excellent book for someone who already knows something about AIDS and needs a comprehensive guide. Part Two: The Clinical Spectrum defines the scope of AIDS infections. The writing is very clear throughout.

Institute of Health, National Academy of Sciences. *Mobilizing Against AIDS: The Unfinished Story of a Virus.* Cambridge: Harvard University Press, 1986.

Journal of the American Medical Association. *AIDS from the Beginning.* Edited by Helen M. Cole, M.D., and George D.

Lundberg, M.D. Chicago: American Medical Association, 1986. This book contains almost every article on AIDS that appeared in that journal from the beginning through the early part of 1986. It also contains three new forewords that are extremely useful. Many of these are highly technical reports on specific aspects of the disease, but they extremely useful in describing treatments.

Kübler-Ross, Elisabeth. *On Death and Dying.* New York: Macmillan, 1969. A groundbreaking and enlightening guide to the phenomenon of death and dying.

Moffat Betty C. *When Someone You Love Has AIDS.* Santa Monica, California: IBS Press, 1986. This is a book about self-actualization and may not be suitable for people not deeply involved in those concepts. Chapter V, in which persons with AIDS talk about themselves, is particularly useful. The chapters on alternative therapies are certainly filled with interesting ideas, but there is too much jargon. Ms. Moffat is very sincere and her love for her son is evident throughout the book. However, her need to apologize for her gay son is disturbing.

Nungesser, Lon. *Epidemic of Courage: Facing AIDS in America.* New York: St. Martin's Press, 1985. This is a book of interviews from an author who has AIDS himself. He has talked to people who have AIDS, their lovers and friends, and has provided some wonderful insights into how people have handled the illness.

Office of Technology Assessment. *Review of the Public Health Service's Response to AIDS.* Washington, DC: U.S. Government Printing Office, 1986. This book, published by the federal government itself at the request of Congress, is the best explanation yet as to why the government has been so slow in responding to the AIDS crisis. There are endless documents here as well as some interesting interviews. The main point is simply that the government told us that AIDS was the nation's first health priority, but they didn't act that way.

Peabody, Barbara. *The Screaming Room.* San Diego, California: Oak Tree Publication, 1986. A moving story, this book tells how the author; her son, Peter, dying of AIDS; and the rest of the family reconciled themselves to Peter's physical, but not spiritual, devastation. A hopeful book, but filled with sadness. A journey to read about if you identify with any of the characters in the book.

ACKNOWLEDGMENTS

David Groff, editor at Crown, recognized good intentions and a very imperfect idea, and molded that idea into a book that we hope will prove to be greatly useful to those for whom it was written. I thank him for his constant and continued encouragement, his suggestions for improvement, and his hard work and important contributions to the development of the manuscript. This book would not exist without him.

Joyce Wallace, doctor and AIDS specialist in New York City, was more than just a doctor to Evan and me, but a friend when we were in need of all her encouragement, inspiration, and caring. And to **Barbara Starrett** for being there when Joyce could not be.

My Carepartners' Group—these men and women, and their friends and lovers—has opened my eyes to a depth of human love and dedication I would not have guessed existed before this crisis.

St. Vincent's Supportive Care Program—Sister Patrice, Sister Pat, Joan Blanchfield, Carol, Cathy, and especially Jim Earley and Roger Smith—have watched over Evan and me, cared for us, and loved us.

L.J.M.

INDEX

231

234

high-grade B-cell non-Hodgkin's
  lymphoma, 75
Hirsch, Martin S., 46
HIV (human immunodeficiency virus),
  5
  in conjunction with other viruses, 8
  in saliva, 30, 205
  T-4 cells and, 5–6
HIV antibodies, 6
HIV-antibody test, 11, 13
  pros and cons of, 201–203
HMOs (health maintenance organizations), 33
Holistic Medical Association, 48
holistic medicine, 48
  for KS, 73
Home Relief, 93
homosexuals:
  anonymous sex among, 8–9
  churches for, 153–154, 163–164
  families of, 143–144
  as high-risk group, 7–8
  response of, to AIDS, 8–9
  wills written by, 80–81
hospice programs, 154
hospitalization insurance, 33–34
  Medicaid, 93–94
  see also health insurance
hospitals:
  choosing of, 38–39
  services provided by, 153–154
housing, 79
  AIDS agencies and, 84, 152–153
  convenience of, 111–112
  maintenance of, 84–85
HPA-23, 45
HTLV-III (human T-cell lymphotropic
  virus)/human immunodeficiency
  virus, see HIV
hydrocortisone, 77

I
ibuprofen, 76
immune-system enhancers, 45
incubation period, 58
Indocin, 76
inheritance, 79
Institute for Immunological Disorders,
  38
insurance, health, see health insurance
Integrity, 154
intercourse, 7, 204–205

interferon alpha, 45, 74–75
interferon gamma, 75
interleukin-2, 75
interstate succession, 79
intestinal parasites, 5, 18, 35
iodine medicines, 18
isoniazid, 72
isoprinosine, 45, 47
IV-drug users, 7, 10, 11, 27
  families of, 142–143
  TB in, 72
  wills written by, 80–81

J
Johnson, Warren, 10
Justice Department, U.S., 88, 89–90

K
Kaposi's sarcoma, see KS
kissing, in transmission of AIDs, 6–7,
  29–30, 204
Krim, Mathilde, 46
KS (Kaposi's sarcoma), 5, 14, 30, 36,
  37–38, 43, 64, 72–74
  chemotherapy for, 44, 73–74, 78,
  165
  in lungs, lung cancer vs., 72
  macrobiotic diet for, 48
Kübler-Ross, Elisabeth, 56–57, 121,
  174
Kushi, Michio, 48
Kuttner, Robert, 34

L
Lambda Legal Defense, 98
LAV (lymphadenopathy-associated
  virus), see HIV
lawyers, 81, 153
legal matters, 79–98
leprosy, 63, 72
leukoencephalopathy, 70
liver, MAI and, 71–72
living wills, 80, 81–82
Lotrimin, 77
lung cancer, KS in lungs vs.,
  72
lymphadenopathy, 11, 68
lymphadenopathy-associated virus
  (LAV), see HIV
lymph glands, swollen, 11, 68

seborrea, 76
semen, in transmission of AIDS, 6–7, 204–205
Septra, 65–66
Shanti Project, 154
shigella, 70–71
shingles, 68
Shyh-Ching Lo, 200
side-effects, 63, 64
    of chemotherapeutic drugs, 72, 74
    of drugs for diarrhea, 70–71
    of drugs for toxoplasmosis, 69
    of fever medicines, 76
skin rashes, 12, 76–77
skin ulcers, 68
sleep, 17
sleeping sickness, 63
smallpox, 63
social workers, 55
spiramyucin, 71
SSD (Social Security Disability), 91, 94
SSI (Supplementary Security Income), 91–92
streptomycin, 72
stress, 18–19
sulfadiazine, 69
sunlight, 18
support systems:
    families in, 139–148
    friends in, 148–151
    organizations in, 151–154
    setting up of, 138–139
    for "worried well," 155
    see also AIDS agencies; therapy
suppressor (T-8) cells, 6
surgery:
    elective, 18
    immunological shock after, 5
symptoms, 11–12, 14–15
    responding to, 16–20

T

taxes, 92
TB (tuberculosis), 72
T-cell ratio, 13, 57, 65
T-8 (suppressor) cells, 6
terminal stage, 156–180
    acceptance in, 174
    anger in, 169, 173
    bargaining in, 173
    changing feelings in, 171–174
    denial in, 167–173

depression in, 173–174
intimacy in, 164–165
pain in, 168
physical decline in, 165–167
separation in, 168
unresolved issues in, 171
T-4 (T-helper) cells, 5–6
therapy, 42–43
    from carepartners, 127
    federally unapproved, 47–49
    group, 138
    nonmedical, 47–49
    selection of, 152
    vitamin, 48
    see also support systems
thrush (candida esophagitis), 14, 43, 66–67
Tinactin, 77
tiredness, 11
toxoplasmosis (toxoplasma gondii) ("toxo"), 43, 69–70, 79
transmission, 6–7
    attitudes about, 24
    kissing in, 6–7, 29–30, 204
    see also safer sex
trimethoprim-sulfamethoxazole, 65–66, 70–71
trips, 18
tuberculosis (TB), 72

U

ulcers:
    decubitus, 77–78
    skin, 68
urine, 205

V

vaginal intercourse, 7
    safer sex guidelines for, 205
Veterans Administration Benefits, 94
vinblastine, 74
vincristine, 74, 75
virus, 5
    as cause of AIDS, 5–8, 201–203
    CMV, 28, 41, 43, 67
    Epstein-Barr, 67
    herpes simplex, 43, 67–68
    HIV, see HIV
    in leukoencephalopathy, 70
    slow-acting, 6
    zoster varicella, 68

237